The richly variegated religious landscape of India in general, and the multiplicity of Christian expressions of the faith in particular, are extremely well served by this painstakingly detailed and thick description, as well as analysis of the life, work, witness and movement around Bakht Singh. Bharathi is to be heartily commended for offering the wider public a thoroughly researched, carefully documented, engagingly articulated, and meticulously evaluated research project that does not over-generalize the word "Indian" and does not undervalue the word "Christian." Rather, she offers us a solid social history of the Indian context in which the Bakht Singh movement emerged, as well as a nuanced understanding of the richness of specific manifestations of Indian Christianity. Religious interconnections between the natal religion and the accepted religion of Bakht Singh are carefully traced, and the living reality of the form and substance of the way in which Christianity was understood, communicated and practiced by Bakht Singh and the movement that grew around him and his teachings is methodically scrutinized.

For all those interested in deepening their knowledge of the varieties of religious experience in the wonder that is India, and for those concerned about indigenous ways in which the Christian faith has been fostered in interaction with inter- and intra-faith realities, this book offers much sustenance to accompany this journey, and I warmly recommend it to practitioners and researchers alike.

Rev J. Jayakiran Sebastian, DTh
Dean of Seminary and H. George Anderson Professor of Mission and Cultures,
Lutheran Theological Seminary, Philadelphia, USA

The history of Indian Christianity is a long and rich one. Historic churches within the Indian context have often been heavily influenced from the West, products of earlier colonial efforts. There are, however, many newer, independent churches that have sprung up throughout India in recent decades. One of the more significant is a group known as the Bakht Singh Assemblies. While employing the latest in post-colonial Indian historiography, Dr B. E. Bharathi Nuthalapati has written an engaging history of this important movement and its founder. She shows quite clearly what its founder shared with several other widely read European and Asian

Christian leaders, while demonstrating how Bakht Singh drew from his Sikh past to establish a truly indigenous movement without compromising the essence of the gospel message. This is one of the more important books to appear in recent years, filling a gap in the contemporary accounting of India's newer, indigenous churches. It should be read by theologians, missionaries, and seminary students alike.

Cecil M. Robeck, Jr, PhD
Professor of Church History and Ecumenics,
Director of the David J. du Plessis Center for Christian Spirituality,
Fuller Theological Seminary, Pasadena, USA

Brother Bakht Singh

Theologian and Father of the Independent Indian Christian Church Movement

B. E. Bharathi Nuthalapati

ACADEMIC

© 2017 by B. E. Bharathi Nuthalapati

Published 2017 by Langham Academic (Previously Langham Monographs)
An imprint of Langham Publishing
www.langhampublishing.org

Langham Publishing and its imprints are a ministry of Langham Partnership

Langham Partnership
PO Box 296, Carlisle, Cumbria, CA3 9WZ, UK
www.langham.org

ISBNs:
978-1-78368-252-2 Print
978-1-78368-253-9 ePub
978-1-78368-255-3 PDF

B. E. Bharathi Nuthalapati has asserted her right under the Copyright, Designs and Patents Act, 1988 to be identified as the Author of this work.

All rights reserved. No part of this publication may be reproduced, stored in a retrieval system or transmitted, in any form or by any means, electronic, mechanical, photocopying, recording or otherwise, without the prior written permission of the publisher or the Copyright Licensing Agency.

British Library Cataloguing in Publication Data
A catalogue record for this book is available from the British Library

ISBN: 978-1-78368-252-2

Cover & Book Design: projectluz.com

Langham Partnership actively supports theological dialogue and scholar's right to publish but does not necessarily endorse the views and opinions set forth, and works referenced within this publication or guarantee its technical and grammatical correctness. Langham Partnership does not accept any responsibility or liability to persons or property as a consequence of the reading, use or interpretation of its published content.

To

My Parents
The late Mr Nuthalapati Joseph and Mrs Lizziemma
Who taught me that life is about faith, character and values.

And to

My Husband
Mr Duvvuru Kamalakar Jayakumar
for sharing that life with me.

Contents

Foreword xi
Acknowledgements xv
Chapter 1 1
   Introduction
      History of Scholarship 2
      Sources and Methodology 6
      Structure 11
Chapter 2 15
   Bakht Singh and the Beginning of the Assemblies
      Biographical Details of Bakht Singh
      (6 June 1903 – 17 September 2000) 16
         Sikhism 17
         Bakht Singh in England (1926) to India (1933) 20
         Beginnings of Ministry in India 22
      The Process of Making Christianity Indian 24
         Leadership 24
         Theology 25
         Worship and Structures 26
      The Situation of the Denominational Churches in the
      1930s and 1940s 30
      The Beginning of the Assemblies 32
      Assemblies 35
      The Spread of the Movement 37
Chapter 3 41
   The Phenomenon of Spiritual Life Churches
      New Testament Pattern 42
      Common Characteristics 43
      Spiritual Life Church Movements 44
         England: Theodore Austin-Sparks (1889–1971) 46
         China: Watchman Nee (Ni Tuo Sheng) (1903–1972) 50
      Commonalities between Austin-Sparks, Watchman Nee
      and Bakht Singh 60

Chapter 4 63
   The Ecclesiology of Bakht Singh
      The Nature of the Church 64
         House of God 66
         Coworkers 70
      The Unity of the Church 72
         Apostles' Doctrine 74
         Fellowship 74
         Breaking of Bread 75
         Prayer 79
      Practices in the Assembly 81
         Baptism 81
         Laying on of Hands 83
         Praying for the Sick 85
         Holy Convocations 86
      Worship and Church Order 88
         Worship (Time of Individual Praise and Adoration) ... 89
         Table Fellowship or "Table Worship" 90
         The Message 91
         Love Feast 94
      Government and Organization of the Assemblies 94
         "God's Servants" or Full-Time Ministers 97
         Elders 101

Chapter 5 107
   Sikh Antecedents of Bakht Singh:
   Their Influence on the Teaching and Practices of the Assemblies
      Religious Background of Bakht Singh 108
      Main Tenets in Sikhism 111
         Guru 111
         Nam 112
         Hukam (Divine Will or Divine Order) 114
         Sangat 115
      Similar Concepts 115
         The Name of Jesus 116
         The Word of God 117
         Voice of God 122
         God's Will 124
      Similar Practices 125
         Worship 125

    Architecture 128
    Music and Musical Instruments 129
    Greetings 130
    Promises 131
    Begging 131
    The Importance of Family and Sharing 133
    The Tithe 133
    Guru ka Langar and Love Feast 134
    Festival Processions 138
    Ritualism 139

Chapter 6 145
The Bhakti Theology of Bakht Singh
    Sources of Authority: Pramanas 146
        The Scriptures 147
        Experience 148
    Hermeneutics 149
    Bhakti 153
        The Meaning of *Bhakti* 153
        Bhakti Movements 156
    Sikhism and *Bhakti* 160
    The *Bhakti* Theology of Bakht Singh 163
        The Spiritual Experience of Bakht Singh 165
        Bakht Singh's Expression of *Bhakti* 167
        Worship (*Aradhana*) 168
        The "Voice of God" and the "Will of God" 171
        Bhavas (Feelings, Attitudes, Sentiments, Moods) 174
    The Indian Christian *Bhakti* Movement 178

Chapter 7 187
Religious Culture of the Assemblies and Its Impact on Christianity in India
    Special Features 188
        The Role of "Promises" from Scripture 188
        Importance of Scripture Memorization 189
        The Development of an Identifiable Subculture 190
        Openness to All People 191
        Holy Convocations 192
        Marriages 196
        Funerals 198
        Evangelism 199

      Nurturing of the Congregations 202
      Assemblies as Centers of Training 206
      Women 209
  Impact of Bakht Singh on Christianity in India 211
      Other Churches 212
      Union of Evangelical Students of India (UESI) 214
  Foreigners as Coworkers 214

Conclusion 217

Glossary 225

Bibliography 227
  Primary Sources 227
  Correspondence 229
  Interviews 229
  Secondary Sources 230

Foreword

For a thousand years the heartland of the Christian movement was located in the West. In 1800, 87 percent of people who identified themselves as Christians were in Europe and North America and accounted for 23 percent of total world population. A century on, Christians made up 34 percent of the world population. Eighty-one percent of the Christian worldwide population was European and North American, and the other 19 percent were in Africa, Asia, Latin America and the South Seas. Few people noticed that an important trend was building, one that would accelerate throughout the twentieth century.

Based on studies in the 1960s, missiographer David B. Barrett startled many people with his prediction in 1970 that there would be 350 million Christians in Africa by the year 2000.[1] Barrett pointed out that already by 1970 the ratio between western Christians and those from the rest of the world had shifted considerably so that 44 percent of the global Christian population was in Africa, Asia, and Latin America. This trend has continued into the twenty-first century.

The second edition of the *World Christian Encyclopedia*,[2] published in 2001, reported that the Christian population in the West was continuing to decline while Christians in other parts of the world now accounted for fully 60 percent of all Christian adherents worldwide. Such a shift happens but rarely. Over the past two decades scholars have been scrambling to catch up with this sea change that will have far-reaching implications for the study of religion in the future.

---

1. David B. Barrett, "AD 2000: 350 Million Christians in Africa," *International Review of Mission* 59 (Jan 1970), 39–54.

2. David B. Barrett, George T. Kurian, and Todd M. Johnson, eds. *World Christian Encyclopedia*, 2 vols. (Oxford: Oxford University Press, 2001).

The discipline of sociology was established to study modern society. The interaction between religion and modernity became one of the important areas of sociological study. Academic sociologists theorized, with considerable self-assurance, that religion was unable to withstand the overwhelming power of secularization. It was clear that religion was fated to decline and disappear. The secularization thesis remained unchallenged until the 1960s. But by 1970 it was no longer possible to ignore the fact that the secularization hypothesis had missed the mark. Religion was thriving round the world. To be sure, there were instances, such as Europe, where religion appeared to be in decline, but both new forms of religion and revitalized ancient faiths were to be found on all continents. The rise of science, technology, and industrialization did not automatically signal the end of religion. Since the vast majority of these sociological studies were conducted in western industrialized societies, these findings could not be said to be representative of the global situation.

Dr Bharathi Nuthalapati's study *Brother Bakht Singh: Theologian and Father of the Indian Independent Christian Church Movement* provides a window through which to study one of the most important sources of religious vitality: indigenous agency. I suggest *indigeneity* is an indispensable clue to the demographic shift in the center of gravity for the Christian movement worldwide. To be sure, the narrative of this outstanding Indian Christian leader and the movement he initiated and led is worth telling for its own sake. But Bakht Singh – the man and his movement – throws important light on the way religion has repeatedly crossed historical, cultural, and traditional boundaries and formed fresh expressions.

The Bakht Singh story is located at the intersection of several religious and cultural streams. He had no choice but to negotiate among competing options and offers. This he did with confident faith. His vision of Jesus Christ and his word, on the one hand, and unshakeable fidelity to indigenous values and resources, on the other, were the framework for thought and action.

The modern mission movement started on the eve of the nineteenth century. Two centuries later we still do not have a firm grasp on the relationship between the gospel and culture. By the 1830s thoughtful mission leaders observed a fundamental flaw in missionary work. Most missionaries were faithfully *replicating* themselves in terms of religious forms. Consequently, missionary-established churches looked "exotic" rather than "native."[3] Such "foreignness" was a barrier far greater than the missionary was ready to acknowledge. In various ways, local people pushed back against missionary domination and control. For example, by the 1860s an initiative was afoot in India to establish the Indian National church. Although this effort did not succeed at the time, the underlying impulse was never fully suppressed. The Bakht Singh Assemblies are living proof of this indigenous dynamic.

Discerning observers of western Christianity point to evidence that it is suffering from an advanced case of syncretism, a condition fostered by the claim that the West is a *Christian* culture, a claim that was false and must be rejected. Absorption of the Christian faith by culture subverts it. The present study makes an indispensable contribution to our understanding of indigenous Christian movements. The kind of indigenous Christian faith studied here does not focus on achieving a secure status in society; rather its goal is to give faithful witness to its crucified and reigning Lord.

Wilbert R. Shenk
Senior Professor of Mission History
Fuller Graduate School of Intercultural Studies, Pasadena, CA, USA

---

3. The terms used in the 19th century.

Acknowledgements

This book was originally written as a dissertation in partial fulfillment of the requirements for the degree of Doctor of Philosophy in Church History, at the School of Theology, Fuller Theological Seminary, Pasadena, California, USA. A work like this is not possible without the help of others. I want to thank all of them even though I may not be able to mention all their names here. I want to thank God for enabling me to do this work and bring it into a book form.

I am indeed grateful to my mentor, Dr Cecil M. Robeck, Jr., for his guidance and encouragement, and my second reader Dr Wilbert Shenk for his enthusiastic support throughout this project. I express my thanks to Dr James Bradley, Dr David Bundy and Dr George Oommen for the thought-provoking conversations and suggestions.

I am grateful to Dr T. E. Koshy, the official biographer of Bakht Singh, for allowing me to use his archives, furnishing me with the sources I needed, and for his encouragement and hospitality. My special thanks go to all the interviewees for not only giving me time to answer my questions, but also extending hospitality when I went to meet them. Thanks to Dr Sheela Swarupa Rani, Dr Earnest Dhanaraj and Dr D. J. Prabhakar for hosting me during my travels.

I am also thankful to the librarians of Bhai Vir Singh Sahitya Sadan, New Delhi, Jawaharlal Nehru University, New Delhi, and United Theological College, Bangalore and last but not least, the librarians of David Allan Hubbard Library, Fuller, Pasadena.

My sincere thanks to John Stott Ministries and PEO International whose support enabled me to complete my studies in Fuller.

I want to thank all my friends, both in USA and in India, who have been a constant source of encouragement all through and have been directly or indirectly involved in this project. The list is too big to mention all the names.

On a personal note, my in-laws Pramila, Sampath and Jayakar were quite supportive of my work. My sisters, Sree Devi, Sree Rani and Sree Vasu, cared for me when I went home for a surgery, and my other siblings, Rayalu, Sree Vani, and Bharath, hosted my stay during the travels. My nieces and nephews Nani, Bindu, Sangeeta, Preethi, Kutty, Sunny, Ronnie, Finney, Soni, Corrie, Carey, Lolly and Molly assisted me in every way during my field trip. They were my hosts, travel partners, photographers and friends. I cannot thank them enough. But for the prayers of my mom, family and friends, especially my husband who took up the responsibility of home, and without his untiring help, this work would not have been possible. I am grateful to each one of them.

My special thanks go to Drs Mrinalini and Kiran Sebastian for their affirmative friendship and encouragement.

I want to thank Dr Anuradha Sudhir, Nigel Fernandes and Babu Elias for working on the manuscript. I also thank David Bollampalli for designing the initial cover page.

I am grateful to Langham Literature for accepting to publish my dissertation in their Monograph imprint.

CHAPTER 1

Introduction

The history of Christianity in India has for over a century been viewed by the historians of Christianity as a field of western missionary activity and the assertion of Indian Christians for a more contextualized and indigenous Christianity. The concept of a church rooted in India has been analyzed in relation to the dominant model of western historic denominational churches. Indigenous churches and movements have been viewed as missiological or theological aberrations, rather than authentic ecclesial expressions. This book investigates the history of the formation of the "Indigenous Churches in India,"[1] the Assemblies established by Bakht Singh as an independent "Indian" church and the dynamics involved in shaping the church in a pluralistic context. It seeks to examine how the western mode of Christianity, biblical understanding, local religiosity, and the local pluralistic context interacted in the evolution of the new church and the movement, and in making Bakht Singh an Indian Christian Theologian.

Notwithstanding the universal interconnectedness of the Christian church by virtue of colonization and the concept of unity, the book will show that the Assemblies established by Bakht Singh in India emerged as an independent "Indian" church rooted in the theological, political, social, religious and cultural soil of India. The book analyzes how pre-Christian elements persisted in the movement and how various aspects of Indian religiosity and western Christianity were adopted, rejected, reinterpreted, or revolutionized by the movement in the process of its formation. It also

---

1. The Assemblies are officially registered as "Indigenous Churches in India."

discusses how the Assemblies addressed the spiritual demands that were religiously and culturally embedded and what characterized them as an "Indian" church movement.

History of Scholarship

Indian historiography and the historiography of Christianity in India were, for a long time, dominated by the nationalist and elitist approach. Later Christian historians adopted the approach of history from below. However, the perspective that has revolutionized both the secular and Christian historiography is known as the subaltern historiography. The benefits of this approach to the writing of Indian history was evidenced in the emergence of the history of the Dalits, the tribals and women, who do not belong to the literary tradition because of their marginalization. The importance given to orality as a legitimate historical resource, by the subaltern historiography, has opened up new vistas of research for these three groups. In the same manner, the nondenominational churches and other Christian movements that were marginalized by the elitist and denominational historians have been able to benefit from the subaltern approach. As a result, the indigenous Christian movements caught the attention of historians only in the later decades of the twentieth century.

Renewed interest in writing about the indigenous churches in India developed because of the growth of the independent churches during the 1980s and a complete detachment of these movements from academic or theological circles. Some individuals however, have worked on independent movements such as the "Bible Mission," and Pentecostal churches.[2] The Mylapore Institute of Indigenous Studies (MIIS) has produced some literature on the indigenous movements in India. Their purpose has been to expose indigenous Christianity to academic research. Most of the studies are dependent on the participant observation and reflection model which now call for a more systematic approach to research. In fact, many of these

---

2. See Michael Bergunder, *The South Indian Pentecostal Movement in the Twentieth Century* (Grand Rapids, MI: Eerdmans 2008); Werner Hoerschelamnn, *"Christian Gurus" A Study on the Life and Work of Christian Charismatic Leaders in South India* (Chennai: Gurukul Lutheran Theological College and Research Center, 1998)

studies are simply introductory articles that are pointers to the areas of research in this field.

P. Solomon Raj's book *A Christian Folk-Religion in India* deals with a local movement in Andhra Pradesh called the "Bible Mission." He calls the indigenous churches "Indigenous Non-White Churches," meaning that they do not have any association with the West. He maintains that the folk religious forms adapted by this church appealed to and attracted people to understand Christianity from their particular perspective.[3] His latest book *New Wine Skins: The Story of the Indigenous Missions in Coastal Andhra Pradesh, India*, is a survey of different local churches and their style of indigenous adaptations. Describing the title of the book, he mentions that "the new wine of the powerful great message should not be delivered in the old bottles of colonial cultural trimmings and the 17th century archaic idiom and methodology."[4] In an Appendix to Solomon Raj's book written by Roger Hedlund that is titled, *The Importance of the Study of India's New Christian Movements*, Hedlund calls for research to be done on such movements and makes a special reference to Bakht Singh's "Assemblies." Hedlund notes:

> Apart from short devotional accounts, little or no history has been written . . . Whatever weaknesses and strengths there may be, the ministry of Bro. Bakht Singh and the Assemblies is a remarkable indigenous Christian witness and a worthy subject for historiography.[5]

The current survey reveals the serious lacunae in the scholarship regarding the indigenous churches in India. Therefore, this work intends to bridge this hiatus not only by viewing these movements as having their roots in the Indian soil, but also by analyzing the mutual interaction of the local culture and faith with the western denominational and universal modes of Christianity in the formation of an Indian church. It will also underscore the diversity and complexity of "Indianness" in the Indian churches.

---

3. P. Solomon Raj, *A Christian Folk Religion in India* (Frankfurt: Verlag Peter Lang, 1986).

4. P. Solomon Raj, *New Wine Skins: The Story of the Indigenous Missions in Coastal Andhra Pradesh, India* (Delhi: ISPCK/MIIS, 2003), xx.

5. Raj, *New Wine Skins,* 151–152.

The history of scholarship on the Bakht Singh movement is very scant. One of the major and most comprehensive works published (in the year 2000) since the death of Bakht Singh is *Brother Bakht Singh of India: An Account of 20th Century Apostolic Revival* written by his coworker and official biographer T. E. Koshy.[6] This book traces the history of the movement and the biography of Bakht Singh. Koshy acknowledges the connections that Bakht Singh had with other likeminded people, and situates him in the national context. Daniel Smith's *Bakht Singh of India: A Prophet of God*[7] is mainly the author's personal impressions on Bakht Singh and his movement. As the titles suggest, both of these monographs are hagiographic and written from within the movement. Lal Rosem's *Brother Bakht Singh* is also based upon the views of an insider.[8]

In his book, *Quest for Identity: India's Churches of Indigenous Origin: The "Little Tradition" in Indian Christianity*,[9] Roger Hedlund introduces various indigenous movements that arose in India with a special emphasis on those that emerged in Andhra Pradesh, South India. Hedlund designates these movements as the "Little Tradition" and also identifies them as "Subaltern," in the sense of belonging to "the weaker sections of the society and arising spontaneously through indigenous initiatives."[10] He shows how these churches are meeting the needs of people and filling the gap left by the churches of the "great tradition." Hedlund provides a brief overview of the Assemblies of Bakht Singh in his book. Because of the claims of the Assemblies of Bakht Singh and their fundamentalist approach to the Scriptures, he identified the movement as having Baptist/Brethren leanings and as being evangelical. Hedlund suggests that the Assemblies are also indigenous and he observes that there are similarities with the *gurudwara*[11] worship. He concludes by calling for further research to be undertaken

---

6. Thottukadavil E. Koshy, *Brother Bakht Singh of India: An Account of 20th Century Apostolic Revival* (Secunderabad: OM Books, 2003).

7. Daniel Smith, *Bakht Singh of India: A Prophet of God* (Washington, DC: International Students Press, 1959).

8. Lal Rosem, *Brother Bakht Singh* (Delhi: ISPCK, 2002).

9. Roger E. Hedlund, *Quest for Identity: India's Churches of Indigenous Origin* (Delhi: MIIS/ISPCK, 2000).

10. Hedlund, *Quest,* 11.

11. Sikh Temple

on the subject. He includes a brief analysis of the theology and leadership of Bakht Singh within the broader framework of Indian Christian leaders. Moses Premanandam's article "God-Chosen Movement for India" in *Christianity Is Indian: The Emergence of an Indigenous Community*[12] is a study on the "life" of the Assemblies. He comments on the present state of the Assemblies and contends that they might become irrelevant in the future if they continue to follow the methods that they are currently following.

There are two unpublished works on Bakht Singh as well. One is a BD thesis titled "A Study of Bakht Singh Movement – Its Origins and Growth especially in Andhra Pradesh" written by Reddimalla Samuel from the United Theological College, Bangalore, in 1971. It is a participant-observer account of the lifestyle of the Assembly members and their beliefs. He focuses mostly on the attitude of its members in terms of their spirituality and practices. Samuel concludes that the movement addressed a basic understanding of spirituality, that is, "experience of God," rather than offering a dogmatic or mere adherence to a set of beliefs and doctrines. It is this spirituality, he reckons, that attracted people to the movement. However, he tends to be dismissive of the Assemblies because of what he views as their sectarian, exclusive and rigid attitude towards other denominations.

The second work is titled "Contextualization of Christianity in India – A Critical Study of the Contribution of Bakht Singh and His Assemblies." It was written by Santha Kumari as an MPhil dissertation in Christian Studies, from the University of Madras in 2006. She situates Bakht Singh with those who attempted to contextualize Christianity in India. Kumari traces some parallels between the practices of the Assemblies and the Sikh religious practices. She deals with the current situation of the Assemblies, and offers some corrective thoughts. She identifies the areas where further research is needed on the subject. Since the researcher relied more on the participant-observer method and was also associated with the Assemblies, she tends to accept uncritically and idealize their claim to be Bible based. The dissertation is a very general narrative, providing more of a survey than an in-depth analysis of the movement. The work lacks proper documentation and fails to substantiate the information that is provided.

---

12. Moses Premanandam, "God-Chosen Movement for India," *Christianity Is Indian: The Emergence of an Indigenous Community*, ed. Roger E. Hedlund (Delhi: ISPCK, 2004).

Neither of these two works is based on in-depth historical research. They are both dominated by historical narrative, rather than critical and analytical study. It is evident that the history of scholarship on Bakht Singh and his movement is scarce, and a critical, in-depth study is needed.[13]

Sources and Methodology

The primary sources on Bakht Singh and his movement are to be found mainly in his writings,[14] and in the magazine, *Hebron Messenger*, published by the Assembly. *Monsoon Daybreak*, an autobiography of Bakht Singh's coworker R. Rajamani, is another important source. It is a first-person account of the beginnings of the movement in Madras and its spread outside Madras. Eleanore H. Llewellyn's article "Bakht Singh of India"[15] is a missionary's account of the ministry of Bakht Singh that covers the period when he was an itinerant evangelist in North India, 1933–1941.

I have attempted to analyze the construct of the primary sources and apply a method of reading against the grain, in order to go behind the text to understand the socio-cultural and religious implications that are embedded in the teachings and the writings. Secondary sources were consulted for the religious and contextual background. Since the movement is from the recent past, it has been possible to conduct interviews with various members of the Assemblies, with persons who worked alongside Bakht Singh, as well as the younger brother of Bakht Singh. The lack of proper documentation in the form of objective, biographical and analytical studies, and the culture of orality, therefore, required that the perspective of the people be captured through their memories.

I have encountered certain limitations in the methods used in the interviews. I found that structured interviews often yielded little more than stereotypical and spiritualized answers. As a result, I changed the method of gathering information from one that included inviting answers to

---

13. A thorough search of dissertations reveals that no doctoral level research has been done on this movement.

14. Most of the booklets published in his name were his sermons in written form.

15. Eleanore H. Llewellyn, "Bakht Singh of India," in *Unforgettable Disciples* (New York, NY: The Board of Foreign Missions of the Presbyterian Church in the United States of America, 1942).

specific questions, to one in which the interviewees were asked to narrate their stories. This approach allowed me to intersperse their narrative with questions, depending on the information provided in the narrative. This method proved to be much more informative and helpful than the earlier approach.

Interviews were conducted in urban and rural congregations, with both individuals who were closely associated with Bakht Singh and with those who never saw him. I attended a convocation, participated in Sunday services, visited the headquarters of the movement, as well as various local Assemblies. I conducted informal conversations and interviews with individuals outside the Assembly circles, in order to gain an objective and critical overview of the Assemblies. The data collected through the interviews and by means of participant observation will be used primarily to understand the religious culture of the Assemblies.

The initial object of this work was to examine from a historical perspective the obvious parallels between Sikhism and the Assemblies, from the beginning of the movement through its development up to the present. As the research progressed, however, it became necessary for me to limit the topic to the period of the consolidation of the movement, that is until the time Bakht Singh was actively involved, and to expand the scope of this study in other dimensions such as the religious and spiritual undercurrents that formed the broader background of the founder and the movement. The complex and multiple identities or experiences of the founder necessitated a more comprehensive analysis and assessment of the historical, contextual, theological and religious dimensions of the teachings of Bakht Singh. Most of the scholars who have written on the subject have identified the Sikh antecedents of Bakht Singh, but typically they made the simplistic assumption that the movement and theology of Bakht Singh were solely evangelical. These interpretations were based upon a superficial understanding of the movement. But the underlying question regarding the basis of this movement requires a critical response. If Bakht Singh's movement is not merely an evangelical movement, then what is it?

A second major question that has guided this research project has been, "what makes the movement Indian?" The context of the founder, and the time and places in which the movement began and took shape, were varied and complex. This complexity has contributed to the conclusion that the term "indigenous" is inadequate if we are to understand the movement.[16] At the same time this complexity has suggested the importance of the assertion of the term "Indian," so that the complexity and diversity of Indianness are maintained.

According to Roger Hedlund, "The Indian independent church movements are expressions of an authentic Indian incarnation of the Christian faith. These movements are demonstrations of the translatability of the gospel." In his book *Quest for Identity, India's Churches of Indigenous Origin: The "Little Tradition" in Indian Christianity*, Hedlund sketched the entire gamut of these movements as well as the various shades and shapes they took over the years. He explains the distinction between the indigenized churches and the indigenous Christian movements or churches in India as follows:

> Indianization, contextualization, and indigenization are expressions of the effort towards change/relevance made by a non-indigenous church (one of alien origin and pattern) – in an attempt to give it an Indian face. None of the mainstream denominations (the Great Tradition) is indigenous except the ancient St. Thomas Christian community which, however, became Syrianized at an early stage in its history. Indigenous Indian Christianity is found in the Little Tradition of the so-called fringe sections largely (not exclusively) of Pentecostal, Charismatic or Evangelical origin.[17]

Thus the terms "indigenization" and "indigenous" were set within the polarities of the classical, Brahminical, high caste, and denominational on the one hand, and the folk, Dalit, tribal, and nondenominational identities and religions on the other. The early efforts of indigenization were viewed as the high caste Christians' affirmation of their identity in the cultural and nationalistic milieu of the larger society. The indigenization of Christian theology was oriented toward the Brahminical traditions of Hinduism and the dominant cultural elements in the society, to the neglect of the Dalit

---

16. The Assemblies are registered as "Indigenous Churches in India."
17. Hedlund, *Quest*, 2–3.

and tribal culture and religion.[18] The current understanding, however, is a theology that is embedded in the subaltern (folk, Dalit, tribal and women's) culture and religion is considered as indigenous. Hedlund identifies them as subaltern both in the sense of belonging to "the weaker sections of the society and arising spontaneously through indigenous initiatives."[19] In fact, the attempt to indigenize and to establish indigenous churches was a recognition of the inappropriateness of the way and form in which the gospel was presented to all the communities in India. It was a collective effort, though it appears to have happened in a community-based manner, to make it relevant to the social and religio-cultural context to make Christianity Indian.

It is essential, however, to embrace in their totality the experiences of high caste, Dalits, tribals and women in order to understand the Indian Christian experience. George Oommen rightly observes, "Indianness is very much related to plurality and diversity. That is what we see in the Indian Christian experience also. In that sense, Indian Christianity was part and parcel of a process of becoming Indian in its own plural way, which is Christ's way." He further affirms, "It is a plurality of experiences that we perceive in the Indian Christian-ness."[20] Thus the term "Indian" encompasses the plurality and the heterogeneity of the cultures and religions that are involved along with foreign contributions to India's heterogeneous culture.[21] By recognizing the heterogeneity of Indian Christianity, it is possible to establish its interconnectedness to the universal or global Christianity.

Bakht Singh and the Assemblies represent the complexity as well as the heterogeneity of Indian Christianity. An in-depth assessment of the movement reveals the complex and diverse religious environment in which Bakht Singh conceived his ideas and applied them to the existing situation. Bakht Singh was associated with Hinduism and Sikhism during his

---

18. Saral K. Chatterji, "Indigenous Christianity and Counter-Culture," *Religion and Society* 36, no. 4 (December 1989).

19. Hedlund, *Quest,* 11.

20. George Oommen, "Is Indian Christianity both Indian and Christian?" (paper presented at the consultation on "How Do People of Other Faiths Perceive Christianity in India," EFI Theological Commission, 4 December 2002), 9.

21. M. E. Prabhakar, "Christians in Andhra Pradesh: Some Issues for Church Growth and Church-Planning," *India Church Growth Quarterly* 12, no. 1 (Jan–Mar 1990): 80.

childhood. He also studied and lived in the West for seven years, so he was not only acquainted with western culture but also tried to imitate it as well. Singh became a believer in Christ in Canada. Hence he became very familiar with Christianity and the church in the West. Working for eight years as an itinerant evangelist throughout India, by the time he started the Assemblies, he understood the nature of Christianity and the church in India. The varied experiences of Bakht Singh, apart from his western exposure, represent to a certain extent, the maze in which an Indian Christian finds himself or herself. The multifaceted and comprehensive knowledge of Bakht Singh, both of the Indian religious and cultural contexts and the western social and religious situation, demands that he should be understood within the context of his antecedents and their likely influences, whose impact cannot be denied, much less ignored.

Given these facts, I will attempt to derive inferences with regard to these religious and spiritual impingements upon the teachings and practices of the Assemblies. Thus, a study of Sikhism and *Bhakti*[22] should render insights into the spiritual undercurrents of the teaching, theology and practices of the Assemblies, and help to identify the continuities and discontinuities of Bakht Singh's pre-Christian worldview and the way he applied it to Christianity. The study should reveal the strong affinity of Bakht Singh with Sikhism and the *Bhakti* tradition. It should also affirm that the sources of his beliefs were the Scriptures and his experience of Christ at the time of his conversion and also in his day-to-day life. These source materials should enable an analysis of the ecclesiology, theology and practices of Bakht Singh and the Assemblies.

The movement can also be located in the global phenomenon known as "Spiritual Life churches" led, for example, by people such as Austin-Sparks, Watchman Nee and Poul Madson, and the context in which they came into being. Mapping the movement within the larger context of global Christianity helps to identify the distinctiveness of the movement and its ecclesiology from similar ones.

---

22. Translated as devotion, or loving devotion, to a personal God.

Structure

The next chapter focuses upon a biographical introduction of Bakht Singh, the background and immediate context in which the Assemblies took root, and a brief sketch of the spread of the movement. It situates the beginnings of the Assemblies within the context of the Indian church's and Indian Christianity's endeavor to find where she belongs spiritually, culturally, theologically and nationally. While efforts to indigenize Christianity in the institutional churches began piecemeal, first in the area of governance, then in theology, worship and architecture, they still remain as replicas of the foreign model brought to India. The alien nature of Christianity, as well as the spiritual and structural inappropriateness that this model brought to India, left the common folk in search of a meaningful spiritual experience outside its confines. The chapter discusses the beginnings of the movement within this context.

The third chapter deals with how Bakht Singh's movement in India was not an isolated event in Christian history. It attempts to show how the Assemblies are a part of the global movements of the early twentieth-century Christianity. During this period, several independent movements arose in different parts of the world. Based on the common characteristics and resemblances to each other, the churches that followed the "New Testament pattern" arose out of a common quest or situation. The churches that were established by T. Austin-Sparks (The Honor Oak Fellowship in London), Watchman Nee (The Little Flock Movement in China), Bakht Singh (The Assemblies in India), and Poul Madsen (the Danish Kristent Fælleskab Movement) could all be identified as "Spiritual Life churches." Although these churches were considered evangelical, it is argued that the local context and spirituality was more important in shaping these churches and movements than was the common ecclesiology that has often been perceived to be the main influence on these churches.

Chapter 4 views the ecclesiology of Bakht Singh as unique in its own right because of the themes and practices he emphasized. True to his biblicist theology and his claim to his dependence on the leading of the Holy Spirit, Bakht Singh asserted the scriptural nature of his teaching. He insisted that the Assemblies were based on the "New Testament pattern" and upon "biblical principles." The study reveals that the ecclesiology that evolved in the Assemblies depended upon the existential need of the Assemblies, and the way that they sought to meet their existential need was based upon both the Scriptures and their immediate situation. In other words, it was the existential need that counted for more than any previously existing theology in shaping the Assemblies' ecclesiology. As much as Bakht Singh was biblical in his ecclesiology, he was just as thoroughly contextual in his approach to his understanding of church and its practices. The spontaneity of blending the biblical with the cultural and contextual elements conceals the struggle of theologizing within the specific context, and the socio-cultural elements embedded in the theology. It is the practices in the Assembly that reveal how his Sikh background also informs his ecclesiology.

Chapter 5 surveys the main tenets of Sikhism and suggests the ways in which they had an impact on Bakht Singh. Attempts to understand the movement of Bakht Singh from a purely theological and biblical perspective obscured the broader religious environment in which he was trained before his conversion, as well as the bearing it might have had on his thought and practices. Bakht Singh's approach to his newly found Christian faith is embedded in various aspects of his contemporary social and religious worldview. His deep observation and analysis of the problems involved both in his religious tradition and his adopted religion is discernable in his approach and application of the biblical teachings in the Assemblies. While personal spirituality is the major emphasis of Bakht Singh, the essence of his spirituality and practice of faith is underscored by his personal quest as a Sikh for the realization of God. Thus, it is necessary to probe the religio-spiritual contours of his teachings that could have been structured on the foundation of his personal spirituality inherited as a Sikh. Some of the major concepts and practices of Sikhism are explained from the Sikh religious perspective. Bakht Singh's concepts and practices that had closer affinity with Sikhism will be analyzed and evaluated to determine how Bakht Singh reinterpreted them within Christianity.

Chapter 6 investigates the theology of Bakht Singh from the perspective of Indian *Bhakti* tradition and identifies Bakht Singh as an Indian Christian theologian who addressed or incarnated the gospel into the core Indian spiritual ethos of *Bhakti*. It also seeks to understand and demonstrate how the movement is a *Bhakti* movement within Christianity, and how the churches are modeled on that tradition. Finally, it also shows how Bakht Singh addressed the common religiosity or spirituality of the people through *Bhakti*.

The final chapter explains the religious culture of the Assemblies, and tries to explore the possible methods and causes that might have contributed to the expansion of the movement and its impact on Christianity in India.

CHAPTER 2

Bakht Singh and the Beginning of the Assemblies

The advent of Bakht Singh and the Assemblies established by him in the mid and later half of the twentieth century marked the emergence of a new form of Christianity and churches in India. They were considered the best examples of Indian-led, independent, well-organized churches, expanding into the non-Christian culture of India.[1] The movement spread all over

---

1. See James A. Bergquist and P. Kambar Manickam, *The Crisis of Dependency in Third World Ministries: A Critique of Inherited Missionary Forms in India* (Madras: Christian Literature Society, 1976), 65, 67.

India and abroad, and the Assemblies have been estimated as being among one of India's faster growing churches.[2] Their critics have described them as Sects, "Brethren" or "Baptistic" groups, indigenous churches, and fellowships led by lay people.[3]

Bakht Singh was popularly known as "Brother Bakht Singh." His biographers named him an "Apostle." He was regarded as "The *'Christian Guru'* with the largest following."[4] His simple lifestyle and exemplary character, financial integrity and life of faith were undisputed.[5] While the leaders of the denominational churches felt the scorn of his eloquence, the common folk felt the appeal of his invitation. With these diverse descriptions, who then was Bakht Singh Chhabra? What factors made him who he was? How did the Assemblies come into being? We now turn to some of the answers to these questions.

Biographical Details of Bakht Singh (6 June 1903 – 17 September 2000)

Bakht Singh was born to Hindu parents in 1903 at Joiya in the region of Punjab (in present day Pakistan). According to family tradition, Bakht Singh, the first male child, was reared as a Sikh. His mother vowed that if she had a male child she would dedicate him to Guru Nanak. Though his parents were Hindus, they were devotees of Guru Nanak, the founder and first of the ten *gurus* in Sikhism. Bakht Singh grew up as an orthodox Sikh, adhering to all the Sikh practices and spirituality. From his early childhood, he asked his mother how he could find the *Satguru*.[6] Bakht Singh used to go out to the riverbed to pray alone in his attempt to find God. As a child he spent more time in the Sikh temples and with the Sikh religious leaders than was typical of his peers. Because of this religious attitude of their son,

---

2. David Barrett, *World Christian Encyclopedia*, 2nd ed. (2001), 365.
3. Hedlund, *Quest*, 47.
4. Hoerschelamnn, "Christian Gurus," 6.
5. P. A. Susheel Rao, "Bakht Singh Movement: A Case Study," *The Community We Seek: Perspectives on Mission*, ed. Jesudas M. Athyal (Tiruvalla: Christava Sahitya Samithi, 2003), 152.
6. *Satguru* means the true teacher. It also means God.

his parents were worried that he would become a *sadhu*.[7] As a result, they pampered him.

According to his brother, Shrichand Chhabra, "A streak of spiritual element was with him from the beginning."[8] Bakht Singh studied in a Christian boarding school, but he kept himself aloof from other Christian students. During his school days he learned about Sikhism from a person named Sundar Singh. Bakht Singh also developed hatred towards Christianity and tore the Bible as a sign of his hatred. He was proud of his Sikh religion. When his mother worried that he might leave his religion after going to England to study, he promised his mother that he would not leave the religion.[9] With this promise Bakht Singh went to England in 1926. He was steeped in his Sikh religious tradition by the time he left India.

Sikhism

Sikhism, the youngest of the world religions, originated in Punjab. Guru Nanak (1469–1539), the first of the ten *gurus*, was the founder of Sikhism.[10] It was believed that all ten *gurus* have the same light or illumination as Guru Nanak, thus making them a single unit or continuation of the same light that originated with Guru Nanak. The tenth *guru*, Guru Gobind Singh, brought an end to the line of human *gurus* by conferring Guruship on the message or hymns known as *gurbani* recorded in the *Guru Granth Sahib*,[11] the Sikh scriptures. The Sikh scriptures were said to be endued with spiritual

---

7. A *sadhu* is a Hindu mendicant – a person who practices mendicancy (begging) and relies chiefly on charitable donations to survive.

8. Shrichand Chhabra, interview by author, tape recording, Delhi, 29 November 2007. Shrichand Chhabra is the younger brother of Bakht Singh. At the time of the interview he was 95 years old.

9. Bakht Singh was married when he was twelve years old. He had a son in 1924. He never mentioned this anywhere. See Koshy, *Brother Bakht Singh*, 64.

10. Some scholars view Sikhism as a syncretic religion of Hinduism and Islam. This notion, however, has been countered by scholars like W. H. Mcleod, and J. S. Grewal, and others view Guru Nanak as the founder of a new faith that had its origins in the medieval Indian local traditions of *Sants* and the *Bhakti*. Sunita Puri views Guru Nanak as the chief proponent of the *Bhakti* movement in Punjab. Most of the scholars are of the opinion that *Bhakti* is intrinsic to Sikhism though the form it took differed from the form found in other Bhakti cults. See W. H. McLeod, *Exploring Sikhism: Aspects of Identity, Culture and Thought* (New Delhi: Oxford University Press, 2000); Jaswant Singh Neki, "Bhakti and Sikhism," in *Encyclopaedia of Sikhism* vol. 1, 335–337.

11. The Guru Granth Sahib contains a collection of hymns written by the Sikh Gurus. It also contains various hymns written by Hindu and Muslim *Bhaktas* or saints.

authority over the Sikh community or congregation, which is called the *panth*[12] or *sangat*. Although from the time of Guru Nanak the *gurbani* carried spiritual authority, the final systematization of the *Guru Granth Sahib* as the ultimate authority in Sikhism took place only in the late nineteenth century.[13] The word "Sikh" is derived from the Sanskrit term *Sisya* meaning "disciple," and the Pali term *Sisya* or *Sikkha* meaning "a pupil" or "one under training in religious doctrine." Today the Punjabi term "Sikh" denotes a follower of Guru Nanak, his nine successors and their teachings now embodied in the *Guru Granth Sahib*, the Sikh scriptures.[14]

Guru Nanak is believed to have had a direct encounter with the supreme reality and from the time of that encounter he started preaching that, "there is neither Hindu nor Muslim and that God is One." Guru Nanak claimed that he was the minstrel of God's message or God's word, *sabad*, and he began to proclaim the *sabad* revealed to him. According to him, the self-existent Creator exists and emanates from his creation. He is all-pervasive, both transcendent and immanent, and with attributes and without attributes. God can never assume any physical form. Thus, there is no room for divine incarnation or for idol worship.

Sikhism believes in the concept of *karma*, which means that one reaps the consequences of the acts he or she performs. *Karma* also denotes fate or predestination or deeds which cause the cycle of births and deaths. Since they believe in the transmigration of souls, salvation means the liberation from the cycle of births and the soul uniting or merging with the Supreme Spirit or God. The merging of the individual with the Supreme Spirit is a spiritual experience that happens through intuition and divine grace. The main impediment to this realization is *haumai* or "egoism." *Haumai* separates the human being from the divine, thereby making a person self-centered (*manmukh*), and an unregenerated individual. When a person abides in or obeys the divine order or "will" (*hukam*) in his or her life, or when

---

12. *Panth* literally means a "path" or "way." It also denotes a system of religious belief or practice; a community observing a particular system of belief or practices. *Sangat* means "holy fellowship"; congregation or group of devotees. The terms *panth* and *sangat* are used as synonyms.

13. W. Owen Cole, *The Guru in Sikhism* (London: Darton, Longman & Todd, 1982), 58.

14. Gurbachan Singh Talib, "Sikhism," in *Encyclopaedia of Sikhism* vol. 4, 148.

an individual lives wholly in accordance with the divine Will, that person overcomes the *haumai*. So one should become *gurmukh* or "God-oriented" in order to cease to be a *manmukh*, that is, a self-centered individual. This state is attained by following the *gurbani*, the message or *sabad*, the Word of the *guru*.

The means to attain a God-oriented life is to love God through devotion. Love of God is expressed by immersing oneself in the repetition of the name of God or *nam simaran*, and the meditation of God's greatness through awe and through singing God's praises. Sikhism does not believe in ascetic life or a ritual form of worship. Instead, it recommends living the life of a householder, a normal family life that is defined not by love of worldly passions but by love towards God. The householder is supposed to earn his living through hard work (*kirat karni*) and honest means. Guru Nanak's followers are to share their earnings (*vand chakna*) with others.[15] Guru Nanak emphasized the idea of *seva* or "self-abnegating deeds of service."[16] He established community living in a village called Kartarpur, where he worked on a farm and maintained a community kitchen (*langar*) where all were served and ate together without maintaining any caste distinctions. Those who became his disciples were called Sikhs. Nanak composed his teachings in the form of songs and hymns that were sung by the community. Thus, the corporate singing of praise (*kirtan*) gained great importance in the *panth* or *sangat*. Wherever he went he established *sangats* or "holy fellowships," congregating for prayer and sitting together and sharing a common meal without any distinctions.[17]

Sikhism took shape as a religion over a period of two centuries from the first to the last *guru*. Although the teachings of Guru Nanak constitute the primary spiritual content of Sikhism, a more formalized structure of the movement took shape during the time of his successors as well as in subsequent reform movements within Sikhism. According to McLeod three events are of fundamental importance in this evolution. The first came in Guru Nanak's selection of a successor to lead the community, which led

---

15. H. S. Bhatia, "Sikhism and Sri Guru Granth Sahib," *Journal of Dharma* 21, no. 4 (October–December 1996): 383.

16. Talib, "Sikhism," 148–152.

17. McLeod, *Exploring Sikhism*, 50–52.

to the continuity of leadership. The second event was the compilation of the canonical scripture by the fifth *guru*, Guru Arjun in 1603–1604. This gave a permanency to the teachings of the *gurus*. The third event was the founding of the *khalsa* by Guru Gobind Singh in 1699.[18] It was a new martial order within Sikhism. Sikhs who joined in the order were expected to maintain a strict code of discipline[19] that touched on outward appearance, social obligation and ritual observances. They are initiated into the order through a special initiation ceremony.[20] Male Sikhs belonging to this order are given the surname Singh. They are also identified by their uncut hair and the wearing of the turban.[21]

Bakht Singh in England (1926) to India (1933)

Bakht Singh was attracted to the European lifestyle in England, and soon he tried to adopt it. With his exposure to western culture and education, he claimed to have become an atheist and a free thinker.[22] He gave up his Sikh identity of uncut hair and turban, and began to live an extravagant lifestyle of smoking, drinking and visiting different places for sightseeing. However, this adopted lifestyle later made him think once again of his life and the need of true happiness. He began questioning people on whether

---

18. W. H. McLeod, *Guru Nanak and the Sikh Religion* (New Delhi: Oxford University Press, 1998), 1–2.

19. A Sikh should rise up early in the morning, and after taking a bath should observe *nam japa* by meditating on God. They are to recite early morning, evening and a concluding prayer every day. Since Gurus' Words are best experienced in a religious assembly, each Sikh should, therefore, join in *sangat* worship, and draw inspiration from the scriptures in the presence of the *sangat*.

20. W. H. McLeod, *Textual Sources for the Study of Sikhism* (Totowa, NJ: Barnes & Noble, 1984), 71.

21. *Khalsa* is a voluntary order and not all Sikhs joined this order. Those who did not join the *khalsa* and did not keep the external code of uncut hair are known as *Sahajdhari* Sikhs. Sikhs with uncut hair are known as *Kes-dhari* Sikhs. Many Sikhs observe the requirement concerning the *Kes* without receiving a formal initiation as a member of the *khalsa*. See Harjot Oberoi, "Popular Saints, Goddesses, and Village Sacred Sites: Rereading Sikh experience in the 19th Century," in *History of Religions* 31, (1992), 363–384.

22. Bakht Singh, *Looking unto Jesus*, 4th ed. (Hyderabad: Hebron, 2005), 45.

or not they were happy, and he realized that culture and education could not solve the problem of evil.[23]

In 1928, Bakht Singh visited Canada with a group of students and he stayed there for three months. In order to join his friends in all their activities and also to see the first-class dining saloon on the ship, he attended a Christian service that was held there. When the congregation knelt for prayer, he did not want to kneel down. He thought, "These people do not know anything about religion. They have exploited my country and I have seen them eating and drinking. What do they know? After all, my religion is the best religion." However, "breaking his national, intellectual and religious pride," he claimed that he knelt down out of courtesy.[24] As he knelt down, Bakht Singh realized that some divine power had entered him. As a result, he was filled with joy, the name of Jesus became sweet, he would later write, and for the first time he felt he was one with the Europeans. After this experience, when he returned to England, the joyless faces of the members of the church he had once attended, kept him from going to a church, or from sharing his experience with anyone.[25]

Bakht Singh returned to Canada for a degree in Agricultural Engineering in 1929. While he was there he borrowed a New Testament from a friend. While reading the Gospel of John chapter 3, he was caught by the words of Jesus, "Verily, verily I say unto you." He was convicted of his sin and heard a voice that said, "This is my body broken for you, this is my blood shed for the remission of your sins." He came to view this personal encounter with Christ as the point at which he truly became a Christian.[26]

From 1930 to 1933 Bakht Singh stayed in Canada with John and Edith Hayward. The Haywards became the first Christians or spiritual mentors that discipled Bakht Singh. They belonged to the Christian and Missionary Alliance church.[27] Bakht Singh made the best use of the Haywards' library. In 1932, he claimed to have had an encounter with God in which he

---

23. Bakht Singh, *The Skill of His Loving Hands* (Bombay: Gospel Literature Service, 1975), 6–11.
24. Ibid., 13.
25. Ibid., 13–15.
26. Ibid., 16–18.
27. Koshy, *Brother Bakht Singh of India*, 91.

surrendered himself for the work of ministry in India. According to his testimony, Bakht Singh heard a voice saying:

> I accept you for my service on three conditions: withdraw all your claims to your father's property in Punjab, and never tell any man about your material and financial needs by letter or by suggestion of any kind. Tell it only to Me. Do not join any society, but serve all people equally, wherever I send you. Do not make your plans, but let Me lead you day by day.[28]

With this divine call, he dedicated himself to the work of the ministry and he began to work among the internationals and nationals, preaching the gospel.

Beginnings of Ministry in India

When Singh returned to India in 1933, his family initially disowned him because of his conversion.[29] He stayed in Bombay for some time, distributing tracts on the streets and doing personal evangelism. While he was there, Bakht Singh met Mr Warner the superintendent of the Methodist Mission in Bombay. Warner received him cordially and gave him a place to stay and invited him to preach in the meetings in several places. Warner also introduced Singh to Bishop Bradley who in turn introduced him in different parts of India and particularly the Sialkot convention held in Sialkot, Punjab.[30] With the invitation of his sister, who did not know about his conversion, Bakht Singh went to Karachi and began his ministry, distributing tracts and gospel portions. Later, he ministered as an itinerant evangelist among the denominational churches in North India. He was well received by most of the denominations at that time, and was invited as a preacher to their conventions and churches. During 1934–1936, Bakht Singh worked

---

28. Ibid., 113.

29. His parents wanted him to keep his conversion a secret. They left him because he declined. His open preaching in Karachi led to a family gathering, and later he was accepted by the family. His wife along with his son left him and never returned. His father became a Christian and was baptized by Bakht Singh. Most of his siblings continued in their own faith.

30. Koshy, *Brother Bakht Singh of India*, 121–122.

as a licensed preacher of the Church Missionary Society (CMS)[31] church in Karachi. With the converts from his ministry he formed a team who worked along with him in their spare time. At the end of 1936, Bakht Singh, along with Chandy, a customs officer from South India, left CMS "because they could not work under the system."[32] Later, he began to work independently with the denominational churches.

While he was ministering in the denominational churches, Bakht Singh became well acquainted with the problems within the denominational churches and the state of Christianity in India. Through his ministry in a Christian village in Uttar Pradesh, a major revival took place where there had been bitter rivalry between two groups in the church. After these meetings, the two groups confessed their sins and were reconciled. This revival soon spread to other villages also.[33]

Bakht Singh became increasingly critical of the denominational church leaders for their callousness in not meeting the needs of their people. As Eleanore Llewellyn described it, "The leaders of the church: pastors, teachers, and missionaries who have become self-indulgent, careless, lazy – who did not feed the sheep – have felt the scorn of his eloquence. His youth has made his criticism hard to take, true though it has been."[34]

Along with these experiences in the churches, when Bakht Singh tried to give a tract to a Hindu in Karachi, he was challenged to show this Hindu one good Christian in the entire town of Karachi. If he could do it, the man said that he would become a Christian. Bakht Singh would later claim that this incident laid the foundation for the focus of his ministry to teach the importance of prayer, the word of God and Christian life. He believed that the lack of dependence upon the Word was one of the causes for strife and spiritual barrenness among Christians.[35] This would become a continuous refrain in his sermons and writings regarding the lack of spirituality in the lives of Christians in India.

---

31. According to Eleanore H. Llewellyn, Bakht Singh was an evangelist who was licensed by the church of India, Burma and Ceylon. Llewellyn, "Bakht Singh of India," 86.

32. Koshy, *Brother Bakht Singh of India*, 137.

33. Bakht Singh, *Return of God's Glory* (Hyderabad: Hebron, 2006), 7–8; See Koshy, *Brother Bakht Singh of India*, 158–167.

34. Llewellyn, "Bakht Singh of India," 87.

35. Bakht Singh, *Return*, 68–69.

During the 1930s when Bakht Singh was personally dealing with the issues in the denominational churches and the state of Christianity in India, Indian Christians at large, and leaders and theologians of the mainline churches in particular, began to grapple with the alien form of Christianity that had been introduced into India. From the 1920s onward, Indian nationalism and its freedom struggle were at their height. The loyalties of Indian Christians were questioned by the general public because of their religious association and identity with the colonizers. Against this backdrop of the national movement in India, Christians felt the tension between their pride of being Indians, and their acceptance of the religion of their colonial rulers. Their identity with the religion of their colonial rulers caused conflict between their new religion, and the inherited indigenous culture and spirituality which determined their Indianness.[36] Along with its image of being foreign, Christianization, viewed culturally, simply meant Europeanization or westernization. Moreover, the awareness of the inappropriateness of worship, theology, structures and leadership of the church in the Indian context brought with it a deep consciousness of the need for a form of Christianity that was distinctly Indian. The process of developing an Indian identity of the church and Christianity resulted in the effort to indigenize the faith. It happened at various levels, from the leadership, which would eventually become Indian, to worship as it came to be practiced in the life and liturgy of the church, to the identity of the Christian community.

The Process of Making Christianity Indian

Leadership

Empowered by the zeal of nationalism and the newly found faith that was defined by the gospel of liberation, Indian Christians began to resist the hegemony and dominance of missionaries in the church. The first person to contest the missionary domination in the 1850s was Lal Behari Day, a church leader from Bengal. Day, who was ordained as a minister in the Free

---

36. J. W. Gladstone, "Mission and Evangelism in India: Historical Perspectives," in *The Community We Seek: Perspectives on Mission,* ed. Jesudas M. Athyal (Tiruvalla: Christava Sahitya Samithi, 2003), 132.

Church of Scotland in India, demanded that he and his Indian colleagues be recognized as having equal status on par with their fellow European clergymen.[37] The assertion of Indian leadership in the mission became one of the Indian identities of the church in the beginning.

The movement that started within the missions as a result of Day's protest, extended to the notion of forming an Indian or national church. This resulted in some initial experiments, such as Christo Samaj, in Calcutta.[38] The movement continued to intensify along with the secular nationalist movement. As part of the assertion that Indian Christians should make Christianity Indian and national, several independent Indian organizations and publications were established.[39] According to T. V. Philip, the "indigenization in church government, in worship, in theology and in several other aspects of the churches life" happened during the first half of the twentieth century.[40]

The Indianization of church government or polity eventually resulted in the formation of the united churches, that is, the Church of South India and the Church of North India, and it contributed to the autonomy of the Indian churches of the "great tradition." In other words, having been liberated from the alien rule of missionaries, which was described as "missionary imperialism," Indians were able to govern themselves. While one group of Indian Christians strove towards self-governance, another group endeavored to make Christian theology Indian.

Theology

With the realization that the creeds, confessions and doctrinal statements of the mainline churches were alien to the Indian religious tradition, Indian

---

37. See Sisir Kumar Das, *The Shadow of the Cross* (New Delhi: Munshiram Manoharlal Publishers,1974), 55–56; George Thomas, *Christian Indians and Indian Nationalism 1885–1950: An Interpretation in Historical and Theological Perspectives* (Frankfurt: Verlag Peter D. Lang, 1979), 66.

38. Thomas, *Christian Indians*, 68–84.

39. For example, "The Bengal Christian Association for the Promotion of Christian Truth and Godliness, and the Protection of the Rights of Indian Christians," and "Bengali Christian Conference"; Newspapers – "The Indian Christian Herald," "The Christian Patriot." See Kaj Baago, *Pioneers of Indigenous Christianity* (Madras: CISRS & CLS, 1969), 2–10.

40. T. V. Philip, "Protestant Christianity in India since 1858," in *Christianity in India*, edited by H. C. Perumalil and Hambye (Alleppy: Prakasam Publications, 1972), 283.

Christians attempted to relate, communicate and understand the gospel by using Indian philosophical categories and thought forms. During the nineteenth century the attitude of the missionaries regarding theology was that "the theology of the sending churches from the West should be reproduced in India and that those who were won over from Hinduism should sever all connection with their former religion."[41] Missionaries like William Miller, and J. N. Farquhar, however, thought that such a severance was not necessary, and that Christianity could be understood in Hindu thought forms.[42]

In the last quarter of the nineteenth century and early twentieth century, Indians such as Brahmabandhab Upadhyaya, A. S. Appasamy, and Sadhu Sundar Singh began to develop an Indian theology viewed through the lens of Indian philosophy and culture. The "Madras Rethinking Group," a group of Indian Christian thinkers, strove especially hard to develop a Christian theology, "which could express the truth and meaning of the gospel, Christian life and experience against the background of indigenous thought and life, independent of western formulations of doctrine."[43] Famous among this group were the Indian Christian theologians, P. Chenchiah, V. Chekkarai and A. J. Appasamy. Thus theologizing from an Indian perspective became an ongoing process as Indians continued to relate the gospel to their own Indian soil. In the 1970s, the assertion made by the Dalit and Tribal Christians, and women in the Indian church, resulted in the development of the respective theologies and forms of Christianity.[44]

Worship and Structures

In the philosophical and religious thought of India, the idea of having an "experience of God" was far more important than any idea of the institution. In fact, "Hinduism never had the consciousness of being a church as it is understood by western Christians. For the Hindus, the creeds,

---

41. Robin H. S. Boyd, *An Introduction to Indian Christian Theology* (Madras: Christian Literature Society, 1969), 88, 89.

42. Boyd, *An Introduction*, 89.

43. Philip, "Protestant Christianity," 291.

44. Since the later developments of theology do not fall in the purview of the dissertation, they are just mentioned. Several monographs have been written in the last two decades on this subject. For example, see A. P. Nirmal, *A Reader in Dalit Theology* (Madras: Gurukul, 1992); V. Devasahayam, *Frontiers of Dalit Theology* (Madras: Gurukul, 1996).

confessions and institutional church represent a low form of religious development."[45] It was into this context that the church was introduced. In addition to the insertion of this new concept of religion as institution, the existence of numerous denominations with their subsequent rivalries, the troublesome emphasis on Episcopal ministry during the union negotiations, and the frequent and innumerable court cases over Episcopal elections, undermined the value of the concept of church. The problems that arose as a result of these new realities also resulted in many converts embracing what might be called "churchless" Christianity as well as other indigenous forms that did not bear the name "church." Thus it was observed, "To the ancient world, the offence of Christianity was the cross, today in East Asia the offence is the church. Its alien character and its intimate association with the West largely account for this attitude."[46] The notion that Christianity was western, the replacement of certain social customs with "customs of questionable value" as in the areas of food, dress and family life, and disregard for certain lasting values of Indian culture and tradition by the Christians, alienated Christians from the social mainstream. In the church, the paternalistic attitude of the missionaries, their hegemony, the structural hierarchy, and formalism reinforced the perception that the church was as dominant and exploitative as the Indian social system was. T. V. Phillip points out:

> (J)ust as the Brahmins defined their own rights and powers, it was the councils or synods of clerics in the church which defined their own powers and privileges . . . Christian ministry in the church and the mission is often associated with power and prestige.[47]

Eddy Asirvatham has also noted that the reaction of second generation Christians to the church hierarchy was that some of them vowed never to enter a mission or church service again.[48]

---

45. T. V. Philip, "Theological Tradition in India," *ICHR* 21, no. 1 (June 1987): 31.

46. Rajah B. Manikam, ed., *Christianity and the Asian Revolution* (Madras: Joint East Asia Secretariat of the International Missionary Council and the WCC, 1954), 216.

47. Philip, "Theological Tradition," 48.

48. Eddy Asirvatham, *Christianity in the Indian Crucible* (Calcutta: YMCA Publishing, 1957), 57.

As aliens, both in the society and in the church, the situation of the Indian Christians became precarious. Within that context they could neither own nor disown the church. P. Chenchaiah, an Indian Christian theologian during this period, advocated "churchless" Christianity, viewing the institutional church as a hindrance to the gospel.[49] He contended that, "an all-powerful organization dominating religious life is repugnant to Hindu instinct . . . Hinduism has rejected after due deliberation the ideas that lie behind the church – as detrimental to true growth in religion – as fatal to the freedom and liberty of the soul."[50] For instance, in the state of Andhra Pradesh in southern India, even before Chenchaiah advocated churchless Christianity, Subba Rao, who became a convert through a vision of Christ, decided that the churches were merely ceremonial, and as a result he totally rejected them. He once commented on his own church attendance, "Had I continued going, I would have forgotten Christ long ago, for the churches won't tell us anything about Christ. They tell us about a religion called Christianity."[51] It is evident that all of them were reacting to the institutional, hegemonic, and hierarchical form of the church.

In order to make the church relevant to the Indian understanding, attempts were made to Indianize worship patterns. The Indianization of worship within the institutional churches was mostly at the experimental level, taking place within the theological seminaries or at Christian conference centers. There was reluctance on the part of the westernized urban congregations to introduce Indian ways of worship into their liturgical life. They continued to maintain western ways of worship inherited from the missionaries.[52] In the village churches, however, Indian music was frequently used. The congregation left their sandals outside, and sat on the floor.

---

49. While Chenchaiah advocated churchless Christianity, a study by Herbert E. Hoefer on Madras Christianity entitled *Churchless Christianity* (Pasadena, CA: William Carey Library, 1991) actually reveals the existence of believers, who he terms as "Non-Baptised Believers in Christ" equal to the number of professing Christians in Madras.

50. Cited, Duncan B. Forrester, *Caste and Christianity* (London: Center for South Asian Studies School of Oriental and African Studies, 1980), 182.

51. Kaj Baago, *The Movement around Subba Rao* (Madras: CLS, 1968), 8.

52. R. H. S. Boyd, *India and the Latin Captivity of the Church: The Cultural Context of the Gospel* (London: Cambridge University Press, 1974), 16.

Certain Indian festivals, and religious and cultural practices were incorporated into their Christian lives and practices as well.[53]

Parallel to the Indianization within the mainline churches, independent Indian churches were soon established.[54] Several individuals started churches based on the Indian religious and cultural traditions. Sattam Pillai established the Hindu Christian Church of the Lord Jesus Christ in Tamilnadu as early as 1857, as an assertion and empowerment of the local Christian community against the ethical and racial discrimination of the missionaries in the churches. According to Vincent Kumaradoss, "Sattam Pillai's first move was to delegitimize western Christianity and to establish it as a counterfeit."[55]

Another such move was made by O. Kandaswamy Chetti, who did not identify himself as a Christian,[56] but founded what he called the Fellowship of the Followers of Jesus, in Madras.[57] Parani Andy's National Church of Madras was an assertion of the Asiatic origin of Christianity, and the irrelevancy of the western denominations that had their roots in the political revolutions and dissensions in Europe.[58] In Andhra Pradesh, Fr. M. Devadas established the Bible Mission, breaking away from the Andhra Evangelical Lutheran Church. With the Bakht Singh movement, the number of independent churches in South India mushroomed, especially in Andhra Pradesh, from the second half of the twentieth century.

---

53. See P. Y. Luke and John B. Carman, *Village Christians and Hindu Culture: Rural Churches in South India* (New York: Friendship Press, 1968).

54. Early indigenous efforts of missionaries like Robert de Nobili, Ziegenbalg and others do not fall in the purview of the study. The concentration of the study is on the Indian churches established by Indians.

55. Y. Vincent Kumaradoss, "Creation of Alternative Public Spheres and the Church Indigenization in the Nineteenth Century Colonial Tamilnadu: The Hindu Christian Church of Lord Jesus Christ and the National Church of India," in *Christianity Is Indian: The Emergence of an Indigenous Community*, ed. Roger E. Hedlund (Delhi: ISPCK, 2004), 7.

56. See O. Kandaswami Chetti, "'Why I Am Not a Christian': A Personal Statement," in *Pioneers of Indigenous Christianity*, ed. Kaj Baago (Madras: CISRS & CLS, 1969), 207–214.

57. Hedlund, *Quest*, 68.

58. Baago, *Pioneers*, 7–8.

The Situation of the Denominational Churches in the 1930s and 1940s

The denominational churches viewed the independent churches as sectarian and labeled them "groups" and "sheep stealers," denying them status as churches. Describing the attitude of the members of the denominational churches towards these independent churches, P. Solomon Raj wrote, "Until very recently, those of us who belonged to the denominational churches had a very guilty feeling if we had anything to do with these groups. Even sitting in their prayer meetings was sometimes considered to be an act of unfaithfulness to one's own church."[59]

The common people in the denominational churches were left in a quandary as to how to respond to all the confusion. To add to the confusion of the common person's faith, the coming of "liberal theology" and the debates over the core issues of faith in some of the denominational churches engendered the teachings of the denominational churches questionable. People began to seek alternate ways of making sense of their faith, either by gathering informally as groups to study the Bible, or by attending other churches,[60] where they found spiritual nurture.

In the mid-1930s, some evangelists visited Madras and conducted "gospel meetings." These meetings were influential in encouraging young men of different denominations to participate in gospel work, particularly street preaching. This resulted in the formation of the "Gospel League" in 1935. The League was an informal group of believers from different denominations, committed to the service of the Lord through street preaching, conducting Bible studies, etc.[61] This movement led to some conversions, and consequently the spread of the ministry in Madras.

One of the issues that created a flurry within the Christian population of Madras was a report that appeared in a daily newspaper. In 1938, a newspaper, *The Mail*, published an article titled, "Doctrine in the Church of England" as though it were the official doctrinal statement of the

---

59. P. Solomon Raj, *A Christian Folk Religion in India* (Frankfurt: Verlag Peter Lang, 1986), 11.

60. The other independent churches are mostly Pentecostal and charismatic.

61. Rayappan R. Rajamani, *Monsoon Daybreak* (London: Open Books, 1971), 45–51.

Church of England. This statement raised questions regarding the cardinal doctrines of the church such as the virgin birth of Jesus. It was actually the report of the Archbishop's Commission on Christian Doctrine. While this report naturally agitated the general populace, the official response from the churches in India was minimal. Although the Bishop of Madras wrote an explanation[62] stating that the position stated in the article was not official doctrine, but rather, was only a report sent to the Archbishops for consideration, the issue triggered doubts in the minds of Christians about the leadership of the denominational churches.[63] Explaining the reaction of the public to this, Rajamani reported, "Many true Christians throughout South India (where they have long been identified as "Bible-folk" by those of other faiths) were profoundly shaken by this report." He further stated that "the impression created on the minds both of Christian believers and of unbelievers was a simple one: the foundations of our faith were being undermined by those who held the positions of highest authority."[64] Added to this, during the Church Union negotiations, the preoccupation of the leaders was more on the structures or episcopacy of the church than it was on the ministry being offered for the needs of the people. Furthermore, the church-centered view of mission and the emphasis on structures and social justice in the 1938 Tambaram World Missionary Conference undermined the importance of evangelism and personal conversion in the ministry of the churches.[65]

When the core doctrines of their faith were questioned by the very teachers of the faith, with the accompanying onslaught of modernism and exposure to liberal doctrines, the predicament of regular church-going Christians was not addressed by the churches. A study on the doctrine of ministry in the denominational churches would later note that, "In fact, it could be argued that the Indian pattern had no doctrine of ministry at all, at least not a doctrine which was in any way consistent with the theological

---

62. See "Report of the Commission on Christian Doctrine," *The Madras Diocesan Magazine* 33, no. 2 (February 1938): 55–56.

63. Rajamani, *Monsoon Daybreak* (London: Open Books, 1971), 55–57.

64. Ibid., 56–57.

65. T. V. Philip, *Edinburgh to Salvador Twentieth Century Ecumenical Missiology: A Historical Study of the Ecumenical Discussions on Mission* (Delhi: CSS & ISPCK, 1999), 97–98.

presuppositions of the sending churches."[66] The ordained ministry in the churches had become more a position of authority and power than a position of function and service. The function of the pastors revolved around the administration of the churches and the administration of the sacraments. The real pastoral work, the work of spiritually nurturing the congregations was grossly neglected.[67] Thus, people began to seek meaning outside the institutional churches by forming into groups where they could devote themselves to Bible study and prayer. The ministry of the itinerant independent evangelists helped to quench their spiritual hunger. Bakht Singh arrived in Madras at precisely the time when the people were most confused and hungry in their spiritual quest.

The Beginning of the Assemblies

In 1938, Bakht Singh went to Madras as a result of an invitation from D. Samuel who belonged to a group called the "One by One Band." Singh met him while he was ministering in North India.[68] Singh preached for nineteen days in the denominational churches where he was initially well received. In these meetings he emphasized the importance of prayer and the word of God. Bakht Singh insisted that all participants should bring their Bibles to the meetings and should not be ashamed of carrying them. He conducted all-night prayer meetings in Madras, which was something new for the churches there. He emphasized personal salvation and the need for every one to be born again. This resulted in a revival within the churches.

As a result of these meetings, Bible study groups were organized and people became involved in open-air preaching and cottage meetings. R. Rajamani and R. P. Dorairaj, who belonged to the denominational churches, were actively involved in the gospel ministry. They had been disappointed and disillusioned both because of problems they faced in their ministries, and because of the Archbishop's report. As a result of the ministry of Bakht Singh, they renewed their commitment to the ministry and joined D. Samuel in the follow-up work that Bakht Singh left for them.

---

66. Bergquist and Manickam, *Crisis of Dependency*, 24.
67. Ibid., 25–27.
68. Rajamani, *Monsoon Daybreak* (London: Open Books, 1971), 61.

D. Samuel also invited Alfred J. Flack and C. Raymond Golsworthy from Nilgiris to help in the follow-up work. Both of these men were missionaries from the Honor Oak Fellowship in London. They conducted Bible studies, retreats, and Saturday night prayers in different churches. As the revival continued, Bakht Singh again visited Madras in 1940.[69]

On this second trip to Madras, Bakht Singh stayed for three months, once again preaching in the churches. Rajamani and Dorairaj worked closely with him and were joined by George T. Rajaratnam who had been born again through the ministry of Bakht Singh. Singh preached in the denominational churches throughout the city. Once again he conducted all-night prayer meetings and gospel processions in the city. He organized a bonfire to burn books, magazines and other things which were considered to be displeasing to God. Bakht Singh emphasized the concept of living a Christian life separated from the world. At the end of his campaign Bakht Singh organized a "love feast" for all the churches.[70]

Two incidents that took place during the meetings in Madras provoked the leaders of the denominational churches against Bakht Singh. Singh required that children sit in the church sanctuary, and he moved the traditional benches aside in the church in order to make room for more people. The people then sat on the floor. This was considered a desecration of the church. Some of the church elders reported it to the bishop, who did not at first intervene. Bakht Singh continued to minister in the church for two weeks. He further challenged the elders by preaching, "Bishop or no bishop, the Lord has sent me to preach and I must deliver his message. Do not you adults smoke and indulge in other vices that defile the house of God far more grievously than does the presence of these innocent children?"[71] Moreover, he vehemently preached against corruption which had entered the churches. The other incident came about when a Hindu girl from Madras who received Christ in the meetings, and some men who traveled

---

69. Ibid., 60–66.
70. Bakht Singh, "A Prepared Place and a Prepared People," *Hebron Messenger (Part IV), Special Issue for Silver Jubilee of "Jehovah –Shammah,"* no. 14 (3 July 1966): 5–6.
71. Rajamani, *Monsoon Daybreak* (London: Open Books, 1971), 67.

with Bakht Singh from Punjab, requested Bakht Singh to baptize them. He baptized them in a Baptist church without making it a public event.[72]

Bakht Singh returned to North India after the Madras campaign. In 1941, on his way to Coonoor, Bakht Singh once again wanted to visit Madras. Enthusiastic about his arrival, Rajamani and his friends wanted to conduct a meeting. They were elders of various local churches. In preparation, they approached a local church pastor for permission for Bakht Singh to once again hold some meetings in a local church building. But this time they were informed by pastors regarding a resolution that stated, "We in the Indian Ministers' Conference have met and passed a resolution never again to make any place available to this Punjabi preacher. Our objection is that he is not an ordained minister, and therefore had no right to baptize anyone."[73] Pained by the denial of a place and after much consideration, three of them tendered resignation to their membership in their respective churches. When Bakht Singh arrived, Rajamani informed Bakht Singh about the resignations. Singh responded with, "You should not have done that." Rajamani's then asked, "What then would you have done?" Bakht Singh knelt and prayed aloud in the restaurant in which they had met.[74] The result was that this small group of men requested that Bakht Singh conduct a gospel campaign in a premises that was not related to the churches. Bakht Singh notes that the opposition of the denominational churches had intensified the zeal of the believers, and their mood was on the verge of developing competition and rivalry.[75] As a result, Bakht Singh declined to hold a campaign. One evening, however, they arranged an informal meeting in a church where the pastor took the risk of giving them permission.

This situation made it clear to Bakht Singh that he should give serious thought not only to his next step, but also about the future of the people who took a stand in Madras for his sake. Bakht Singh then proceeded to Coonoor where he spent two months seeking God's guidance regarding "his [God's] solution to the problem of follow up, and especially, his perfect plan for his work in Madras." Fred Flack and Raymond Golsworthy

---

72. Ibid., 69–71.
73. Ibid., 76.
74. Ibid., 77–78.
75. Singh, "A Prepared Place," 6.

joined him in prayer along with some of his friends who accompanied him from North India. Bakht Singh had known Flack and Golsworthy before. In 1940, when he went to Coonoor for a YMCA meeting, Flack and Golsworthy met him. Lady Daisy Ogle, another missionary from the Honor Oak Christian Fellowship, was in charge of a missionary center in Coonoor. She invited Bakht Singh for tea. This acquaintance with these missionaries turned in to a spiritual partnership in the ministry.[76]

Describing how God convinced him about his future action, Bakht Singh wrote:

> We continued waiting upon the Lord; but for many days He gave us no answer. Then, one sleepless night, I prayed, "Lord, I promise Thee I will pay the price and obey Thee fully . . . Though every avenue of my present ministry close, and I be misunderstood on every hand, I am ready, at any price, to do Thy will." As I uttered these words, I heard a voice, "Behold I make a covenant, I will do marvels!" (Exod 34:10).

Bakht Singh was further convinced of his next step when he read Acts 26:19 – "I was not disobedient unto the heavenly vision" and Acts 28:30–31, "Paul dwelt two whole years in his own hired house and received all that came unto him, preaching those things which concern the Lord Jesus Christ, with all confidence."[77] Shortly thereafter, Singh arrived in Madras along with his friends. They initially rented a small house and conducted Sunday gatherings and informal meetings with people who came to see them. Later they moved to a place that is now called Jehovah Shammah, which means "The Lord is there" (Ezek 48:35), on the 12th of July 1941. Thus, the Assembly came into being.

Assemblies

The Assemblies claim that they were established according to the pattern of the New Testament church, based upon Acts 2:42. The apostles' doctrine, fellowship, the breaking of bread, and prayer are the four main features

---

76. Alfred J. (Fred) Flack, telephone interview by author, 16 November 2006.
77. Singh, "A Prepared Place," 6–7.

emphasized by the Assemblies. These four aspects of the community are viewed as the binding factors for their unity.[78]

The prominence that Bakht Singh gave to the Bible was unparalleled in the Indian church. Bakht Singh and the congregation members were known for their knowledge of the biblical text. Bible verses are written on the walls or hung as banners in and around the prayer hall. Assemblies are centered on the word of God because Bakht Singh always claimed the authority of the Bible over the church. He emphasized the need of having a personal experience with God and a life that is controlled and led by the voice and will of God.

Most of the practices in the institutional church, which the Indian Christians recognized as offensive to Indian religious worldview and mindset, were addressed by Bakht Singh in very practical ways. Before entering the Assembly congregation members were invited to leave their footwear outside the worship area at a separate place allotted for it. The congregation sat on mats or carpets spread on the floor in the prayer hall. Indian musical instruments were used. Lyrics were composed, based on biblical texts and set to Indian tunes. The order of the service was generally divided into three parts: worship (a free time of individual praise and adoration), Table fellowship, and the message. Most of the time, the service lasted two to three hours. Bakht Singh introduced the practice of love feast following the Sunday service. The Assemblies also became the main training centers for members, and especially for those who dedicated themselves to full-time Christian ministry. Physical work in the Assemblies like cooking, cleaning, and serving was done by the members. Irrespective of their status, all were expected to take part in this activity as part of their training in service, fellowship, and humility. The members were known for their piety and devotion to the word of God.

The architecture of the Assemblies was Indian and does not follow the architectural pattern of the western church. Buildings were plain, ordinary buildings with a big hall for worship. The congregation took part in the construction of their Assembly buildings. No religious art or symbols were to be kept in the Assembly, but the walls were decorated with Bible verses.

---

78. Bakht Singh, *God's Dwelling Place* (Mumbai: Gospel Literature Service, 1957), 122.

These practices, first implemented by Bakht Singh, continue more or less unchanged in the present.

The Spread of the Movement

Bakht Singh was fully supported by the local leaders who joined him. Most of them were employed in secular jobs, but they joined with him in the evenings for evangelistic work and the development of the ministry. They became involved in open-air preaching, gospel campaigns, and in conducting Bible studies. In December 1941, Bakht Singh organized a holy convocation in Madras in order to bring people from different parts of the country to a common place for fellowship. He always understood these holy convocations as being one of the sources that stood behind the spread of the ministry. He affirmed:

> The fellowship and ministry of the Word during those meetings were so strengthening and refreshing that people began begging us to conduct similar Holy Convocations in other places. People of all classes coming from so many different places and countries enlarged our vision and understanding of His Church, and opened doors to us for ministry in almost every country of the world.[79]

The "Gospel raids," which he conducted in different places outside Madras, furthered the movement. Bakht Singh would take a team of believers, both men and women, to a particular village where they engaged in open-air preaching. They would go in a procession carrying cloth banners with gospel texts in bold letters stitched on them. They sang songs, knelt on the streets for prayer, shared the Word at different corners in the main streets of the village, sold gospel portions, and distributed tracts. Seekers were invited for a gospel meeting in the evening, or they were ministered to more personally. Some of the team members stayed back to do follow-up work by conducting Bible studies and prayer meetings. Thus the group

---

79. Singh, "A Prepared Place," 7.

that was formed in that village would initially gather for Bible study, and eventually take the shape of an Assembly.[80]

People from other parts of the country who visited Jehovah Shammah began to invite Bakht Singh to their places for ministry as well. Those who had experienced spiritual blessing or physical healing were especially persistent in their requests that he should go to their places. Along with the "Gospel raids," ministry in Andhra Pradesh started through the invitation of individuals who were blessed by his ministry. In 1944, Bakht Singh went to Cuddapah, a town in Andhra Pradesh, to visit a family that had been inviting him for a long time. His ministry to them resulted in conversion of the entire family. With this contact, Bakht Singh conducted a "gospel raid" in the town, which eventually resulted in the starting of the Assemblies in Andhra Pradesh.[81] The work in Hyderabad was the result of a persistent invitation of one family and some believers, who were born again through the ministry, and praying that he should visit that place.

In 1950, after he had completed the campaigns in several parts of Andhra, Bakht Singh and some of his team proceeded to Hyderabad. The people who invited Bakht Singh arranged meetings in a Baptist church in Secunderabad. After few days of meetings, Bakht Singh baptized some believers who had already been baptized as infants in the denominational churches. This caused contention with the denominational churches in the area and they refused to allow him to use their premises for any further meetings. Bakht Singh continued his ministry for some more days in the grounds that were usually used by the Nizam, the ruler of Hyderabad state, at that time. To support the believers in the area who had cast their lot with him, Bakht Singh rented a small house and began to conduct Sunday services there. Later they moved on to a larger facility. It was here that Bakht Singh became convinced that the place was given to him for the ministry, not merely for Hyderabad, but for the whole of India. The name given to the first Assembly building there was "Elim."

In 1959, the Assembly moved to a permanent place which they named "Hebron." This became the headquarters of the movement and the

---

80. Bakht Singh, "The Work is Great," *Hebron Messenger, Special Issue (Part II) for Silver Jubilee of "Jehovah-Shammah,"* (24 July 1966): 6.

81. Bakht Singh, "Write the Vision," (Unpublished Manuscript), 17.

Assemblies.[82] The largest number of these Assemblies is in Andhra Pradesh. The movement continued to spread throughout India and to other countries such as the USA, Australia, France, and certain Middle Eastern countries. In the latter half of the twentieth century, Bakht Singh Assemblies were considered to be the fastest growing churches in India. As already mentioned, the movement began as a collective endeavor of lay Christians or Christians from the historic denominational churches, who were seeking for meaning and nurture in their spiritual journey, under the leadership of an evangelist whose primary focus until then had been leading people to Christ through a born-again experience. Now, Bakht Singh was confronted with the challenge of establishing a church, which also meant that he had to study and understand the meaning of the term "church."

Having been exposed to Christianity and the churches in the West and also to Christianity and churches that had been transplanted into India, Bakht Singh searched the Scriptures in order to find an Indian form of Christianity that was devoid of the elements of foreignness and structures that bound the spirituality of the people. He turned towards what he believed to be the New Testament pattern of churches, and to his own Indian spirituality. It appears that Bakht Singh was aided by his personal religious upbringing to equip the Assemblies with Indianness that was missing in the historic denominational churches. Bakht Singh strongly emphasized the spiritual life, both in the Assemblies and in the individual believer. In developing his ministry, he sought the help of Flack and Golsworthy, who assisted him in the follow-up work. They also assisted Bakht Singh in his understanding of the concept of the church.[83] Bakht Singh claimed that he followed the "New Testament pattern churches" based upon the Scriptures. Was Bakht Singh the only person who believed that he followed the New

---

82. Koshy, *Brother Bakht Singh of India*, 285–295.

83. In his letter to Koshy, Golsworthy mentions how Bakht Singh always appreciated their role in "confirming and clarifying that larger "CHURCH–VISION" which God was *already* putting in *his* heart, and which later found such a fuller expression throughout the land." Raymond Golsworthy, Carina, Australia, to (T. E. Koshy, Syracuse, USA), 6 April 2000. Flack mentions that they had assisted him in shaping the church but it was a totally indigenous work where they were privileged to work. A. J. (Fred) Flack, Sidmouth, Devon, UK to (Bharathi, Pasadena, CA, USA), 13 December 2006. He also mentioned in the telephone interview that Bakht Singh was the leader and they only followed him. A. J. (Fred) Flack, interview by author, telephone, 16 November 2006.

Testament pattern for the church and for spiritual life? If there were other similar churches and movements, were they related to him, and if so how were they related to him? Finally how were the Assemblies unique? It is to such questions that we now turn our attention.

CHAPTER 3

The Phenomenon of Spiritual Life Churches

Bakht Singh's movement in India was not an isolated event in Christian history. It was part of the global movements of the early twentieth-century Christianity. During the same period, several independent movements arose in different parts of the world. These movements were connected to each other by virtue of cross-fertilization of ideas as well as extensive evangelistic and missionary activity that took place during this time.

The Keswickian or higher-life spirituality, as well as the Plymouth Brethren form of ecclesiology, were the two dominant teachings that were transmitted around the world, beginning with the late nineteenth century and continuing to the present. Their spread came largely through the literature these communities produced. Ian Randall comments, "The Keswick idiom shaped the prevailing pattern of evangelical piety for much of the twentieth century."[1] Most of the movements that arose during this period could be traced to the influences of either one or the other of these two traditions. The diffusion of ideas through literature and conferences, the general dissatisfaction towards the institutional churches, and the call for an alternative and meaningful Christian and congregational life were all part of the global Christian phenomena during the period. While each of these concerns influenced the other, the theology that was transmitted through the literature was questioned, reflected upon, and applied if appreciated or modified according to the different contexts in which it appeared.

---

1. Ian M. Randall, *Evangelical Experiences: A Study in the Spirituality of English Evangelicalism 1918–1939* (Carlisle, Cumbria: Paternoster, 1999), 14.

The denominational identities of the various authors became immaterial as long as the theology was appealing. This also led to the need to return to the Scriptures not only to verify the claims being made by these authors, but also to counter the claims made by the historic denominations. The search of the Scriptures and the importance given to the word of God, in turn, resulted in the claim that they could establish "New Testament pattern" churches, counter to the pattern of those found in the denominational churches. Within this common landscape, both movements and individuals that addressed a specific need or had a specific emphasis expressed within a specific context sprang up. For churches in the West, the changes seemed to be mostly about bringing in an alternative model to the denominational structures. But for the churches in Asia, it was a quest for a church that was born from within the culture, a church that was believed to be closer to the one represented in the Scriptures than it was about an alternative political model.

New Testament Pattern

Basing themselves on the common characteristics and resemblances to one another, the churches that followed the "New Testament pattern" arose out of a common quest against a common situation. One can notice the pattern of events that led to the call to "go back" "restore" and "renew" the "New Testament pattern" churches. The context and environment, especially in terms of the administration, structures, doctrine and polity of the denominational churches, were at their lowest ebb. The thorough dissatisfaction and growing discontentment of the people towards the denominational churches, made people view what they experienced as oppressive church structures and nominality in the Christian life, especially as hindrances both to the furtherance of the gospel and to the growth of the individual Christian.[2] The alleged secularization of programs within the churches,[3] the emphasis on what many viewed only as ritualism, and the acceptance

---

2. See James Patrick Callahan, *Primitivist Piety: Ecclesiology of the Early Plymouth Brethren* (Langham, MD: Scarecrow Press, 1996).

3. See David G. Fountain, *Contending for the Faith: E. J. Poole-Connor – A Prophet amidst the Sweeping Changes in English Evangelicalism* (London: Wakeman Trust, 2005).

of higher criticism, in a way, each came to be viewed as undermining the authority of the Scriptures in the life and ministry of the church.[4] The enhanced significance of prophecy and latter-day prophetic events, the place and work of the Holy Spirit, and above all, the need and the thirst for a deeper/higher Christian life or for holiness,[5] all worked one upon the other to turn people to the Scriptures, and especially to the New Testament, for an alternative to the existing situation.[6] In other words, the reaction of people seeking an alternative model that met their spiritual quest was to be free from all that appeared to be both a scandal and a hindrance to the "true" or "pure" form of church.

Common Characteristics

Some of the common counter-measures[7] that are adapted by most of the churches which claim to be established on the principles of the "New Testament Pattern Church" are:

- their claim that the movement is of divine initiative.
- their appeal to the authority of Scripture, and not to any human institution.
- their view of the church as a gathering of believers and the body of Christ.
- their refusal to give a name to the church (they will only call themselves either an "Assembly" or a "Gathering" or a "Fellowship").

---

4. See David W. Bebbington, *Evangelicalism in Modern Britain: A History from the 1730s to the 1980s* (London: Routledge, 1989), 146ff; Adrian Hastings, *A History of English Christianity 1920–1990* (London: SCM Press, 1991).

5. See E. J. Poole-Connor, *Evangelicalism in England* (London: Fellowship of Independent Evangelical Churches, 1951).

6. The Pearsall Smiths from America, who were the pioneers of the Keswick movement and convention in England, had a Brethren background. Charles Price and Ian Randall, *Transforming Keswick* (Carlisle, Cumbria: OM Publishing, 2000), 22; cf. Bebbington, *Evangelicalism,* 158. An early source, however, states that they had Quaker origins; cf. John C. Pollock, *The Keswick Story* (Chicago, IL: Moody Press, 1964), 13.

7. These characteristics are gleaned from all the above readings. Since these are mentioned in most of the sources in different ways, I am not giving elaborate footnotes for each one of them.

- their refusal to acknowledge a centralized authority (at least in the beginnings).
- their emphasis on personal salvation and holy living that includes a call to "come out" and be separate from both the world and non-believers. At times, this is a call to come out of the denominational churches, which are viewed as evil, unspiritual and unscriptural.
- their advocacy of the priesthood of all believers and their rejection of ordination and of seminary training as a prerequisite for pastoral ministry (anti-clericalism).[8]
- their giving a central place to the word of God and the Lord's Supper in Sunday worship.
- their emphasis on believer's baptism through immersion, which at times results in those who have taken infant baptism, being baptized again.

While these were the common features, shared by various groups of the time, these groups also differed substantially in their understanding and implementation of each of these features. By this means, they maintained their uniqueness. In their uniqueness, the churches that were established by T. Austin-Sparks and The Honor Oak Fellowship in London, Watchman Nee and The Little Flock Movement in China, Bakht Singh and The Assemblies in India, and Poul Madsen with his Danish Kristent Fælleskab Movement, could all be identified as "Spiritual Life churches." Although each of them claimed to follow the "New Testament pattern," like most of the free churches of their time, the uniqueness of these churches was their emphasis on spiritual life and the manner in which they connected to each other, while maintaining their own independence.

Spiritual Life Church Movements

All of the Spiritual Life churches had a local place of origin, but all were connected in terms of their spiritual association with other similar movements

---

8. Shuff mentions, F. F. Bruce recalls hearing the aphorism: "Clerisy is the sin of sins Godward, as socialism is manward, a reflection also of the political preoccupations of the era." Roger Shuff, *Searching for the True Church: Brethren and Evangelicals in Mid-Twentieth-Century England* (Carlisle: Paternoster, 2005), 34.

that developed outside their respective countries. Because of the affinity of the pattern of these churches with the Brethren churches, these churches have been identified as the descendants of the Brethren churches. A closer examination of the Spiritual Life churches, however, reveals that in spite of the similarities they have with the Brethren churches, each of them has developed an ecclesiology of their own, and their theological emphases differ depending on the context where they have taken root. By placing them under the category of the Brethren or, more broadly, as emulators of Keswick spirituality, assumptions have been made that has led the academic community to miss the unique characteristics of these spiritual life church movements. In fact, they have been marginalized and treated as insignificant groups. Now it is recognized that these movements are to be given due importance since they have had a much greater impact at the grass-root level than was initially assumed.

Gier Lie has identified the Spiritual Life churches as "individuals and groups characterized by a combined doctrinal affinity with Holiness (i.e. Keswickean) anthropology and Plymouth Brethren ecclesiology."[9] Miles J. Stanford classifies the movements of Watchman Nee, Austin-Sparks, Bakht Singh, Poul Madsen and Stephen Kuang as Plymouth Brethren emulators. He maintains, "The motivating factor of these bodies is to hew as closely as possible to the New Testament pattern as they see it, for worship, instruction, and service."[10] Basing his conclusions on the faith principles of Watchman Nee and Bakht Singh, and their association with the associates[11] of Anthony Norris Groves, Robert Bernard Dunn has categorized these churches as the outgrowth of the vision of Anthony Norris Groves.[12] There is no evidence, however, that either Nee or Singh were ever influenced or directly acquainted with Groves.

---

9. Geir Lie, "Poul Madson and the Danish Kristent Fælleskab Movement," *The Journal of the European Pentecostal Theological Association* 28, no. 1 (2008): 34.

10. Miles J. Stanford, *Plymouth Brethren Emulators (circa 1970)*, 4; available from www.withchrist.org.

11. R. R. Rajamani, one of the coworkers and cofounder of the Bakht Singh Assemblies, was the great grandson of John Christian Arullappan, a direct disciple of Anthony Norris Groves. See R. R. Rajamani, *Monsoon Daybreak* (Fort Washington, PA: Christian Literature Crusade, 1971).

12. See Robert Bernard Dunn, *Father of Faith Missions: The Life and Times of Anthony Norris Groves* (Wayensboro, GA: Authentic, 2004).

By classifying these movements based solely on their theological affinities, scholars have ignored the immediate context and culture that gave rise to them. The development of these movements took place in a theologically, politically and culturally complex situation. Tracing the confluence of these threads throughout their development leads to the individual setting of the various movements as well as to their connections.

England: Theodore Austin-Sparks (1889–1971)

Austin-Sparks was the founder of the Honor Oak Christian Fellowship in London. From 1912–1926 he worked as a pastor in both Congregational and Baptist churches.[13] He was associated with some of the Keswick leaders like F. B. Meyer, G. Campbell Morgan and others. He was associated especially with Jessie Penn-Lewis and worked alongside her during 1923–1926. They parted ways over the issues of the Lord's Supper and baptism. Austin-Sparks advocated an interconfessional Lord's Supper and believer's baptism through immersion, while Penn-Lewis was against the administering of sacraments. Still, Austin-Sparks continued the teachings of Penn-Lewis regarding the centrality of the cross. He also conducted conferences modeled on those of the Keswick Movement.[14] It was through the periodical *A Witness and a Testimony* that he published, however, that he was able to pass on his teachings more broadly.

Around 1922, Austin-Sparks became the pastor of the Honor Oak Baptist Church. In 1923, he underwent a spiritual crisis. He began to preach the experience of the cross and Christ in the life of believers and he observed that the denominational divisions went against his understanding of the New Testament church. In 1926, accompanied by some of the members of the Honor Oak Baptist Church, Austin-Sparks left the Baptist Union and started the Honor Oak Fellowship and conference center. He opened the work on a faith basis and based it upon his understanding of the church as the body of Christ.[15] The conference center and hostel

---

13. Angus Gunn, *Theodore Austin-Sparks: Reflections on His Life and Work* (Toronto, Canada: Clements, 2001), 3.

14. Geir Lie, *T. Austin-Sparks: A Brief Introduction* (article online); available from www.reflekspublishing.com.

15. Rex G. Beck, *Shaped by Vision: A Biography of T. Austin-Sparks* (Cleveland, OH: Greater Purpose Publishers, 2005), 34–47.

were used to hold training programs for leaders and missionaries from time to time. People from all denominations attended the training. Some of them went out as independent missionaries to different parts of the world.[16] Lady Daisy Ogle, Fred Flack and Raymond Golsworthy went to India as missionaries from Honor Oak. Lady Daisy Ogle was in charge of the Honor Oak hostel before she left for India.[17] Later, these three associated themselves with the ministry of Bakht Singh in India. Austin-Sparks also ministered among the Assemblies of Bakht Singh.

Watchman Nee in China was introduced to the writings of Austin-Sparks and of Jessie Penn-Lewis by a woman missionary named Margaret Barber (she was with CMS initially although later she became an independent missionary). When Nee went to London in 1933, on the invitation of the Taylor Brethren,[18] he visited the Honor Oak Fellowship and participated in sharing the Lord's Supper with them. This led to the Taylor Brethren's breaking up with Nee. Later in 1938, Nee used the Honor Oak hostel as a base and he continued to share fellowship with Austin-Sparks. Kinnear mentions that Nee sought the counsel of Austin-Sparks regarding his understanding of the "practical working of the body of Christ." During this trip Nee published his books, *The Normal Christian Life* and *Concerning our Missions*.[19] As a result of this visit, a permanent bond was established between the two fellowships. Austin-Sparks would later visit Taiwan and Hong Kong where he ministered in the churches established by Watchman Nee and Witness Lee.[20]

---

16. Ibid., 72–78.

17. Ibid., 69.

18. This is an exclusive group of Brethren called the "London Group" in England and "Taylor Brethren" in USA after the name of their leader James Taylor. They fence themselves off from attending other Christian meetings. They do not maintain fellowship, including ordinary social relationships with other Christians. Outsiders are allowed only if they agree to be within the group and would be expelled if they go against the restrictions. See Angus Kinnear, *Against the Tide: The Story of Watchman Nee* (Fort Washington, PA: Christian Literature Crusade, 1973), 120–127.

19. Angus Kinnear, *Against the Tide,* 152–154.

20. Beck, *Shaped by Vision,* 202–206. Stephen Kuang and Witness Lee, coworkers with Watchman Nee, established assemblies in the USA. These Assemblies were identified as local churches in the USA. See J. Gordon Melton, "Local Church Movement" *Encyclopedia of American Religions,* 5th ed., available from www.localchurches.org. C. J. B Harrison, who was associated with Austin-Sparks, also established an Assembly in Los Angeles. Bakht Singh ministered in some of these local churches when he visited the USA. Brinda McCumber,

Teaching of Austin-Sparks

Austin-Sparks believed in the tripartite anthropology of the body, soul and spirit. He differentiated between life that was controlled by the soul as being "soulish" or "natural" and life that was controlled by the Spirit as being "spiritual." Life in the Spirit helped one to realize the difference between the soul and the spirit. The soul, being the seat of intelligence, will, feeling and energy, could not discern the spiritual purposes of God. He wrote, "It is not in our souls or ourselves that the Holy Spirit dwells, but in our spirits, and the renewed and indwelt spirit is the organ of divine knowledge, purpose, and power. Life in the Spirit is only possible as this distinction is made."[21]

Along the lines of the Keswick understanding of a crisis experience that can occur in one's life following conversion,[22] Austin-Sparks' emphasis was on the inward working of the cross. He viewed the cross as being operative in the sinful nature of a person as well as in the experience of dying to the self. While the initial working of the cross in the life of a believer delivers him or her from the bondage of sin, judgment, death, and damnation, the subjective working of the cross in a person's life following conversion delivers him or her from the bondage of "self."[23] One's realization of the bondage to "self" is understood to be both a crisis and a process. It does not effect one's standing before Christ, but "self" is understood to be an impediment to entry into the fullness of Christ.[24] God's final goal is to make one spiritual and that happens through the working of the Holy Spirit in one's life. This spiritual life is experiential and sometimes it cannot be explained. It has to be an ongoing experience of the Holy Spirit in one's life, an experience thought to take place in a very practical manner.[25] This

---

email correspondence to author, 31 August 2006. See "Background and development of the Geftakys Assemblies" available from www.geftakysassembly.com.

21. T. Austin-Sparks, *Explanation of the Nature and History of "This Ministry"* (Tulsa, OK: Emmanuel Church, 2004), 11–12. (Reprinted from the original magazine *A Witness and A Testimony* in 1956).

22. See Randall, *Evangelical Experiences,* 27ff.

23. Austin-Sparks, *Explanation,* 8.

24. Ibid., 11.

25. T. Austin-Sparks, *The Nature of the Dispensation in Which We Live,* (online library of T. Austin-Sparks); available from www.Austin-Sparks.net.

is brought about through suffering, and suffering is understood to be part of the working of the cross in one's life that is intended to bring forth the nature of Christ in the believer.[26]

Church

For Austin-Sparks, the church is Christ: "The Church, the House of God, is simply Christ Himself in undivided oneness found in all those in whom He really dwells. That is all. That is the Church . . . You and I are not the Church. It is Christ in you and in me that is the Church."[27] He goes on to explain, "It is Christ in living union with His own. That is the Church."[28] The church as the body of Christ, then, is viewed as organic. It symbolizes the oneness of believers, "interrelated, interdependent, by the power of a common life and the government of a common head in the anointing of the Holy Spirit."[29] Austin-Sparks stressed the mystical body of Christ and the freedom of the Holy Spirit to give the church today a variety of expressions on earth.[30]

Because of his emphasis upon the governance and guidance of the Holy Spirit, Austin-Sparks viewed the church as being a spiritual entity, and the Christian life was defined by its spirituality. Since the Holy Spirit directs the life of the church, any other external control was viewed as being under a tradition, and therefore under a system and a form of bondage. Accordingly, being under such a system also impedes one from following the Spirit or from being truly spiritual.[31] Austin-Sparks contended that if one tries to do God's work with the "natural" man, "there is bound to ensue a static system of teaching, a fixed horizon of vision, a legal bondage to tradition, a fear of man, a deadening domination of the 'letter' as separated from the 'spirit,' and division, and spiritual pride."[32] So he believed that

---

26. T. Austin-Sparks, *What It Means to Be a Christian* (Tulsa, OK: Emmanuel Church, n.d.), 66.

27. T. Austin-Sparks, *God's Spiritual House* (Tulsa, OK: Emmanuel Church, n.d.), 22.

28. T. Austin-Sparks, *What Is the Church*, (online library of T. Austin-Sparks); available from www.Austin-Sparks.net.

29. Beck, *Shaped by Vision*, 142.

30. Kinnear, *Against the Tide*, 155.

31. T. Austin-Sparks, *Worship*, (online library of T. Austin-Sparks); available from www.Austin-Sparks.net.

32. Austin-Sparks, *Explanation*, 10.

the church should be continually ordered by the Holy Spirit. For practical purposes, however, he did recognize the need for organization. At the same time, all decisions were supposed to be taken by the leading of the Spirit through prayer.[33]

By emphasizing the organic nature of the church as the body of Christ consisting of those who are true believers, he refused to view the fellowship as a church. At the same time, Austin-Sparks understood that wherever two or three believers gathered in Christ's name, they would constitute the church.[34] This "local company" would therefore, represent the whole body of Christ. These believers would also be connected to the rest of the believers in the world because of the organic and universal nature of the body of Christ.[35] For Austin-Sparks, the church was "the aggregate of *such* believers, in which what was true of Christ is true of it – deity apart . . . So spirituality, which is a heavenly other nature and endowment, is the first basic principle of the Church."[36] For him, the transformed nature of the born-again person represented spirituality and he understood this as a mystery. Moreover, this presence of Christ in a company of believers gathered together constitutes a local church. Since Christ in living union with his own is what the church is or represents, for him a church cannot be founded on the basis of locality.[37] Since Austin-Sparks viewed the development of spiritual life in the believers as the end of the church, he concentrated on the growth of believers, rather than upon evangelism.

China: Watchman Nee (Ni Tuo Sheng) (1903–1972)

Watchman Nee was the son of Christian parents from Foochow, China. He was trained in the Confucian Classics and was later sent to Trinity College, Foochow (Anglican), for theological education.[38] By 1920, Nee

---

33. Beck, *Shaped by Vision*, 68.

34. T. Austin-Sparks, *The Cross, the Church and the Kingdom* (Tulsa, OK: Emmanuel Church, 2008), 30. (Reprint of the original articles from 1948–1949 from the magazine *A Witness and a Testimony*).

35. T. Austin-Sparks, *The Church Which Is His Body* (Tulsa, OK: Emmanuel Church, reprint, 2000), 21.

36. Austin-Sparks, *Worship*.

37. Beck, *Shaped by Vision*, 229–231.

38. Leslie Lyall, *Three of China's Mighty Men* (Dunton Green, Sevenoaks: Hodder & Stoughton and Overseas Missionary Fellowship, 1980), 52.

had become disillusioned with the failure of Christianity in his own family. That year he attended a revival meeting conducted by Dora Yu, a Chinese preacher. Nee's mother, who had a new experience of Jesus Christ in these meetings, confessed to Nee that she had wrongly punished him over a certain incident. This gesture, which was unusual for a mother to confess to her son, drew Nee to attend the meetings. Nee also had a similar experience in these meetings and he committed himself to be faithful to Christ. Nee went on to spend a year in a school run by Dora Yu in Shangai. From Dora Yu, Watchman Nee learned to trust God in faith and to depend upon the word of God. Dora Yu introduced Nee to Margaret Barber, an independent missionary from England. Over the years, he visited Barber frequently and she became his spiritual counselor and mentor. Barber introduced Nee to the writings of the Keswick leaders.[39]

Both Watchman Nee and Austin-Sparks were mentored by women who were independent. Grace May has observed that Nee's understanding of the church as well as the "breaking of bread" gave a new sense of home to him because the faith was passed on to Nee by women in a home setting.[40]

Nee began to explore the Scriptures on his own in order to find ways by which he could make Christ more relevant to the Chinese context. Along with his friends, Nee began to spread the gospel in neighboring villages. They used posters and wore shirts printed with Bible verses. They held meetings in homes and rented halls.[41] In 1922, Nee held his first worship service in which he broke bread or celebrated the Lord's Supper in the house of man named Leland Wang. This was, in fact, considered the beginning of the Little Flock movement.[42] Nee was not acquainted with the Brethren at that time, nor does it appear that he or Wang as yet had a good sense of what their ecclesiology might be. Later, Nee recalled this incident: "I will not forget that night until death even in eternity," he wrote. "We

---

39. Kinnear, *Against the Tide*, 42–52.

40. Grace Y. May, "Watchman Nee and the Breaking of Bread: The Missiological and Spiritual Forces That Contributed to an Indigenous Chinese Ecclesiology," (ThD Thesis, Boston University School of Theology, 2000), 102.

41. Lyall, *China's Mighty Men*, 55.

42. The name "Little Flock" was given to them by observers, basing on the title of the hymnal used by them, "Hymns of the Little Flock." The churches are also known as "the Assembly Hall," and "the Local Churches."

never felt that we were so close to heaven that evening. That day heaven was so near to earth! All three of us were so joyous that we cried."[43]

It may well be the case that this experience had a greater impact on Nee and his understanding of the nature of the church and the breaking of bread than did any of his reading of other literature. It might also be the case that this experience only confirmed his understanding. In either case, in 1928, Nee started his first congregation in Shanghai, based upon his understanding of ecclesiological principles. He did not give any name to this congregation but called it simply a "Christian meeting place" or "gathering of believers" with the name of the city affixed to it. All subsequent congregations started mainly as house churches. Ultimately, however, they grew to be an important movement all over China.[44]

Conditions That Prompted Nee to Start the Churches

It is generally understood that Nee's ecclesiology and spirituality were strongly influenced by Keswick and Brethren thought. By emphasizing this understanding, the immediate spiritual context that prompted Nee to think the way he did as well as the factors that attracted him to these ideologies were largely ignored. Nee merely claimed that his theology was based on the Bible, and even he almost ignored the context that actually shaped his understanding. Grace May rightly points out:

> While the social and political context of his day played an undeniable factor in much of his theologizing, Nee made little conscious effort in his articles or his messages to suggest the connection. True to his fundamentalist leanings, Nee strove to back all of his preaching and teaching with the Scriptures, not the circumstances in which he lived and struggled.[45]

A closer look at the origins of the Spiritual Life churches reveals the multifaceted struggle that the various founders had gone through and the dynamics involved in their development. While Austin-Sparks, Watchman

---

43. Watchman Nee, "Narration of the Past," in *Notes on Scriptural Messages, The Collected Works of Watchman Nee*, vol. 18 (Anaheim, CA: Living Stream Ministry, 1992), 308, quoted in May, "Watchman Nee," 100.

44. Lyall, *China's Mighty Men*, 64.

45. May, "Watchman Nee," 309.

Nee and Bakht Singh, were each reacting to the doctrinal concerns and the ecclesiastical structures of their day, the contexts of Nee and Singh were different from that of Austin-Sparks. Nee and Singh were addressing not only the theological issues that had developed in China and India, but also the political and cultural issues associated with their faith. Christianity in Asia was associated with western colonialism and imperialism. Since the missionary enterprise and the colonial enterprise became synonymous, "in the eyes of the Asians, Christians were perceived to be a danger to the security of the nation both political and cultural."[46] Christian identity within their homeland became precarious. While Christians were alienated from the main stream of public life, they were also not given freedom of expression in the mission organizations and the churches to which they belonged. Nee and Singh, who were initially associated with the historic denominational churches, had to bear the constraints of these structures. Nee was vocal in expressing his frustration that the Chinese were not given enough freedom in their churches.[47] Bakht Singh's experience of being turned down by the denominational churches because he was not ordained and yet had performed baptisms provides a clear example of their frustration.

Culturally, too, church structures presented a form of religion that was alien to the thinking so prominent in Asian spirituality. Wickeri notes:

> Structurally, it is important to understand that religion in traditional China tended to be diffuse and non-institutional. Just as it was non-exclusive in the realm of belief, so Chinese religion has been loosely structured. Religious organizations

---

46. T. V. Philip, *Reflections on Christian Mission in Asia* (Delhi: ISPCK/CSS, 2000), 70.

47. May, "Watchman Nee and the Breaking of Bread," 311. Nee's letter to Norman Baker, a missionary of the China Inland Mission, illustrates his attitude to the missions: "You may argue that the Chinese Churches are so young and they do not know much; therefore, missionaries have to decide for them; but do you mean to say that because of the immediate babyhood of the Chinese churches you try to make a regulation for their permanent immaturity? Brother, in the Principles and Practice there was no provision made for the Chinese churches in case they do get into maturity. It is taken for granted that they will always continue to be babes, and hence the form of Church Government instituted by the first missionary is the permanent form. There is not even a suggestion that some day they would be otherwise, and that they could decide for themselves. Do you never expect the Chinese churches to grow out of their infancy?" (Nee, London, to Mr Norman Baker, London, 19 September 1938), quoted in May, "Watchman Nee," 311.

were seldom able to attain dominance over other institutions in traditional China.[48]

The mode of Christian worship also posed a challenge to the Asian Christians. Grace May has noted that, "The shadow of imperialism seemed to hover over every communion service. The elements tasted foreign. The table setting looked unfamiliar. And the prayer honoring the crown of England sounded like a betrayal of China."[49] In this situation the test for the Asian Christians was not only to maintain their local identity, but also to incarnate Christianity into the local cultural format. The Asian Christians responded by establishing independent indigenous churches of their own. In 1917, "The True Jesus Church" and in 1921 the "Jesus Family" were established by Chinese Christians in China.[50]

The challenge could not have been more intense for both Nee and Singh because of the times in which their movements arose. During the 1920s, China saw the anti-Christian movement reach its height. From the 1920s to the 1940s the Indian Independence movement grew dramatically. Both Nee and Singh were products of their times, with their nationalistic zeal and their equally intense religious fervor. The combination of these two factors must have brought both of them to the Scriptures to seek an alternative. Naturally they chose an ecclesiological understanding, which did not represent the denominational churches, but rather, represented the Bible or the New Testament church, that is, spirituality.[51] They found a kindred spirit in Austin-Sparks who did not belong to any denomination, nor did he claim to be establishing a new one. Instead he viewed the church as a universal church, that is, the body of Christ. Leslie Lyall has observed,

> His [Nee's] visit to the West was an almost pathetic search for fellowship, and the one man not involved in the missionary enterprise who was able to enter into his thinking was Mr

---

48. Philip L. Wickeri, *Seeking the Common Ground: Protestant Christianity, The Three-Self Movements and China's United Front* (Maryknoll, NY: Orbis Books, 1988), 30.

49. May, "Watchman Nee," 13.

50. Lyall, *China's Mighty Men*, 62.

51. See Kinnear, *Against the Tide*, 136–138; Peterus Pamudji, *Little Flock Trilogy: A Critique of Watchman Nee's Principal Thought on Christ, Man, and the Church* (Ann Arbor, MI: University Microfilms Int'l, 1986), 181.

Austin-Sparks . . . Meanwhile another interesting figure had appeared on the Indian scene and the ministry of Bakht Singh and the assemblies which he created formed a third point in the triangle of similar ministries in England, China and India.[52]

Watchman Nee must have also found an authentication of his own understanding in Austin-Sparks. However, Nee's theology was neither a total duplication of that found in the West, nor did he adopt a totally Chinese ideology. Nee appears to have blended these two together. While this understanding stood on the theological side, the nationalistic spirit that propelled him toward making Christianity Chinese also led him to adapt the biblical teaching to his own cultural context. He accomplished this by discarding everything that represented the "Imperial" "foreign" "colonial" or "alien." Leslie Lyall aptly summarizes it as follows:

> As with the other movements, it was the combination of old biblical principles and the new ardent nationalism that influenced Watchman Nee to develop his independent policies. Pragmatic motives and the spirit of Chinese nationalism, in other words, as much as doctrinal distinctiveness without question lay behind all these movements. Consciously or unconsciously they were an attempt to escape the stigma of association with "western missionary imperialism."[53]

The Teachings of Watchman Nee

Basis of the church

As we have already noticed, Watchman Nee has often been portrayed as having followed the Brethren ecclesiology. Nee's search for an alternative model to denominational Christianity, one that would be more appropriate to the Chinese context, must have endeared the Brethren model to him. Nee did not however, adopt the Brethren ecclesiology uncritically. Nee clearly states:

---

52. Lyall, *China's Mighty Men*, 73.
53. Ibid., 63.

> It was not until 1927 that we began to learn of this movement in other countries. Through books and magazines we found that it is a large movement which has made its influence felt all over the world . . . At that time a question arose in our mind: what does the Bible say? Are children of God supposed to join a movement?[54]

It is obvious that Nee was questioning this system, even as he was seeking an alternative to the existing systems and saw that this Brethren movement as one possibility. Pamudji has observed,

> Some people thought that Watchman Nee simply imported Plymouth Brethrenism to China. But Watchman Nee is too complex to be labeled as an importer or plagiarizer. . . . Nee himself was critical of the Brethren and labeled them as "Laodecia" according to Revelation 3.[55]

Angus Kinnear argues that Nee sought the Scriptures in the light of variances he found in the churches in the West during his visit between 1933–1939, and that he was confirmed about his own conviction regarding the nature of the church.[56] Moreover, during the time of the dispute with the Brethren in England, the Chinese assemblies established by Nee declined to affiliate themselves with the denomination. Grace May concluded that this was because the Assemblies understood themselves as a family and they refused to be associated with a foreign denomination. She notes:

> To maintain the emphasis on close-knit fellowship and informal worship Assembly leaders refused to join any official organization or affiliate with a wider movement. The Assembly's position promoted a maximum degree of autonomy. Freedom from western leadership and administration permitted the Assembly to preserve its Chinese distinctives and its sense of

---

54. Watchman Nee, *The Orthodox Tradition of the Church* (Taiwan: Gospel Boon Room, 1963), 85, quoted in James Mo-oi Cheung, *The Ecclesiology of Watchman Nee & Witness Lee* (Fort Washington, PA: Christian Literature Crusade, 1972), 34–35.

55. Pamudji, *Little Flock Trilogy*, 181.

56. Kinnear, *Against the Tide*, 128.

self-rule in a country where foreign missions and Christianity had often become synonymous.[57]

Thus, Nee was able to maintain his own emphasis on what constitutes the church.

Nee believed that the church is by nature both heavenly or spiritual, and earthly. His understanding of the church is based upon two fundamental issues that he considered to be biblical. According to him, the church was based on the authority of the Holy Spirit and the boundary of locality. He wrote, "(O)nly that which is able to express the mind of the Holy Spirit can be called the church."[58] The authority of the Holy Spirit was to be realized through the mature, spiritual, elderly brothers within the congregation. The second ground was the boundary of locality. According to him, in the Bible, only one church existed in each locality or city, like the "Church in Jerusalem" or the church in Corinth. From this, he concluded that there can be only one church in one locality or administrative unit. Each local church is to be autonomous.[59]

Nee proposed the concept of locality in order to avoid denominational divisions. His desire for unity nearly drove him to the other extreme of claiming that there can be no church apart from the ground of locality.[60] He sought to promote locally autonomous and nondenominational congregations independent of any external control. He did not give a name to these congregations but called them "assemblies." For some time they were known simply as the "Christian meeting place," although later they added the name of the locality to the church. The chief medium of spiritual instruction that Nee adopted were his writings and his publication, the magazine called *The Present Testimony*.[61]

---

57. May, "Watchman Nee," 142–143.

58. Watchman Nee, *Further Talks on the Church Life* (Los Angeles, CA: Stream Publishers, 1969, reprint, 1974), 12.

59. Later in his ministry, Nee modified the principle of autonomy of the local churches. He advocated the Jerusalem principle where he supported that the work should be centralized. See Nee, *Further Talks*, 153–170. This aspect of Nee's ecclesiology is attributed more to the influence of Witness Lee than to Nee. See Dana Roberts, *The Newest Book on Watchman Nee: Understanding Watchman Nee* (Plainfield, NJ: Haven Books, 1980), 134–137. Kinnear, *Against the Tide*, 55–58, 186ff.

60. Nee, *Further Talks*, 45–48.

61. Cheung, *Ecclesiology*, 17.

Nee argued that the unity of the church was based upon the concept of the body of Christ. He taught that the body of Christ was not a doctrine, but was something living. As one body that is living, every believer had a spiritual responsibility of serving the other. He strongly advocated the priesthood of all believers and excluded the role of pastor in these congregations. "The service of the church is a spiritual coordination," he wrote, "a coordination of the saints in life and in the Holy Spirit."[62] He advocated the idea of obeying the elders in the church, because they had more experience in the Christian life, so it would be easier for the Holy Spirit to speak through them.[63] This emphasis might, in fact, be derived from his Confucian background where obeying or respecting the elders is one of the five virtues taught by Confucius.[64] The emphasis on demonstrated character and experience, rather than professional skills, manifested a strong work ethic, which Watchman Nee acquired from Confucianism and his own strict upbringing.[65]

Spiritual life

The sustaining factor of Watchman Nee's ministry was his stress on the spiritual life of individual believers as well as on the corporate body, the church. He questioned the intellectualism of western Christianity and he opposed the systematic rendering of doctrine. He viewed doctrine as a static tool that catered to mental apprehension, but which did not give room to the dynamic leading of the Spirit through the word of God.[66] For him, it was not the doctrine that was important, but experience and life of the Christian. He argued that what was important was, "First the experience of Christ, then the doctrine of Christ. First the life of Christ, then the teaching of Christ . . . It is God who carries you through. First experience, then the doctrine."[67] Because it is through the experience of new birth that

---

62. Nee, *Further Talks*, 137f.

63. Ibid., 14–18.

64. Pamudji, *Little Flock Trilogy*, 156.

65. Joseph Tse-Hei Lee, "Watchman Nee and the Little Flock Movement in Maoist China," *Church History* 74, no. 1 (March 2005) (journal online); available from http://proquest.umi.com.

66. Cheung, *Ecclesiology*, 39.

67. Watchman Nee, *The Body of Christ: A Reality* (New York: Christian Fellowship Publishers, 1978), 40.

one becomes a part of the church, one has to live that new life of Christ: "Therefore there is a need for us to live, behave, and act according to this life, the life of Christ . . . It is not many "men"; it is a *life*."[68]

Like Austin-Sparks and Bakht Singh, Watchman Nee also adhered to the tripartite anthropology of body, soul and spirit. He gave more importance to the ongoing work of the Holy Spirit in a believer's life. He concluded that it was the carnal nature that brought about divisions and defeat in the life of the believer and the church. He gave importance to "life in the Spirit" without giving room for the flesh. According to Nee's understanding, the differentiation of acting in the flesh and in the Spirit could be attributed to the Asian concept of viewing the body as evil and the Spirit as good.[69]

Nee reckoned that the deepening of the spiritual life of the believers would happen largely through the dependence on the word of God. Thus, he claimed to derive his religious authority and his teaching directly from the Word and gave his congregations intensive training in the word of God. Nee's decision to follow the Bible, instead of finely honed doctrines and theology, was in consonance with the Chinese tradition of strict adherence to Scripture.[70] Pamudji has described Nee as acting like a *guru* or sage to the believers who followed his teaching by imparting his teachings and also by trying to apply these teachings in practical ways to everyday life. Since the Chinese attribute more importance to duty in life and they believed that religion was for life and not vice versa, Nee emphasized the practical Christian life than speculative theology. In that sense, "Nee's theologizing was uniquely Chinese."[71]

---

68. Watchman Nee, *The Glorious Church* (Anaheim, CA: Living Stream Ministries, 2nd Indian ed., 2005), 31–32.

69. Stephen C. Johnson, *The Spirituality of Watchman Nee, Its Sources and Its Influences* (book online), 21; available from www.tren.com.

70. Lee, "Watchman Nee."

71. Pamudji, *Little Flock Trilogy,* 180–181.

Commonalities between Austin-Sparks, Watchman Nee and Bakht Singh

In a way, the three movements of Austin-Sparks, Watchman Nee and Bakht Singh are each independent movements. The founders were each seeking an alternative to the existing denominational system and to the emphasis of dogma in the churches within their time and place. In order to do away with denominational identity, all of them adopted the "assembly" system without giving a specific name to them. They also discouraged any centralized authority and encouraged autonomy of individual churches. They tried to focus their followers on the word of God as the ultimate authority and ongoing normative revelation from the Word.[72] They tried to shift the focus of the congregation from doctrine to experience. This was one of their major emphases.

Each of them called for a spiritual life based upon the personal experience of salvation and a persistent relationship with Christ in day-to-day life of the individual. The common issues that all the three of them were addressing within their own context were, the prominence given to doctrines in the place of Scriptures, and the barriers to a common identity for the church, a universal church that was based upon the Scriptures that were set by the existing denominational structures. To each of these men, the adherence of the historic denominational churches to a set pattern that was then imposed upon their people, mitigated against the personal relationship of the individual to God and a life controlled by the Holy Spirit. In other words, they believed that being in a denominational structure or institutional church only brought people under the control of the individual denomination's doctrine and system. It did nothing to bring them under the control of the Spirit of God. As a result, they concluded that being led by the Spirit and being under the Lordship of Jesus were the alternative to denominational, doctrinal dominance. For them, leading a spiritual life or being under the authority of the Spirit defined the life of the believer as well as the nature of the church. Thus, they advocated the concept that the church was largely to be understood as a spiritual reality. All those who were born of the Spirit were, therefore, members of the church, and the

---

72. Johnson, *Spirituality*, 12.

earthly or local representation of the church was simply the company of believers who gathered together.

While spiritual life is what defines these movements, they differed in their specific emphases. Austin-Sparks emphasized the centrality of the cross in the life of the believer and the mystical nature of the church. Watchman Nee stressed the ground of locality as the basis of the church, and the obedience of believer and the church to the Holy Spirit. Bakht Singh emphasized the word of God and doing the will of God in the believer's life. On the one hand these three movements – of Austin-Sparks, Watchman Nee and Bakht Singh – maintained their independence, while on the other hand they were able to associate with one another on the spiritual level. Fred Flack, the Honor Oak missionary and a coworker of Bakht Singh in India, describes the relationship of these churches as "individual, autonomous, not any one under the other. It is a Spiritual Life relationship."[73] The unique contributions of Bakht Singh and his Assemblies will be set forth in the following chapters.

---

73. A. J. Flack, Sidmouth, Devon, UK to (Bharathi, Pasadena, CA, USA), 13 March 2007.

CHAPTER 4

The Ecclesiology of Bakht Singh

The ecclesiology of Bakht Singh evolved as the movement progressed and encountered different issues in the theology and administration of the Assemblies. Bakht Singh strove to maintain the biblical principles of a "New Testament pattern" as he perceived it. As much as Bakht Singh was biblical in his ecclesiology, he was thoroughly contextual in his approach to the understanding of the church and its practices. The spontaneity of blending the biblical with the cultural and contextual elements, conceals the struggle of theologizing within the specific context, and hides the sociocultural elements embedded in the theology. True to his biblicist ideology and dependence on the leading of the Holy Spirit, Bakht Singh asserted the scriptural nature of his teaching. In that sense the Scripture clearly informs the ecclesiology of Bakht Singh.

The concept of the church as the "house of God" is strongly emphasized along with the themes of the, "spiritual nature of the church," the "unity of the church," "submission to the headship of Christ," and the "autonomy of the local churches." Similar to the practice followed in the Brethren tradition, as well as that embraced by Austin-Sparks and Watchman Nee, Bakht Singh gave special emphasis on worship and to the breaking of bread. Contending against the existing denominational structures and models, Singh highlighted the role of each individual's spirituality and role that individuals had as coworkers and partners with Christ in the building of the church.

Bakht Singh's Sikh background informs his preference for viewing the church as the "house of God," and practices such as the "love feast" and "Holy Convocation" that are unique to the Assemblies. Bakht Singh did not have a systematized administrative structure for the governance of all the Assemblies. The local Assemblies were autonomous and were loosely connected to each other. This pattern has evolved depending on the needs dictated by the context, and the Assemblies continue to function independently from each other while at the same time they maintain a spiritual affiliation. Bakht Singh's strong belief in the sovereignty and the will of God and the need to depend on God on a daily basis informs the organizational and administrative pattern in the Assemblies.

The Nature of the Church

Bakht Singh strongly claimed that the pattern of the church, which he followed, was based upon the word of God, and that it was revealed to him through prayer and meditation on the Scriptures. His primary understanding of the church was that the church was a spiritual reality. According to Bakht Singh, the church was brought into being through the blood of Jesus Christ or through his work on the cross. Those who are born again and have experienced the salvific work of Christ become members of the church. The church is composed of a group of people who have been redeemed by the Lord Jesus Christ and received the Holy Spirit. Bakht Singh defined the Greek word *Ecclesia* as "drawn out or pulled out" (Eph 1:22) arguing that "It refers to those who have been drawn out of the world by Christ" (John 15:16).[1] He held that the church was heavenly and that the pattern of the church already existed in the Scriptures.

Bakht Singh's emphasis on the church as a spiritual reality appeared to have stemmed from his premise that the term "church" was misunderstood or misused as an earthly building by the members of the mainline churches. His rhetoric was intended to differentiate between the meaning of the church that was in common usage and what he believed to be the correct meaning of the term. He continuously reminded his followers that earthly buildings are not churches, and that a building should never be given a name like the Baptist church, the Methodist church, etc.[2] Bakht Singh was emphatic in his teaching that a physical building could never be a church.

---

1. Bakht Singh, *My Chosen* (Hyderabad: Book Room, 1964), 2.
2. Bakht Singh, *God's Dwelling Place* (Mumbai: GLS, 1957), 2.

At the same time, he sought to clarify the meaning of the church by using similar images like the church as "the house of God," "the building," "the sanctuary," "the habitation," "the temple," and "the dwelling place" of God (Eph 1:22–2:21).[3]

Contending that mainline denominational churches sought to build the church with their own knowledge, he argued that they failed to give the true meaning to the concept of the church. He believed that one cannot build God's building with human knowledge, but one must follow the word of God and God's guidance completely.[4] He argued that as Moses and David were given a plan to construct the tabernacle and the temple respectively, God has also given a plan for the construction of the church. As Moses and David had been instructed to follow every detail of the plan and not to change anything, so too should the plan given by God not be changed in the building of the church.

Although Bakht Singh believed that God had a definite plan for building God's church, he also pointed to the fact that God would not always reveal his entire plan at one time. One needs to depend on God day by day, to seek God's guidance, so that he or she might implement what God wants done. He taught:

> The Lord Jesus Christ as the Chief Engineer knows the plan of the Heavenly habitation, but He will not show us the entire plan at a time. We have to receive instructions from Him day by day. It is a daily exercise. But many times we fail to seek God's help, wisdom and guidance for our daily tasks and ministry.[5]

Another reason Bakht Singh did not accept the model of the mainline churches was, for him, they were fixed in their understanding and did not leave room for subsequent change. He believed in the dynamic and continuous revelation and guidance from God for every action.

---

3. Singh, *Return*, 64–65.
4. Ibid., 63–72.
5. Bakht Singh, *Unsearchable Greatness of the Salvation*, 2nd ed. (Hyderabad: Hebron, 1984), 25.

House of God

Bakht Singh's approach to the understanding of the church emerged from the framework of the Old Testament. Corresponding to his view that the Old Testament was the shadow of the New Testament, he interpreted the Old Testament allegorically, by which he believed it to be possible to understand the New Testament church. Taking the Old Testament examples of Jacob (Gen 28:14–17), the tabernacle (Exod 24, 25), and David's temple (1 Chr 28), he explicated the purpose and the vocation of the church. In the images of the tabernacle and the temple he found a parallel to his conception of the church as the abode of God. These structures were the abode of God's glory and they were built by God. For Singh, Jesus Christ, who is the chief architect of this building or sanctuary, builds the church which acts as God's resting place.

Basing his argument on the typology of the tabernacle, Bakht Singh understood the church as "the house of God" and the "dwelling place of God." Although he used these metaphors from the Scriptures, Bakht Singh's spiritual roots must have struck a familiar chord with these images and made him more at home with them. Bakht Singh's brother explained how they were taught in their childhood to respect both the *Mandir*[6] and the *gurudwara* as places of God, without arguing or questioning what the basis of this understanding was.[7] Bakht Singh used the metaphors of the "house of God" and "dwelling place of God" to signify two things: (1) the people of God are the house of God, and (2) they are also involved in the building up of the house of God (1 Pet 2:5; Heb 3:6). Like any other building, the church also needs a plan, material and personnel for its construction. Believers are not only coworkers and partners in the construction of this building, but also the material with which it is built. Since the church is both heavenly and earthly for Bakht Singh, so also is the function of the church both heavenly and earthly.[8] Bakht Singh emphasized strongly that the purpose of the church was to manifest the glory of God (Eph 5:27) in the same way that the glory of God filled the tabernacle (Exod 40:34)

---

6. Hindu Temple.

7. Shrichand Chhabra, interview by author, tape recording, Delhi, 29 November 2007.

8. Singh, God's Dwelling Place, 101.

and the temple of Solomon (1 Kgs 8:2). Similar glory was witnessed on the day of Pentecost when "the house" was filled and the church was born (Acts 2:3).[9] Singh maintained that just as God had given a clear plan to Moses and David for the building of his house, God also had a clear plan for the church. This was because these buildings were meant for God and not for people:

> The details of that Pattern [given to David] were of heavenly origin, because the temple was neither for man's use nor to attract man's attention nor to show forth any man's skill. Every dimension, every material, even the windows doors and colours were to show forth not an earthly building, built for man's habitation, where money is collected and lectures are given. It is a spiritual building, in which is to be revealed the love of God in Christ for man's salvation.[10]

Bakht Singh underlined that building the house of God was the vocation of the church. The prerequisite was that the hearts and homes of the believers should be the dwelling place of God. He stated that, "If we want to build the house of God, first of all our bodies must become the temple of God (1 Cor 3:16–17)" and "If we want to take [a] share in the building of the house of God, we must keep our bodies clean and holy, fit to be God's dwelling place."[11] Bakht Singh did not separate the individual's spiritual life from the church's life. Whatever happens in an individual's spiritual life has implications or effects on the church at large. Thus, every individual member is responsible for maintaining the wellbeing and growth of the church. Conclusively, the believer's personal spiritual life becomes a determining factor in the building up of the church.

Just as stones were shaped for the temple in the Old Testament (1 Kgs 6:7), Singh observed, so also is every individual believer shaped to fit into the building in order to become part of it.[12] Bakht Singh maintained that the metaphor of "God's Temple" has two functions for the people of God:

---

9. Bakht Singh, *What Happened on the Day of Pentecost* (article online), 2; available from www.brotherbakhtsingh.com.
10. Bakht Singh, *The Joy of the Lord* (Hyderabad: Book Room, 2003), 42–43.
11. Bakht Singh, *Fullness of God*, 4th ed. (Hyderabad: Hebron, 2003), 33.
12. Singh, *Return*, 46–47.

(1) that they might listen to God, and (2) that God would dwell among them. He wrote:

> These two are great features of the sanctuary: God speaking to His people from between the Cherubims, and the Divine Presence leading them by a cloud (Num. 7:89). Without the sanctuary these would not have been possible. For that reason, God asked the children of Israel to build Him a sanctuary. In Heb 8:5 we are told that all these serve unto the example and shadow of heavenly things . . . We also have no right to be called God's House unless the two great features of the sanctuary we have mentioned already are found in our midst, that is, God speaking to us and revealing His will, and God's presence going before us in power and glory.[13]

He stressed the importance of knowing the will of God as well as the importance of being willing to obey it. In other words, only when a believer was willing to be controlled by the Lord, would God dwell in him or her, work and reveal his glory through that person.

Singh viewed the participation in the building of the church as a double vocation. It is a heavenly vocation as well as an earthly vocation. Viewing the church as an earthly replica of the heavenly tabernacle he explained that the "sanctuary in the wilderness was a shadow of the true Heavenly Sanctuary of which the High Priest is our Lord Jesus Himself" (Heb 8:1, 2).[14] The material used in the construction of the tabernacle signified the character or qualities that are essential in the work of the church. He taught:

> The outer part of the Sanctuary, the Holy Place, speaks to us of the earthly vocation of the Church. The inner part, or Most Holy Place, tells us of the heavenly vocation of the same Church. The Church of the Lord Jesus Christ has that double service. We have to do some work upon the earth at the same time we have to fulfill a heavenly vocation.[15]

---

13. Bakht Singh, "Studies in Ephesians," *Hebron Messenger* 21 (11 October 1987).
14. Singh, *God's Dwelling Place*, 102.
15. Ibid., 103–104.

For him, living a Spirit-filled Christian life and working towards a Spirit controlled life was to be engaged in the "heavenly vocation." Living a Christian life itself was heavenly vocation. One cannot do God's work through "human strength, wealth and intellect." It is possible only through the Holy Spirit for a person to do this. The work is done through the abiding Spirit. The task is not easy, for there are enormous temptations and trials on the way. Suffering, trials and temptations are part of following God and intended for believers to learn from him at every step and become spiritually mature and responsible. This school of suffering alone prepares a person to be a servant of God.[16]

On the one hand, Bakht Singh interpreted the heavenly vocation as the spiritual journey of the believer. On the other hand he envisioned the eschatological function of the believers in heaven quite literally. He inferred that the believers who lived the victorious life on this earth would be seated on the throne with Christ in heaven (Rev 3:21) where they would ultimately judge both humanity and Satan. He assumed:

> We may often ask why God did not destroy Satan on the very day he rebelled, and why there is this long delay in judging him. The answer is God wants His judgments to be carried out through His Church; His love for His people is so great that He wants to give them His authority in this. But to exercise that authority, we must ourselves be constantly tested and proved by fire and so refined. It is in the furnace of affliction that we are chosen (Isa 48:10).[17]

The earthly vocation is to reach spiritual maturity through overcoming the trials and tribulations on earth. As Singh explained, "Spiritual maturity does not come by head knowledge. You may have much true knowledge, but it only after hardships, trials and tribulations that you become spiritually matured, and your life here on earth is your training ground."[18]

The second aspect of the earthly vocation is to make the church the dwelling place of God. Here again Bakht Singh concentrates on the

---

16. Ibid., 142.
17. Ibid., 109.
18. Ibid.

individual's personal spiritual life and church life. Believers become the material in the building as "living stones" (1 Pet 2:5) because they possess eternal life. At the same time they must be willing to be chiseled or shaped by God so that they may fit or become the right stone to be set in the right location. As God works internally in an individual, one has to engage in work externally for God, by living a life that shows forth the love of Christ and by participating in the activities of the church.[19] He goes on to explain:

> We can build the Church of God by recognition of the headship of the Lord Jesus Christ, by the power of the resurrection, by the word of God given with authority, by serving and helping others, and by learning to worship together. It is by all these the Church becomes God's dwelling place. As we take our share in building the dwelling place of God, we shall experience God's presence very near to us.[20]

Coworkers

Bakht Singh's understanding of the believers' role in the church was unique. He emphasized more the concept of believers as coworkers and partners with Christ (1 Cor 3:9; 2 Cor 6:1) than he did the priesthood of all believers. He noted that God needs us in order to build his church. He contrasted this status of the believers with that of the angels in order to emphasize both the responsibility and the privilege of the believer. Since most of his writings were delivered originally as sermons, the repetition of these themes must have come across strongly for the congregation. He explained that, "Nowhere in the Scriptures are the angels called God's coworkers or partners. But we believers who are purchased by the precious blood of the Lord Jesus Christ have become His partners, so that we may build for Him, His everlasting habitation. This is [a] great mystery."[21] He exhorts that even the weakest believer has something to share in the building of the church: "The mystery is, for such an everlasting habitation, God needs you and me. However weak and foolish we may be, God wants us for such a house."[22]

---

19. Singh, *High Way to Victory*, 26.
20. Singh, *Fullness of God*, 34.
21. Singh, *Unsearchable Greatness*, 8.
22. Ibid., 9–10.

The Ecclesiology of Bakht Singh

Bakht Singh described how believers become partners with Christ in different ways: first, by accepting the Lordship of Christ in the personal, family and corporate life. He maintained that, "If we want to take any share in the building of God's House, first of all, we must keep ourselves under the headship, Lordship and Kingship of the Lord Jesus Christ." Coming under the Lordship of Christ helps one to fulfill the will and purpose of Christ in the church. Thus he reiterates:

> When our personal life, family life, and the church life are brought under the complete Lordship, headship, and Kingship of the Lord Jesus Christ we can hear God's voice day by day for our guidance.
>
> . . . we can know God's will. Then we will become partners in building God's everlasting habitation. At the same time we can enjoy God's fullness in His House. God's love is fully expressed at home.[23]

Second, according to Bakht Singh's understanding, the calling of all believers is to be focused on building the house of God. He came to this conclusion through an allegorical interpretation of the blue robe mentioned in Exodus 28:31–35. Bringing in the practical aspect of this conclusion, Bakht Singh asserted that "the church is being built by the Lord Jesus Christ, with those who are of one mind and are free from jealousy. Only then you can be a coworker with the Lord Jesus Christ in building his church"[24] Becoming a coworker with God, however, is accomplished through prayer. Bakht Singh claimed that, "When one talks to God, God acts in other places and in this way we are his coworkers." By encouraging his followers to develop a personal prayer life, he insisted on the need of a praying church.

Third, every individual in the church has a specific role to play or task to do. At the same time, he noted, individuals cannot simply be independent. Their individual roles are best accomplished when they keep in mind that they are part of a community. As a result, they come under or function within the church because only in and through the church is the power

---

23. Ibid., 11.
24. Singh, *Fullness of God*, 34.

of Christ manifested and the mind of Christ discerned. When believers function as the church, they experience a victorious life and are able to overcome trials and temptations. In turn, the fullness and the glory of God are revealed through the church.[25]

The Unity of the Church

One of the prominent teachings in Bakht Singh's ecclesiology was regarding the unity of the church. At the spiritual level the metaphor of the church as the "body of Christ" informs this concept. On the practical level, his teaching was based upon Acts 2:42, which is the "New Testament pattern" that he claimed to have been revealed to him in the establishment of his Assemblies. Bakht Singh's constant appeal to the biblical basis for his teachings authenticated the practices that he followed in the Assembly. Considering unity as being essential to the nature of the church, he taught that the "body of Christ" represented oneness, unity, equality, interdependence and corporate life of the church. Bakht Singh explained that the human body was the most perfect example of unity. All believers were already united in the "one body" when they were regenerated by the Holy Spirit, and at the same time baptized by the Holy Spirit into one body (1 Cor 12:13). The church is therefore one, and all believers throughout the world and throughout the ages belong to one another.[26]

The principle of the life of Christ is the common binding factor in the oneness of the church. For Bakht Singh:

> Christ and His people were one great Resurrection Life together. What we believe was the beginning of the whole revelation that Paul had been chosen to share with the then – emerging church – and with us all. We say it again. – Christ and His born – again Christians ARE one Living Organism! This IS God's glorious "Mystery"![27]

---

25. Bakht Singh, *The Lamb upon the Throne* (Hyderabad: Hebron, 2005), 20.
26. Koshy, *Brother Bakht Singh of India*, 432–433.
27. Bakht Singh, *Fellowship of the Mystery or All One in Christ Jesus* (message online), 3–4; available from www.brotherbakhtsingh.com.

While Austin-Sparks emphasized the organic nature of the church, most often in a mystical way,[28] Bakht Singh stressed the practical aspect of its implementation at the local level. For Singh, unity was not merely a spiritual principle. It had to be realized in the form of the functioning of the church. Bakht Singh concluded that the pattern or the order of the church should unite people to God and to one another.

Once again, Bakht Singh explained this concept with an allegorical interpretation using the items in the tabernacle. He interpreted the five tie-rods that bound the tabernacle together (Exod 26:26–29) as the five spiritual bonds that keep the whole church together. While the central hidden rod is the life of Jesus Christ that binds together all Christians in the world, the external rods that bind the church are found in Acts 2:42 where it was recorded, "They continued steadfastly in the apostles' *doctrine*, and *fellowship*, and in the *breaking of bread*, and in *prayer*."[29] While comparing the Christian life to that of a ship and a journey full of storms, Singh taught that these four principles should function as anchors in the daily life of the believer.[30] Thus believers were exhorted to follow these four principles steadfastly. In other words, these principles supplied the reason and need to attend and participate in the church services regularly.

Bakht Singh's contention that the four principles form the basis for the unity of the church appears to have stemmed from the backdrop of his understanding of the historic denominational churches and their move towards unity in the early and mid-twentieth century. This was the period when Church Union negotiations were going on among these denominational churches. Bakht Singh maintained that the movement towards church unity was futile and humanly devised. He argued:

> Some people are trying to bind Christians together by man-made constitutions. No church constitution – not even the constitution of the Church of South India – and no man-made constitution whatever can truly bind together the Church of

---

28. Kinnear, *Against the Tide*, 155.
29. Singh, *God's Dwelling Place*, 112. (Italics added.)
30. Singh, *Fullness of God*, 7; *Return of God's Glory*, 50.

God. It is the inward flow of abundant life in the heart of the believer which binds us, and nothing else can.[31]

Because he perceived that the historic denominational churches failed to implement the biblical pattern, his explanation of the four characteristics of the church developed from a comparative evaluation of the existing denominational churches and the biblical principles.

Apostles' Doctrine

Bakht Singh argued that the pure word of God should not be adulterated by man's wisdom. For this reason he advocated that people must read God's word more than other Christian literature.[32] He asserted that the apostles did not preach by appealing to human wisdom (Gal 1:10–12, 1 Cor 2:3–5), but they proclaimed "God's message with God's wisdom and God's power."[33] Bakht Singh argued that the apostles travailed on their knees for the message of God, while some preachers and seminary graduates prepare their messages without even referring to the Bible. In this way he maintained that some seminaries and preachers had undermined the word of God by giving more importance to extra-biblical messages and literature.[34] Bakht Singh's understanding of the word of God and the primacy of the Scriptures, which is explored in detail in the next chapter, may be viewed within the larger context of his Sikh background. His contention was that the cause of division among the churches came as a result of their failure to give teaching based on the entire Bible. He maintained that preaching and teaching from the entire Scriptures, instead of teaching some favorite passages or pet doctrines, would bring forth genuine unity among believers.[35]

Fellowship

The second characteristic that he claimed binds the church together is fellowship. For Bakht Singh, the basis of the fellowship in the church is one's fellowship with God, the Father and the Son (1 Cor 1:9; 1 John 1:3). A

---

31. Singh, *God's Dwelling Place*, 112.
32. Singh, *Return of God's Glory*, 106.
33. Singh, *God's Dwelling Place*, 114.
34. Ibid., 114–116.
35. Ibid., 116.

personal relationship with God and one's personal spirituality and maturity are continuous refrains found in Bakht Singh's teaching. According to him, "The more we walk with God and the nearer we live to God, so much the more we long to enjoy fellowship both with God and with His people; the two go together, they cannot be separate."[36] He encouraged the believers, therefore, to meet together as often as possible. Taking the example of the Roman Catholic nuns and monks who practiced individual spirituality, apart from the community, he reminded his followers that God dwells and expresses his power through the church. Since an individual alone cannot fulfill the purposes of God, he opined, every individual believer should be in fellowship with other believers (1 Chr 29:17).

Singh further observed that "in love and fellowship there is power and strength. By coming together as one body we forget our sorrows and poverty. By bearing each other's burdens we fulfill the law of Christ. By praying together in His name we bind Satan (Matt 18:18, 19)."[37] He maintained that believers could not have the kind of fellowship about which he spoke, genuine fellowship with unbelievers or worldly people is not advised and one could only be kind and polite to them: "Our fellowship should be only with God's people even if they are poor or illiterate, because they are our people."[38] This statement reveals two important points: First, it reveals the exclusivist and separatist tendencies of Bakht Singh and the Assemblies; second, it reveals the important point that in Christ, the only thing that matters in relationship is being in Christ and all humanly constructed barriers no longer have meaning. Ultimately the fellowship among believers brings about unity in the church.

Breaking of Bread

When it comes to the "breaking of bread," Bakht Singh shared theological convictions that were similar to those found among the Brethren. Like the Brethren as well as Watchman Nee,[39] the Lord's Supper is observed every Sunday. The location of the Table, which is placed in the center of the

---

36. Bakht Singh, *David Recovered All* (Hyderabad: Hebron, Reprint, 2002), 96.
37. Singh, *God's Dwelling Place*, 118.
38. Bakht Singh, *The Strong Foundation* (Hyderabad: Hebron, 1983), 8.
39. May, "Watchman Nee," 318ff.

Assembly to signify its centrality in the worship, is another of their common features. The invitation to participate in the Table comes with the exhortation that only believers, or those who are born again, are welcome.

Although the breaking of bread is central in the Sunday worship service, Bakht Singh did not give as much importance to it as the Brethren do or Nee did. Brethren ecclesiology is centered on the Lord's Supper, and for them the way of being the church revolved around the weekly "breaking of bread" service.[40] For Watchman Nee, the existence of the church is signified by the ceremony of celebrating the Lord's Table: "(T)he establishment of a bread breaking service constituted a group of brothers and sisters as the church." In fact, it was not the number of people who attended the church that constituted the core of the church but the number in attendance at the "breaking of bread" service.[41] Singh, along with the breaking of bread, gave equal importance to the preaching of the Word. For him, the significance of the breaking of bread is associated more with the spirit of worship, and as a result was viewed as the culmination of worship and fellowship.

Singh underscored the significance of the Lord's Table as being the place where the visible oneness or unity and equality of believers is manifested. He emphasized the believer's personal, ethical, and moral worthiness as a prerequisite to participation in the breaking of bread. He advocated quite forcefully the concept of equality between all believers at the Table. "There is no magic in the bread and the cup," he wrote:

> They merely testify to us that we are the Lord's. When God's children take part worthily, there will be unity and love amongst them. It is the Lord's Table and not man's (1 Cor 10:16) . . . At the Lord's table all believers are equal . . . In this way at the Lord's table, all the believers understand the one life, one body, one Church, in which all share. Every man-made difference is broken and we have a bond which keeps his children together. . . . God wants oneness, and that bond of

---

40. Shuff, *Searching*, 8.

41. May, *Watchman Nee*, 335. Originally the bread breaking service was held separately on Sunday evening. In the celebration, the practice of covering the elements was avoided, because he believed that the biblical instruction that the "Table was meant to reveal the Lord's death, not conceal it." May, *Watchman Nee*, 332.

unity should be peculiarly manifest at the Lord's Table. There all believers become one and Christ alone is preeminent. . . . The true and strong bond which binds us together is the bond of mutual love springing from our common life in Christ. That bond is for eternity, and by it believers are bound together throughout the world, whatever their nationalities may be.[42]

It is extremely important to understand Bakht Singh's insistence on the aspect of equality within the Indian socio-religious context. Here, he seemed to have attempted explicitly to demolish the socio-cultural barriers of caste and class that were prevalent throughout the Indian churches. Bakht Singh remarked that in the initial days of the movement he had to learn about caste barriers among believers in South India.

(M)any were very proud of their various castes, like Nadars, Pillais, and Vellalas; they were more conscious of their past status in a Hindu society than of their new status as members of the heavenly family of God. . . . The Lord burdened us to expose all this. We realized that unless all these things were set right, mere Bible knowledge would not bring life and revelation and fullness of blessing.[43]

In some churches in South India, the holy communion was served separately to Christians from a high caste background as opposed to those from a Dalit background. This discrimination has resulted in the formation of different congregations, which can be described as "caste" churches even within the same denomination. At the same time people from lower caste background have sought to move out of some of the historic denominational churches in order to form independent churches, once again, mostly based upon caste. Separate caste churches continue to exist, where people from certain castes normally do not attend.[44]

---

42. Singh, *God's Dwelling Place*, 121–122.

43. Bakht Singh, "The Work Is Great," *Hebron Messenger, Special Issue (Part II) for Silver Jubilee of "Jehovah –Shammah,"* (24 July 1966): 4.

44. See V. V. Thomas, "Subaltern Historiography and Post-Colonial Theory: The Case of Dalit Pentecostalism in Kerala," *Religion and Society* 49, no. 2 & 3 (June & September 2004).

As a corrective to this kind of system, Bakht Singh provided a theological imperative that outlined the need for maintaining oneness and equality between believers. It may well be the case that Bakht Singh's Sikh background, where people of all religions are treated the same at the food fellowship, might have also contributed to his perspective and ultimately to his practice.[45]

Participants in the Lord's Supper were warned not to partake unworthily, and to set things right both with God and their fellow believers. Unbelievers were also warned not to participate. More in keeping with the practice of the open Brethren and Austin-Sparks, Bakht Singh and the leaders of the Assemblies claimed that they were inclusive and universal because they opened the Table fellowship to all those who are born again, irrespective of denominational affiliation.[46] According to them, excluding any one on the basis of their denominational affiliation would amount to sectarianism. Bakht Singh explained it this way:

> Again we saw that this service must be expressive of the Church as "one body." Though there would be the local churches, these would only be true to the universal church of Jesus Christ if sectarianism was avoided and universality was clearly expressed. We were convinced that we must welcome all true children of God to partake with us at His Table without reference to or acknowledgement of any caste, creed, nationality or sectarian label they might have.[47]

Perhaps this position was adopted in response to the practice found in certain denominations, where the Table was shared only with those who belonged to that particular doctrinal or church affiliation.

Singh emphasized the ethical implications that impinged upon one's participation at the Lord's Table. He noted that participating unworthily in the Table would incur judgment (1 Cor 11:29, 30). Being right with God and with one's neighbors was assumed as a precondition for participating

---

45. This issue will be dealt in detail in the following chapters.

46. On the issue of an open celebration of the table, Austin-Sparks broke away from Jessie Penn-Lewis, and Watchman Nee from the Exclusive Brethren.

47. Singh, *Write the Vision*, 9.

in the Supper. Thus, each Sunday members were exhorted to examine themselves and to set things right both with God and their neighbors. By locating the Supper as the pinnacle of worship and fellowship with a moral imperative, Singh sought to restore reverence both for the ceremony and for the participation.[48] He criticized the historic denominational churches for having undermined its sacredness and significance in his instructions on the proper understanding of the Lord's Supper, by pointing to the formal and perfunctory ways in which it was conducted.[49]

In consonance with his ideology of intense personal and interior religiosity or *Bhakti*, he described the significance of breaking the bread as one of drawing "to our Lord and see Him."[50] Bakht Singh went on to assert that the believers meet the Lord face to face at the Table and declare that they are waiting to meet him at his coming. When one understands the love of Christ at the Table, it is but natural that they should share that love with their fellow believers. Thus they manifest the life of Christ that brings about unity in the church.

Prayer

The fourth principle that creates unity in the church is prayer. Bakht Singh believed that prayer was the lifeblood of the believer and of the church. He asserted that regular prayer was the practice of the early church. His emphasis on the importance of prayer both in the personal and the corporate life was unparalleled. Prayer would not only bring about solidarity among believers, but also has the potential to bind all believers around the world. He declared that believers all around the world maintain fellowship and oneness through prayer.[51] Bakht Singh believed that effective prayer stood behind every conversion and every revival. He illustrated, "Go to Ireland, Wales, Assam or to any other part of the world where there has been a revival," he charged, "and you will find that it was a prayer revival."[52] For him, participation in prayer was the priestly duty of every believer and it

---

48. Singh, *Return*, 54.
49. See Singh, *God's Dwelling Place*, 120.
50. Ibid., 119.
51. Bakht Singh, "Editor's Letter," *Hebron Messenger* 7, no. 3 (2 February 1969): 2.
52. Singh, *Return*, 31.

was a duty that could be exercised by all, however inadequate they were to perform other tasks. Citing the example of the early church as it withstood persecution and trials through prayer (Acts 16:25), he also taught that prayer was the most effective weapon available to conquer their enemies.[53]

Bakht Singh not only taught about prayer, but was also well known as a man of prayer himself. George Verwer, the founder of Operation Mobilization (OM) and a close associate of Bakht Singh in India, testified, "Here is a man I greatly admire, not that he was perfect, but he fulfilled the things that I had seen in the word of God, especially the emphasis on prayer, care for handling the finance and a simple lifestyle."[54] Daniel Smith a biographer of Bakht Singh wrote, "Over all is cast a life of prayer which I myself have never seen equaled in any man, and I have moved around the world a good deal . . . His is a true life of prayer."[55]

Although Bakht Singh claimed that he was following the New Testament, prayer was not a new concept that he learned after his conversion to Christianity. Prayer was also one of the important religious tenets in Sikhism in which Bakht Singh had been reared. Sikh children are taught to say their morning and evening prayers at home and Singh often mentioned how he used to pray to God in his childhood days.[56] Prayer is also a major element in Sikh worship. It is part of the Sikh spirituality and lifestyle, and so it appears that Singh was already religiously predisposed to lead a life of prayer even before his conversion to Christ took place.

Bakht Singh not only modeled an individual prayer life, but also gave equal importance to corporate prayer within the Assemblies. Consistently, he emphasized the need for a praying church. Bakht Singh believed that prayer was the only earthly weapon that one could exercise in order to gain personal strength and to use against the enemy (Acts 16:25). For him, this was again a model he took from the early church, which the Assemblies adopted. He taught the church to pray in order to know the mind of God in everything she did. All-night prayers, fasting prayer, Saturday preparation prayer for Sunday service, and prayer for guidance in every aspect of

---

53. Singh, *God's Dwelling Place*, 122.
54. Koshy, *Brother Bakht Singh*, 506–507.
55. Smith, *Bakht Singh of India*, 85.
56. Bakht Singh, *The True Salt* (Hyderabad: Hebron, 2003), 37.

life and ministry were common features of the Assemblies. He believed in the power of corporate prayers. He acknowledged that he learned the importance of all-night prayer in the Mukti Mission of Pandita Ramabai at Kedgaon, Maharashtra: "It was here that the Lord taught me the value of all-night prayer."[57]

When Bakht Singh first visited Madras, his preaching and practice of prayer had attracted many to his ministry. R. Rajamani testified that the thing that endeared Bakht Singh to him was the prayer that Bakht Singh uttered when he heard him for the first time. He wrote, "I was so much impressed with that closing prayer that I decided to come again. 'If a man can pray like that,' I thought, 'he must truly be a man of God.'" He went on to indicate that, "It was through prayer, and this preacher's strong emphasis on prayer, that the Lord captured me."[58]

During Bakht Singh's first trip to Madras, where he conducted revival meetings, he announced a whole night of prayer, which was a new concept to the churches there. Rajamani again observed that this led to all-night prayer meetings in several places and ultimately to a prayer revival in Madras.[59] Bakht Singh taught that the more the church prays, the more unity and peace would prevail. For him, disharmony and disunity were the cause of Satan, and fervent prayer would bind the power of the evil one.

He believed in the spiritual unity of the church through the life of Jesus Christ. He envisioned unity in the church being manifested through the practice of preaching the whole Scriptures, breaking of bread every Sunday, fellowshiping with the children of God and prayer. All these characteristics, for him, were constituent of the New Testament pattern of the church.

Practices in the Assembly

Baptism

Bakht Singh gave primacy to baptism both in the life of the believer and in the life of the church. According to him, baptism was one of the

---

57. Bakht Singh, "Editor's Letter," *Hebron Messenger* (2 February 1969): 2.

58. Rajamani, *Monsoon Daybreak* (Fort Washington, PA: Christian Literature Crusade, 1971), 60, 62.

59. Rajamani, *Monsoon Daybreak* (London: Open Books, 1971), 62–63.

"foundational and fundamental principles of salvation."[60] He viewed baptism as being part of the process of salvation. He held that there were actually two baptisms. The first baptism took place when a person was born again and was baptized into one body by the Holy Spirit (Heb 6:2; 1 Cor 12:13). The second one was the baptism of water.

The first type of baptism, which happens when a person is born again, does not mean that one is filled by the Holy Spirit, rather a person's spirit is washed or cleansed, surrounded and covered by the Holy Spirit (Matt 3:11). A person is united with God, Father, Son, and Holy Spirit. Subsequently, the Holy Spirit within the person protects, keeps, preserves and guides him or her. The Spirit also enables one to listen to the voice of God every day, because the Lord lives in the believer and the believer lives in the Lord (Matt 3:16–17).[61]

Writing about the significance of the water baptism, Bakht Singh explained that "in baptism we are immersed into water by which we testify that the Lord Jesus Christ has completely washed all our sins away. Secondly, through baptism we declare our union with the Lord Jesus Christ in His death burial and resurrection (Rom 6:3–5, John 1:4)."[62] Daniel Smith has summarized Bakht Singh's understanding of baptism as a fourfold testimony:

> First before God, that the believer has now a good conscience (1 Pet 3:21); secondly before the devil, that he has left his service (Col 2:12); thirdly, before the world, that he is crucified unto it (Rom 6:3); and fourth, before the Church, that he has become a living member of it (1 Cor 12:13).[63]

Bakht Singh held that baptism was more a testimony than a ritual. He taught that "those who do not obey in baptism live defeated lives."[64]

The Assemblies advocate believers' baptism and contend that baptism should only be administered after a person is born again. It should never

---

60. Singh, *Strong Foundation*, 7.
61. Bakht Singh, "*Baptism*." Message delivered in 1950.
62. Singh, *Strong Foundation*, 6.
63. Smith, *Bakht Singh of India*, 60.
64. Singh, *Strong Foundation*, 7.

precede that experience. Because of this understanding, individuals who were baptized as infants in the denominational churches are "re-baptized" in the Assemblies. The Assemblies also insist on full immersion during the baptism. Singh's practice of "re-baptism" triggered the initial conflict between Bakht Singh and the historic denominational churches,[65] because it invalidated the baptismal practice of the historic denominational churches of India. Moreover, those who were re-baptized joined the Assemblies. This practice of "re-baptism" also meant a separation from other Christians who did not profess their faith in similar way. Further, by allowing elders and lay leaders to administer baptism he added another contentious issue between the mainline churches and him.

Although "believer's baptism" is practiced in other Pentecostal and independent churches, insistence on the necessity of immersion baptism after a born-again experience or "believers' baptism" has become an identifying marker of Bakht Singh Assemblies. The concept of born again Christians being separate from other Christians was, in fact, popularized by the Assemblies in India. The terminology that distinguished between "believers" and "unbelievers" and "nominal Christians" came into widespread usage within the Assemblies. Some Christians, who had a born-again experience, attended the Assembly services, though they did not sever their relationship with the historic denominational churches. Classifying Christians in this manner created a separate group of Christians who developed a "holier than thou" attitude, which led to a kind of exclusivism. By claiming their born-again status, the members of the Assemblies actually looked down upon the Christians belonging to other denominations. While on the one hand this attitude became an entry point for evangelism, it also kept other Christians from associating with them and vice versa.

Laying on of Hands

The "laying on of hands" is another of the special practices, practiced within the Assemblies. This is considered another cardinal principle of salvation and associated closely with baptism. It is usually practiced on two occasions. Following baptism in water, the elders lay their hands on the new believer and pray for her or him (Heb 6.2). Bakht Singh taught that this

---

65. Bakht Singh, "The Work Is Great," 8.

laying on of hands signified a spiritual oneness or relationship with other believers. It expresses the believers' spiritual identification with the death of the Lord Jesus Christ (Lev 1:4). It also shows the spiritual equality and oneness of all believers (Acts 8:14–17; Gal 3:28).[66] Singh explained it this way: "We lay our hands on behalf of the whole church scattered all over the world and declare that we belong to one family, the Church of the Lord Jesus Christ."[67] It is, therefore, an expression of the catholicity of the church. He further noted that through this action "it was not to make the relationship, but to declare that the relationship exists."[68] This explains how Bakht Singh viewed the presence of the whole church being represented in each local Assembly. The whole church is a single body. This practice of the "laying on of hands" at the time of baptism was one that Bakht Singh learned from the Honor Oak Missionaries. Raymond Golsworthy and Fred Flack taught this concept to Singh and practiced it with him.[69] Fred Flack, a missionary associated with the Honor Oak Fellowship, claimed that it was he, who first introduced this practice into the Assemblies.[70]

Though today "laying on of hands" is a common practice in some churches, especially many Pentecostal and independent groups, Bakht Singh acknowledged that in the beginning of his ministry this practice has led to various misunderstandings and accusations.

> "We have been accused of teaching that those upon whom hands had not been laid were not in the body of Christ," he acknowledged, though he went on to argue that this "of course is quite false. Others have thought that it was by this means that believers were reckoned to belong to us or not. Nothing of that kind! All believers belong to us and we to them; there is only one body . . . No practice must be made a basis of fellowship. That would immediately make us another sect."[71]

---

66. Singh, *Strong Foundation*, 7–11.
67. Ibid., 12.
68. Singh, *Write the Vision*, 9.
69. Koshy, *Brother Bakht Singh of India*, 435.
70. A. J. Flack, Sidmouth, Devon, UK to (Bharathi, Pasadena, CA), 13 December 2006.
71. Singh, *Write the Vision*, 9.

Thus the practice of "laying on of hands" became one of the unique features of the Assemblies.

The second occasion for the practice of the "laying on of hands" came at the time when a worker was commissioned. All elders in the Assembly are set apart or consecrated through the practice of "laying on of hands." Koshy has clarified that this was not to be misunderstood as the means by which one receives the Holy Spirit.[72] At the time of the consecration of the elders, Bakht Singh declared, "Before they were set apart by fasting and prayer and laying on of hands they were proved and tested. By laying on of hands upon them scripturally we expressed our oneness and relationship with them as believers and members of the body of Christ."[73] Thus, in this case also it was understood to be a symbol of oneness and of relationship.

Praying for the Sick

Bakht Singh taught that the Assemblies would also pray for the sick. Elders and "God's servant" anoint the sick with the oil and pray. They base this practice on the Scriptures (Mark 16:18; Jas 5:14–15). It was widely believed that Bakht Singh had the gift of healing. Bakht Singh's younger brother, who is a Hindu, has reported that, "God had gifted him the most wonderful touch of healing. He would go to lepers and sit on their bed, have lunch in a lepers' house and evening tea at a governor's house . . . He was a healing Sadhu." He also mentioned that he had been a witness to healings when his brother prayed over the sick.[74] However, Bakht Singh was cautious in using this gift. The practice of healing never became a dominant feature in the Assemblies.

Bakht Singh gave more significance to the preaching of the gospel and to explaining the need of salvation. His conviction was that he should follow the Lord's example with respect to healing, and that the healings and deliverances which the Lord gave should neither be proclaimed nor published, nor should undue attention be given to them or to healers. Accordingly, he taught that "the greatest 'miracle' of all was the new birth." He emphasized

---

72. Koshy, *Brother Bakht Singh of India*, 437.

73. Bakht Singh, "Letter for Praise and Prayer," *Hebron Messenger* (6 March 1983): 3.

74. Shrichand Chhabra, interview by author, tape recording, Delhi, 29 November 2007.

that nothing should be allowed to eclipse or to distract from that fact. It was not bodily healings which would give entrance to the kingdom of God. He went on to note that "neither healings nor deliverances could prove a movement to be of God as strongly as the evidences of transformed lives."[75] Yet, many testify to have experienced physical healing in their lives through the prayers of Bakht Singh.[76]

Holy Convocations

Based upon his understanding of Leviticus 23, Bakht Singh came to believe in the importance of what he called "Holy Convocations." The first "All India Holy Convocation" was organized in Jehovah Shammah from 14 December 1941 to 1 January 1942. This would subsequently become an annual event. The number of days was later reduced from nineteen to nine. The reason for this yearly gathering was to bring people from all over the country to a common place for fellowship.[77] Holding such conventions was already in practice in Northern India. Earnest Dhanaraj notes that in the Sikh tradition people from different villages gather together at one place on the first day of the month. They listen to their *guru* and celebrate a meal together.[78] Bakht Singh also participated in the Sialkot convention that

---

75. Singh, *Write the Vision*, 10.

76. In 1975 when Bakht Singh visited the USA, he visited an Assembly associated with George Geftakys in Tuscola, Illinois. Jim and Brinda McCumber, members of the Assembly, had a son who was sick at that time. They asked Bakht Singh to pray for their son. Bakht Singh anointed the child and prayed over him. Details from an email correspondence with the mother, Brinda McCumber: "Stephen was diagnosed with malignant Astrocytoma grade 2 just before his 3rd birthday. He had a brain tumor that was slow growing. The doctors were unable to remove it as it was growing up out of the brain stem and gave him 6 mo to 1 year to live. No chemo was given but they did give him accelerated linear treatments every weekday for a month simply because they didn't have any other treatment. We had a Christian evangelist from India named Bakht Singh come to visit our fellowship. We asked him to pray for Stephen. He said we should always ask for God's healing but then leave the results to Him. He prayed very simply and anointed him with oil. God heard his prayer." Brinda McCumber, email correspondence to author, 26 March 2009. "Stephen will be 37 March 23, 2009. He has a seizure disorder possibly from the scar tissue in his head and the accelerated linear treatments, so his life has been difficult. We praise God for bringing Bakht Singh to pray for Stephen. He also had cancer when he was 9 and had surgery in his lumbar spine. Currently there is no evidence of cancer in his body, for which we praise God." Brinda McCumber, email correspondence to author, 23 March 2009. See Brinda McCumber. "Midwest and Tuscola History." Available from http://www.geftakysassembly.com/Articles/PersonalAccounts/MidwestAndTuscola.htm.

77. Singh, "A Prepared Place, 7.

78. Earnest Dhanaraj, interview by author, Vellore, India, 12 December 2007.

was held every year in Punjab by the Presbyterian Church. Members of all denominations from many parts of the country attended this convention.[79] It is quite likely that Bakht Singh had a Sikh or North Indian Christian convention model in mind when he began to hold such convocations.

Because of the expansion of the Assemblies across India and abroad, convocations are now held regionally. The specialty of these convocations is that the delegates are accommodated in temporary bamboo booths and provided food for the entire nine days. About two thousand people were accommodated in the booths at the regional convocation of Kalimpong, West Bengal, held in December 2005, and every day about three thousand people were fed. Delegates came from Nepal, Myanmar, Bhutan, as well as different parts of India. At that time, delegates from Pakistan were denied visas to attend the convocation.

The entire work was done voluntarily. No offering was taken except on Sunday. No appeal was made nor was the need indicated at any other time or in any other form. Bakht Singh consistently insisted that a Christian should depend on God alone and should not look to any human agency for material resources. He labeled those who expressed their need to others as "Beggars." Importantly, here also unbelievers were warned not to present their offerings before they had offered themselves to God. A continuous chain of prayer was maintained throughout the convocation. Special sessions were conducted for women, youth, men and children.

The day began with a group of volunteers going around the campus at about 5:00 a.m. singing praise songs. There were two main preaching sessions for the delegates, one in the morning and the other in the evening. In the afternoon the congregation participated in an open-air preaching session. They ended the day with family prayer in the booths.

Songs were sung simultaneously in different languages. They were composed by members of the Assembly and were based on the theme of the convocation. Bakht Singh was wary that the annual event should not become what he called a "tradition." There were times when the convocations were not held. After Bakht Singh became ill in 1986, the convocation typically held in Hebron, Hyderabad, was not convened for several years. Still,

---

79. Llewellyn, "Bakht Singh of India," 8.

Bakht Singh attributed the expansion of his ministry and the Assemblies to the convocations. Delegates, who were blessed in these convocations, went back to their native villages and started gathering together for fellowship, eventually leading to the establishment of new Assemblies.[80]

Worship and Church Order

Understanding that the unity and foundation of the church is based upon the four principles, the apostles' doctrine, fellowship, breaking of bread and prayer, the Assemblies sought to emulate the practices of the early church. Disassociating themselves from the traditional patterns of worship found in the denominational churches, the Assemblies adopted a pattern that was partly biblical and partly cultural (social and religious). Bakht Singh's insight into the Indian spiritual culture as well as that of historic denominational or western Christianity helped him to integrate what he came to view as the "biblical pattern" for the life of the church in an indigenous format.

The denominational churches, which may in some respects be viewed as clones of their western partners, did not strictly follow the Indian religious practice of leaving the foot wear outside the place of worship. U. Meyer rightly observed that in India "the walking in of worshipers into the sanctuary with their shoes on is claimed to be the 'most conspicuous breach of reverence.'"[81] In keeping with the Indian tradition of honoring the place of worship, before entering the assembly hall, the congregation of any assembly leaves its footwear outside the worship place. Being a biblicist, Singh provided a biblical basis to this practice of removing of the footwear. In some of the Assemblies, Exodus 3:5, "Remove the sandals from your feet, for the place on which you are standing is holy ground," has been boldly inscribed at the place where the foot wear is safeguarded. Volunteers not only oversee this process, but also protect the footwear during the time of worship. While entering the sanctuary without footwear is a common

---

80. Bakht Singh, "Editorial Letter," *Hebron Messenger* (21 June 1964): 2.

81. U. Meyer, "Indigenisation – A Critical Review of the Discussion in India 1942–65," *Indian Church History Review* 7, no. 2 (1973): 103.

religious practice in India, safeguarding the footwear is purely a Sikh religious practice.[82]

The order of service is generally divided into three parts: worship (a time of individual praise and adoration), "the breaking of bread," and the main sermon. While the service almost parallels the Brethren form of worship as well as that found in other local indigenous groups, the emphasis is more contextual. Most of the time, the service lasts at least two or three hours. After the service concludes, the congregation joins together for a love feast.

Worship (Time of Individual Praise and Adoration)

In some of the historic denominational churches the order of service has been based upon a written liturgy that was read aloud by the congregation. In some congregations, no specific time of praise and adoration (other than through singing) was allotted during the service. Though the Brethren Assemblies included a time of individual praise and adoration, women were not allowed to participate in it.

A unique feature of the Assemblies has been that both men and women participate in a time of voluntary, audible, individual worship, which is a time of praise and adoration. As the congregation takes their seat on the mats or carpets that are spread on the floor the service begins with a prayer, followed by songs of praise. A short homily is given that is related to worship, most commonly on the attributes of God or on the work of Christ on the cross and in the life of a believer. This is usually considered the first sermon. Then the congregation kneels and enters into a time of individual praise and adoration of God. Often, this time is designated as a time of "worship." Alternating between a male and a female, individuals exalt and praise God as they are led by the Spirit, either through a very short prayer of praise or through a chorus or through reading a Bible text. Exalting the attributes of God, alongside praise and adoration with a deep sense of gratitude for the work of Christ in the life of the believer, are the usual features of this part of the service. Depending upon the size of the congregation, they generally spend at least an hour engaged in this form of worship. Bakht Singh held this concept or form of worship in very high regard. Although Fred Flack claims that he was instrumental in introducing

---

82. The cultural nature of these practices will be dealt in detail in the following chapters.

this time of worship into the Assemblies,[83] Bakht Singh's passion for the praise and worship of God can be understood as extending from his Sikh *Bhakti* tradition.[84]

Table Fellowship or "Table Worship"

The "breaking of the bread," which occurs in the second part of the worship service, is central to the Sunday worship service. This is called a time of "Table fellowship" or the "Table worship." Departing from the traditional practice of the historic denominational churches, with only ordained persons serving the elements, Bakht Singh advocated that believers who gathered together for Sunday worship, however small the group, should not hesitate to break the bread. An elder or "God's servant" typically exhorts the congregation against participating unworthily in the Table. This short exhortation is considered to be the second sermon. Then the congregation partakes of Indian bread, chapati, and a common cup of grape juice (sometimes made out of dried grapes). The elders or male members in good standing, in the Assembly distribute the elements, and women were not allowed to do the same.

Bakht Singh started this practice in a most informal way. In 1941, before starting his first congregation Jehovah Shammah, Bakht Singh along with some of his coworkers, met on top of the Pallavaram Hill, near Madras, to pray for their future course of action. According to the narration of Dorairaj (one of the original participants), after praying all through Saturday night, on Sunday morning the group gathered again for prayer. Bakht Singh seemed to have confessed that they were not observing the breaking of bread:

> Then the brothers said, "If God wants us to observe this we will do it now." Immediately one brother rolled a stone which was there nearby, another brother covered the stone with his big towel. Another brother went to the shop nearby and brought

---

83. A. J. Flack, Sidmouth, Devon, UK to (Bharathi, Pasadena, CA, USA), 13 December 2006.

84. Bakht Singh's theology of worship will be explored in detail in the next chapter.

one bun and two glasses of lime juice. They kept these things on the stone. Again they read 1 Cor 11.[85]

In this manner, then, they partook in the breaking of bread. This account signifies that there was a total break from the traditional formal pattern of breaking the bread. As a result, they adopted the practice of using a type of Indian bread called chapati and juice made from dry grapes. They are prepared fresh at home by the "God's servants" or by an elder's family.[86]

In practice, the celebration of the Table fellowship by a new group of believers signifies the birth of a new congregation or new Assembly. The movement essentially spread by means of house churches. Individuals, who were associated with the Assembly and were transferred in their jobs to different places, or who were born again in the convocations, often started to gather together for Bible study. These Bible studies led to times of worship on Sundays. These Sunday times of worship together would eventually lead to the practice of Table fellowship every Sunday, and in this way, the Table fellowship became symbol of the birth of a new Assembly.[87] Bakht Singh believed that a testimony is established, wherever a new congregation is started.

The Table fellowship is followed by a time of intercession for the universal church. This prayer is interpreted as a prayer for the "church around the world, which we saw symbolized in the bread that remained before us."[88]

The Message

The third sermon, which is the final message, is a time of teaching and exhortation from the Bible. Before the main message, the congregation holds their Bibles up and sings what they call the "Bible chorus."[89]

---

85. D. R. Devadoss, *And They Continued Steadfastly . . . Acts 2:42* (article online), 4; available from www.brotherbakhtsingh.com.

86. I have observed the whole process of making this bread and grape juice in one of the "God's servant" families. The wife of the "God's servant" used to take a bath before preparing it. She prayed before preparing it and did not allow the children to go near or handle it. Thus they maintained the sanctity of the elements.

87. Bakht Singh, "*Editorial Letter*," *Hebron Messenger* (9 July 1967): 2.

88. Rajamani, *Monsoon Daybreak* (Fort Washington, PA: Christian Literature Crusade, 1971), 93.

89. The chorus: "The best book to read is the Bible; if you read it every day, it will help you all the way; Oh! the best book to read is the Bible."

The rationale given for placement of the message at the end of the service was, "when God's people take part in the table worthily their conscience becomes clean and will receive the word with readiness of heart. Then you can give a message."[90] Bakht Singh believed in the priesthood of all believers. As a result along with "God's servant," the elders are also invited to participate in preaching. Claiming the sovereignty and the leadership of the Spirit in all matters of the church, Bakht Singh also believed that expounding the Word should be totally under the control of the Spirit. Thus, in a way it was the collective responsibility of the church to participate in this aspect of life together.

The name of the speaker was not announced ahead of time. Bakht Singh reasoned that by not giving the speaker's name the people would look up to God for the message rather than to the speaker. He explained:

> From the beginning the Lord led us to recognize our mutual responsibility towards Him and towards His people in that we should all be exercised about the message. He may want to

---

90. Devadoss, *They Continued Steadfastly*, 5.

speak through any one of us. . . . We felt "one man" ministry was wrong. We equally felt "any man" ministry was wrong. In every church there would be more than one able to minister helpfully something from the Word. . . . Towards this end our practice has been for those responsible to meet together for prayer before every meeting and then enquire from each other who had a word from the Lord.[91]

While Bakht Singh diligently followed this practice, over time the Assemblies have neglected to follow it. The role of "God's servant" in preaching started to take prominence. However, the fundamental departure from an ordained pulpit ministry to an open lay ministry was Singh's attempt towards a more democratic form of polity. It is reminiscent of the Sikh *gurudwara* system which does not have an ordained priesthood. The practice equipped lay leaders to preach, but at the same time it has brought theological and seminary training into discredit. The practice also helped in establishing house churches in different places. Wherever the congregation members were transferred, it led to a genuine potential for the lay leaders to establish Assemblies. As a result, the Assemblies as movement, has grown. In the urban Assemblies messages are usually given in English and translated into one or two local languages. Bakht Singh viewed this method as a unifying factor and a sign of equality among all believers. He explained:

> In some places, they have Hindi service and an English service. To my mind this is wrong. It makes divisions. In our experience, we have always refused this distinction . . . with the view to maintaining this oneness of living together and serving together; and overcoming every barrier together.[92]

After the message, an offering is taken. This is considered to be a public act of worship. Only born-again Christians are invited to participate in the giving of an offering. A box is placed in front of the congregation and the congregation goes forward in an orderly manner singing as they offer their gifts to the Lord. They believe in making the amount of their offering a

---

91. Singh, *Write the Vision*, 10.
92. Singh, *Return*, 121.

secret so they do not show their offerings to others. Giving to the Lord is considered as a part of their offering of praise to God. The offering is then followed by benediction.

Love Feast

The "love feast" is a special feature of the Assemblies. Initially it was started as an evangelistic measure. Even when Singh was serving as an evangelist in North India during the 1930s, he recognized the celebration of the love feast as a mark of the Lord's visitation in their midst.[93] This has as much to do with the Punjabi culture as it does when one considers the Sikh model of *langar*, which will be addressed below.[94] Later, when the Assembly was formed, the love feast came to signify the fellowship of believers along with the breaking of bread (Acts 2:42, 46; 1 Cor 11:20–30). In a caste-ridden society, however, partaking in meals alongside people of different castes in a social gathering, even in churches, was a rare occasion in the 1940s. Thus, Rajamani has pointed to the liberating character of such meals in which "many new converts too took at the outset this public step of sitting together to eat a communal meal. Thus, they overcame their former caste and social distinctions."[95] They all sit in rows on mats spread on floor and partake in the meal. Practically speaking, it also helps those who have traveled from long distances in order to attend the service.

Following the "love feast" the congregation goes out in a procession for open-air preaching. In the evening, a gospel or evangelistic meeting is conducted in the Assembly for those who were contacted during the open-air ministry.

Government and Organization of the Assemblies

Bakht Singh started the Assemblies with a few coworkers. From the beginning of his ministry Singh worked with a team, and he tried to function alongside them. He believed that functioning corporately would help not only in discerning the mind of God, but also in the smooth functioning of

---

93. Llewellyn, "Bakht Singh of India," 82.
94. This issue will be explored in detail in the next chapter.
95. Rajamani, *Monsoon Daybreak* (London: Open Books, 1971), 93.

the ministry. That did not work for long. Slowly but surely, the movement spread all over India and abroad. As a result, Bakht Singh took the whole burden of maintaining these Assemblies upon himself. He ultimately became the sole authority and the leader of the Assemblies. His functioning even came to be viewed by some as being autocratic.[96] Though it was generally agreed that he was authoritarian in certain ways, it has also been observed that his style was fully in consonance with the Indian leadership style of the *guru*. Most of the leaders, who were interviewed for this project, were of the opinion that it was the people who turned Bakht Singh into the *guru*. He never claimed such a title or position for himself.

A spiritual person within the Indian context is usually obeyed and revered, but hardly ever questioned. If their spirituality and their life are exemplary, their word carries the weight of God's word. In such a context, those who worked with Bakht Singh never questioned him or his leadership. They simply followed him. Thus, the entire ministry was centered around his leadership, although he worked with many coworkers. Records of the number of churches, which are affiliated to the movement, are not maintained. In the city of Hyderabad itself, the Assemblies comprise the third largest Christian presence.[97]

Singh's leadership style is now emulated by "God's servants" in the local Assemblies. Since some of them did not have a similar moral or spiritual authority, but tried to function in the way he did, it has led to problems between them and some local leaders. Eventually it resulted in a leadership crisis in the critical years when Bakht Singh became sick.[98] This led Bakht Singh to give serious thought to the possible consolidation and the development of a structure for the Assemblies. It was during this time that he once again turned to the model of the early church where he believed he found a solution by reinforcing the concept of elders as the main leaders in the local Assemblies.

---

96. Premanandham, "God-Chosen Movement," 350.

97. Hedlund, *Quest*, 206.

98. M. Santha Kumari, *Contextualization of Christianity in India – A Critical Study of the Contribution of Bakht Singh and His Assemblies* (M Phil dissertation, University of Madras, 2006), 84.

Bakht Singh did not have a well-defined doctrine regarding the polity of the church. In a sense, his approach was more pragmatic. As the movement expanded it evolved as new needs arose. Bakht Singh wrote:

> We ourselves were only learning, but it was as we studied the Word daily that His plan for His Church became increasingly clear to us. We could see that we must obey the Word of God implicitly fully determined to give up everything that proved to be a hindrance, whether it be tradition, method or doctrine, anything that could not be justified and supported from the Scriptures.[99]

Bakht Singh asserted that the biblical pattern to be followed was the model of the Antiochian congregation (Acts 11:23–29). Paul and Barnabas were sent out by this congregation through prayer and consecration, and they in turn reported back to the congregation. According to Bakht Singh's understanding, the church functions with the fivefold gifts that were given to different people. All of these gifts were essential in the work of the church. They included apostles, prophets, pastors, evangelists and teachers (Eph 4:8–11). While the apostles were given the authority to establish churches, the prophets expounded the mysteries in the word of God. They moved from place to place reviving the believers. Evangelists were needed to bring people to God. Their burden should be for the whole world. Teachers were to explain the Word in simple language, while pastors were to take care of the flock as a mother would her child.[100]

Although all of these people were needed in the ministry of the church, Bakht Singh pointed out, Paul had appointed elders in every church to shepherd the congregation. The role of the apostles was to train the congregation to the level of maturity where they could govern themselves (Acts 14:22, 23). From then on it was the duty of the elders to teach and to shepherd the flock. However, Paul also appointed Titus to ordain elders in different churches (Titus 1:5). The task of Titus was only to ordain them and then to move on, whereas the elders became main leaders or shepherds

---

99. Singh, "Prepared Place," 7.

100. Bakht Singh, "Letter for Praise and Prayer," *Hebron Messenger* 21, no. 3 (6 February 1983): 2.

of the congregations. As a result, he concluded, there should never be a single elder in a congregation, but a number of elders depending on the size of the congregation. All of the elders, he concluded, must ultimately function under the headship of Christ and the leading of the Holy Spirit.[101]

"God's Servants" or Full-Time Ministers

In the beginning, the Assemblies functioned under the oversight of the elders with no single person being in charge or serving as a pastor. Elders were the main leaders of the church, shouldering all the responsibilities. No single person was given prominence over any other. All those who were dedicated to full-time ministry lived as a community, sharing the responsibilities equally, depending upon their gifts. Those, who dedicated themselves to the full-time ministry, were trained in the main centers. As the ministry expanded, however, there arose a need for full-time workers who had the ability to care for new congregations. At the request of local congregations, Bakht Singh sent those who were dedicated to full-time ministry to shepherd and oversee these congregations. Those who were appointed like this, have been called "God's servants."[102] Their main function was to build up the local believers into maturity and to develop local leadership so that they could carry on the ministry with elders. They were not paid a fixed salary. They had to depend on the respective local Assemblies for their support. The local congregations, however, were autonomous and were free to choose the elders for their congregation. Thus, a kind of hierarchy came into existence. Koshy observed, "Just as the Apostle Paul sent Timothy, Titus and others to various local churches for *a period of time* to strengthen the believers, Bakht Singh, too, practiced the same principle by sending . . ."[103]

Bakht Singh tried to clarify his concern that the elders were to be the main leaders in the Assemblies, shepherding the congregation, teaching, and protecting the flock from false doctrines. But he failed to specify the role and place of "God's servants." He did not explain the relationship

---

101. Ibid.

102. It is not essential that a "God's servant" should be present unless the congregation asks for one. Sometimes local congregations are maintained by the elders.

103. Koshy, *Brother Bakht Singh*, 443.

between "God's servants" and elders in the local Assemblies in a practical manner. In the guidelines he devised for the appointment of elders, the role of "God's servant" was to "watch and observe the prospective elders and deacons and see whether these men have the 'mind of Christ.' Once the God's servant feels strongly the men are ready to take the responsibilities he should inform us."[104]

Bakht Singh did not state clearly whether the office of "God's servant" is equivalent to that of the apostles in church planting, who move on after training the congregation towards maturity and self-sufficiency. When Bakht Singh became ill, C. D. Benjamin, one of the elders of the Hebron local Assembly, wrote the editorial column of the *Hebron Messenger*. Reporting the appointment of elders and deacons for the Hebron local Assembly, he described the role of the apostles and the elders in the following way:

> The Word of God nowhere speaks of apostles managing the affairs of a local assembly. It nowhere speaks of elders managing the affairs of several local Assemblies. The apostles were ministers of all the Assemblies, but they had control of none . . . The duty of apostles was to found Assemblies. Once an assembly was established all responsibility was handed over to the local elders, and from that day apostles exercised no control whatever in its affairs. All management was in the hands of the elders.[105]

In reality the role of "God's servants" did not correspond to the role of the apostles as it was described here. Bakht Singh's movement continued to spread and the Assemblies multiplied because of the work of local believers coming together and establishing local congregations. "God's servants" were sent from the headquarters to bring these congregations into maturity. Thus, in a way, they became synonymous with pastors of the denominational churches, which ultimately led to the division of clergy and laity.

---

104. Bakht Singh, "Guidelines for Appointing Elders." This is a manuscript on the decision taken in a meeting during the last week of January 1983.

105. C. D. Benjamin, "Letter for Praise and Prayer," *Hebron Messenger* 24, no. 9 (27 April 1986): 2.

The lack of a clear job description for "God's servants," ultimately led to confusion and power struggles in various congregations.

Although Bakht Singh did not believe in the central control of all the churches, the growth of congregations and the appointment of "God's servants," who were under the local Assemblies as full-time workers, automatically brought the Assemblies under the umbrella of Hebron, the headquarters of the Assemblies. Consequently, they took on more power, which led to friction with the elders. Bakht Singh intended that the practice would be temporary and the full-time ministers would be transferred from one congregation to another according to need. But in due course, these "God's servants" stayed in the same congregations for longer periods and essentially became the "owners" of the Assemblies they had been asked to serve.

Bakht Singh tried to alleviate the tension by giving a spiritual response to the problem. He exhorted the church by pointing out that the responsibility of the smooth functioning of the church was on the shoulders of the entire congregation and not merely on the shoulders of the servants. He advocated joint responsibility between the servants and the congregation. The servants should report what they were doing and the church should pray for the servants (Acts 13:2, 3; 14:21–28; Acts12:12).[106] Claiming that the problems in the churches were the doings of Satan, Bakht Singh called the church to pray together in order to bind the evil one (Matt 18:19; Eph 3:10). His teaching did not seem to have had much influence on the local congregations. Since the local congregations were autonomous, in some Assemblies the full-time ministers took over the churches, disassociated themselves from the main Assembly and began to establish their own congregations. This led to splits in some of the local Assemblies. In some local Assemblies the congregation refused to continue to support a full-time worker, and the local leaders took over the Assemblies forcing "God's servants" to leave. This became one of the major issues in the Assemblies from the late 1980s onwards.

As mentioned previously, "God's servants" became the sole leaders of some of the Assemblies and they began to take on a new level of independence.

---

106. Bakht Singh, "God's Plan for God's Work," *Hebron Messenger* (1991).

Some severed relations with the headquarters of the Assemblies and established their own Assemblies or congregations. Koshy has noted that "this has adversely affected the testimony of the Lord in some places, leading to conflicts between local believers and 'God's servants' and the subsequent breakup of some local Assemblies and in a few places had led to court cases."[107]

Since the local Assemblies are autonomous, they do not have an organized or official affiliation to a central office or headquarters. Under Bakht Singh's leadership they believed in maintaining a spiritual relationship between the various congregations. As Koshy described it, "The affiliation is purely spiritual. It is not an ecclesiastical unity but a spiritual unity. When the 'God's servants' or local believers separate, we meet with them and counsel them, but we do not have any authority over them. Continuing the affiliation is their own decision."[108]

Bakht Singh did not have a specific system or structure in mind when he transferred "God's servants" from one place to another. He adapted his own method of depending upon God and seeking God's will to transfer "God's servants" as needed. They were not given any written or direct verbal orders. Each year the holy convocation at Hebron was followed by two days of "workers meetings." At the end of the meetings, Bakht Singh would pray aloud "Lord, thank you for transferring so and so to such and such a place." This prayer was the only order that "God's servants" received. While some accepted it, others began to refuse it, thereby producing yet another crisis in the Assemblies.[109]

Since Bakht Singh was the sole authority in the Assemblies, it became difficult for him to handle everything. His failing health necessitated the development of a model to share the responsibility and to give a proper structure to the Assemblies. In the end Bakht Singh did not set up a clear, cohesive administrative structure for the Assemblies. To a large extent, the Assemblies remain loosely connected and are independent from one another.

---

107. Koshy, *Brother Bakht Singh*, 444.
108. T. E. Koshy, interview by author, Syracuse, USA, 13 September 2007.
109. Koshy, *Brother Bakht Singh*, 444.

Elders

One of the identifying marks of the local church, for Bakht Singh, was the fact that it functioned under the leadership of elders. He specified that a single elder or leader was never the New Testament principle. Since the term "elders" is plural, only when there was more than one elder in the congregation could it be recognized as a local church. As he explained, "if there are two functioning together in the shepherding responsibilities then the company has 'fathers' and can be regarded as a local church."[110] The elders were to be the main leaders in the Assembly. There were two principles that were followed in appointing the elders. The first was made clear in Acts 14:23, where the apostles appointed the elders; and the second was outlined in Titus 1:5, where the apostles delegated others to appoint elders.[111]

Bakht Singh strongly opposed the system of electing the elders by vote in the Assemblies. He was conscious of the fact that leadership issue was one of the main problems in the historic denominational churches. He wrote:

> (I)t is entirely unscriptural to appoint elders by vote. They all know that by having elections in their system, they bring strife in the churches. It begins by election. One party wins, the other party loses. How can we justify that practice when we know it is unscriptural.

Probably in order to avoid such divisions in the Assemblies and to follow an alternate or a pattern that he deemed to be scriptural, Bakht Singh advocated the method of appointing elders.

Singh taught that the congregation and the leaders should pray for the elders, and according to the guidance of the Holy Spirit they should set apart the elders in the Assemblies.[112] Though in principle elders were to be appointed in the local Assemblies, many Assemblies did not function with elders until the 1980s, resulting in a crisis in the Assemblies. In 1983 Bakht Singh confessed that he had failed to ordain elders in the local Assemblies and invited "God's servants" and elders of local Assemblies to enter into a time of prayer. In the *Hebron Messenger*, the official magazine

---

110. Singh, *Write the Vision*, 10.
111. Ibid.
112. Singh, *Return*, 39.

of the Assemblies, he wrote a series of articles[113] in which he exhorted the churches and gave the biblical principles on the qualities, duties and the procedures for ordaining the elders. In these articles, instead of clearly mentioning the specific duties of elders in a practical manner in the local context, he simply pointed to examples from the Scriptures. Thus, to a certain extent, he was vague in defining the role of elders and deacons in the Assemblies. Recognizing the need to bring order to the Assemblies, Bakht Singh began to take measures towards that end. Thus, he wrote:

> This work cannot be done by one man. Brothers with spiritual maturity, wisdom, vision and discernment are needed to help in this extremely important task of choosing and appointing elders and deacons for God's glory and for the edification of the Church . . . While we were praying the Lord showed me that according to Titus 1:5, before appointing elders and deacons we have to appoint men to help us in that work just as Paul appointed Titus. After much prayer the Lord has led me to set apart six men to assist me in appointing elders and deacons and also to help me in other important jobs of the Assemblies in Andhra Pradesh. Their responsibilities will be local in nature.[114]

In the report that was published in the *Hebron Messenger* the following month, however, Bakht Singh went on to mention that, "They will shoulder various responsibilities in the work of the Lord worldwide as the Lord leads."[115]

Although the six men were to assist Bakht Singh in appointing elders in local congregations, Bakht Singh delegated the oversight of his Trust, "The Society of Trustees of Indigenous Churches in India," the official registered body of the Assemblies, to them.[116] With this move, a central society

---

113. See *Hebron Messenger* (January 1983–April 1983).

114. Bakht Singh, "Letter for Praise and Prayer," *Hebron Messenger* 21, no. 3 (6 February 1983): 3.

115. Bakht Singh, "Letter for Praise and Prayer," *Hebron* Messenger 21, no. 5 (6 March 1983): 3.

116. Minutes of the proceedings of the Principal Trustee, Bro. Bakht Singh, of the Society of Trustees of Indigenous Churches in India, Hebron, Golconda Cross Roads, Hyderabad 500020, 24 February 1983.

came into existence apart from the autonomous local Assemblies. These six men would become "elders" who were in charge of different individual Assemblies in India and abroad. While the local Assemblies were still autonomous in their support, governance and ministry, these elders became their overseers in providing counsel and sending "God's servants," if the need arose.[117] The role of these six men and their relationship to the local Assemblies became one of the most contentious issues in the Assemblies while Bakht Singh was still alive and more so after his death.[118]

Because of the leadership crisis in the Assemblies, the shape that the movement will take in the future has been subject to substantial speculation. Roger Hedlund suggests:

> The Movement which once was viewed as a potential "model" Indian church is expected to continue but the direction is uncertain. The Movement may become a denomination. It may dwindle under less capable leadership. It might divide. Smaller believers' groups may break away. The former movement might transmute as a monument in memory of Bakht Singh.[119]

Moses Premanandham has offered that crystallization has already taken place in the movement.[120] Along with these kinds of speculations, Bakht Singh was generally accused of failing to build up leadership to succeed him. Santha Kumari has observed that, "One of the reasons for this unfortunate situation that is prevailing now is the failure to appoint reliable men of character as leaders at different levels and the failure to follow the biblical model of shared or group leadership."[121]

From the perspective of having or maintaining a hierarchical, structured, centralized leadership or control and authority in the form of a denomination or to form a denomination, this argument holds ground.

---

117. Rosem, *Brother Bakht Singh* (Delhi: ISPCK, 2002), 146.
118. Leadership crisis in the Assemblies and the current state of affairs are beyond the purview of the dissertation and are essential areas for further research.
119. Hedlund, *Quest for Identity*, 156.
120. Premanandham, "God-Chosen Movement," 350.
121. Kumari, "Contextualization," 85.

However, having a centralized control or authority was not the vision of Bakht Singh.

At the time of Bakht Singh's death in the year 2000, the movement was sixty years old. Bakht Singh was bedridden and totally incapacitated for almost fifteen years before his death. Most of the coworkers and leaders he appointed, died before him, leaving a vacuum at the top level.[122] Bakht Singh never envisioned a centralized structure. In fact he was against it. He wrote:

> Federation of local churches will lead to centralized control, however well disguised. There will gradually come about formulation of policy or adoption of resolutions which would be circulated among the churches and they would be expected to conform to them. However sincere and lofty the motive, the result is that the local church loses the edge of its autonomy; the Holy Spirit is replaced as the initiator of activities, thereby marring what Satan hates most of all – the living expression of the headship of Christ in the Church.[123]

This statement reveals Bakht Singh's predicament as he tried to be true to his biblical principles and to his conviction of the view that structures would replace divine authority. According to his principle of faith and depending on God for every move, Bakht Singh did not either consciously form a structure, or find his successor. Equipping "God's servants" and local elders to preach and govern themselves on their own, however, Bakht Singh left a workable model of independent, self-sufficient, self-propagating and self-governing Indian house church movement in India. Thus he could be called the Father of the independent Indian church movement.

Bakht Singh's ecclesiology reveals the complexity of his context and thought, as well as his personal struggle to interact with and reconcile the biblical principles, the immediate church context, and his personal religiosity or spirituality. Although Bakht Singh was undoubtedly sincere in his approach to implement the biblical principles in his ecclesiology, the lenses he wore to understand those principles disclose his internalized Sikh

---

122. Rosem, *Brother Bakht Singh*, 146.
123. Singh, *Write the Vision*, 26.

spirituality. Some of the practices he implemented in the Assemblies, and the way he understood the Scriptures point to his Sikh background and ideology. This necessitates some understanding of Sikhism.

CHAPTER 5

Sikh Antecedents of Bakht Singh: Their Influence on the Teaching and Practices of the Assemblies

If we were to limit our understanding of the movement founded by Bakht Singh solely to a theological and biblical perspective, it would obscure the broad religious environment in which he was trained prior to his conversion and it would mask whatever influence it might have had on his thought and practices following his conversion. Bakht Singh's approach to his newly found faith is embedded in various other aspects of his contemporary social and religious worldview. His deep observation and analysis of the problems involved both in his inherited religious tradition of Sikhism and his adopted religion of Christianity were discernable in his approaches to and application of the biblical teachings in the Assemblies. While personal spirituality was Bakht Singh's major emphasis, the essence of his spirituality and practice of faith was underscored by his personal quest as a Sikh for the realization of God. Roger Hedlund has noted:

> What is not often recognized is the Punjabi nature of the Movement with its worship pattern borrowed from the Gurudwara. Cultural practices have been Biblicised, and North Indian cultural forms adapted and followed throughout a Movement which is largely South Indian in composition.[1]

Thus, it is essential to probe the religio-spiritual contours of his teachings that could have been structured on the foundation of his personal

---

1. Hedlund, *Quest*, 178.

spirituality that he inherited as a Sikh. It is essential therefore, to understand Sikhism and how it has a bearing on the life and teachings of Bakht Singh and the Assemblies.

Religious Background of Bakht Singh

Bakht Singh's father, Lala Jawahar Mall, was a government contractor and one of the richest persons in the surrounding villages of Joiya in Punjab. The family, though it was Hindu, had a tradition of dedicating the eldest male child to Sikhism. This tradition of dedicating the firstborn male child had begun four or five generations before the birth of Bakht Singh. They were devotees of Guru Nanak. His great-grandfather was a *bhai*[2] in the Sikh religion and was called a saint.[3] Bakht Singh's parents did not have children for a long time after their marriage. They prayed for offspring and Bakht Singh's mother, who was later blessed with a female first born, vowed[4] that if she had a son, she would dedicate him to Guru Nanak. As the eldest male child in the family, Bakht Singh was dedicated and brought up as a Sikh.[5] Bakht Singh later described his parents as being "very, very orthodox Sikhs."[6]

Before the birth of Bakht Singh, someone (possibly a *sadhu*, a Hindu mendicant)[7] told his mother that she would have a son, but that he would not live with her.[8] His parents were afraid of this possible separation from

---

2. The term "*bhai*" literally means "brother." Though every Sikh is considered to be a brother in the congregation, this term serves also as a title given especially to the devout Sikhs and a few other Sikhs who earn a substantial reputation for their piety or religious learning. See Gurnek Singh, "*Bhai*," in *Encyclopaedia of Sikhism* vol. 1, 4th ed., ed. Harbans Singh (Patiala: Punjabi University, 2002), 331–333.

3. Amar Nath Chhabra, email correspondence to T. E. Koshy, 16 February 2001. Amar Nath is one of Bakht Singh's brothers.

4. It was common practice for Hindu women to make a vow to raise a son in the family as a Sikh within certain communities in Punjab. See Sushil Narulla, "Striking New Roots," *Indian Journal of Gender Studies* 6, no. 2 (1999); Harjot S. Oberoi, "From Ritual to Counter-Ritual: Rethinking the Hindu-Sikh Question, 1884–1915," in *Sikh History and Religion in the Twentieth Century*, ed. Joseph T. O'Connell et.al. (New Delhi: Manohar Publications, 1990), 147ff.

5. Shrichand Chhabra, interview by author, Delhi, 29 November 2007.

6. Singh, *Looking unto Jesus*, 52.

7. Koshy, *Brother Bakht Singh of India*, 62.

8. Bakht Singh, *Forty Mountain Peaks* (Hyderabad: Hebron, 1971), 48.

their son, so they pampered him, lest he would run away from home or become a *sadhu*. During his childhood Bakht Singh spent time in the Sikh temples and with the Sikh Granthis, the priests or readers in the Sikh religion.[9] Unlike other children playing in the streets, Bakht Singh was so confined to the temple that his parents worried he would become a *sadhu*. Bakht Singh mentions that he used to ask his mother: "Who is Sat Guru? How to find him? Where to find him?" She told him that he could accept one of the Sadhus. However, as the desire to find the Sat Guru deepened, he spent hours reading the Guru Granth Sahib.[10] In Gujaranwala where Bakht Singh attended school, he spent much time with Sikh religious teachers. Sunder Singh, a Sikh who was working there with an advocate or attorney, used to talk to the boys about God.

In 1915, at the age of 12, Bakht Singh was married to a 15-year-old girl named Ram Bai. Bakht Singh's father celebrated the wedding extravagantly for several days so that it became the talk in neighboring villages. He matriculated in 1919 and joined the Government College at Lahore where he earned a degree in Bachelor of Arts. That same year, his family moved from Joiya to Sargodha. After his graduation, Singh worked in his father's new cotton mill.[11]

Bakht Singh strongly affirmed his Sikh identity. Living in the city of Lahore, he was one of the emerging new elites. His ambition, as with any other rich kid in those days, was to go to England for higher studies.[12] His father expected him to help in his business and was not supportive of the idea of Bakht Singh going to England. At this point his mother intervened and said that she would support him were he to go to England, if he promised her that he would not change his religion after going there. With this promise Bakht Singh went to England in 1926 for his mechanical engineering course.[13] He enrolled in the City and Guild's College, London, and

---

9. Sikh priests or readers are called Granthis. Women as well as men can perform Sikh religious functions.

10. Bakht Singh, interview by T. E. Koshy, notes 1970.

11. Koshy, *Brother Bakht Singh of India*, 64–66.

12. Harjot S. Oberoi, *The Construction of Religious Boundaries: Culture, Identity, and Diversity in the Sikh Tradition* (Chicago, IL: University of Chicago Press, 1994), 260–262.

13. Singh, *His Loving Hands*, 6.

stayed as a paying guest of one Miss Kemp, at No. 34, Denmark Hill. In 1928, he completed his course within two years.[14]

For a long time, Sikhism was not considered to be a religion independent from Hinduism. It was identified as a sect within Hinduism. The religious affiliations of the Sikhs and Hindus and different traditions within Sikhism in Punjab were ambiguous, and the identities and boundaries were fluid. This blurred identity was contested by the Sikhs in the latter half of the nineteenth century. In addition to this ambiguity, in 1873, four Sikh students attending a mission school in Amritsar converted to Christianity. Arya Samaj, a Hindu fundamentalist organization, claimed that Sikhism was a sect in Hinduism. All these resulted in the renaissance within Sikhism, through the Singh Sabha movement, that aimed at protecting the Sikh faith as a distinct religion.[15] The leaders of this movement were urban, western-educated elites of the community. Through this movement, the Sikhs affirmed their own identity and established their creedal and ethical codes. Later, the *gurudwara* movement grew up in order to maintain purity in places of worship. Both these movements brought in the consolidation and institutionalization of the Sikh religious administration.[16]

Bakht Singh grew up in an environment where he was exposed both to the Sikh and to the Hindu ideology, and especially when the Sikh identity was asserted by the Singh Sabha movement. Bakht Singh asserts that he was very proud of his Sikh religion.[17] In a way, his assertion of the distinct Sikh faith confirmed his identity and the influence of the times on him. To understand the movement Bakht Singh founded, one must probe into the particular background and religion of Bakht Singh before his conversion to Christianity that first molded and conditioned his outlook and his worldview.

---

14. Koshy, *Brother Bakht Singh*, 76.

15. McLeod, *Exploring Sikhism*, 93.

16. Kushwant Singh, *The History of the Sikhs: Volume 2:1839–1974* (Delhi: Oxford University Press, 1977), 136–147.

17. Singh, *His Loving Hands*, 6.

Main Tenets in Sikhism

Guru

The *Mul Mantra*[18] is the opening statement of the *Guru Granth Sahib*. It is the creed of Sikhism. It defines the nature of God and states that God is realized through the grace of the *guru*. Since God is known through *guru's* grace, it is only right to ask, "who is the *guru*?"

Sikhism is based upon three fundamental concepts: *Guru, Sabad* and *Nam*.

The term *guru* is an extremely ambiguous term in Sikhism. Sikh faith almost revolves around the concept of *guru* and the way it is interpreted. In the Sikh tradition, the term carries similar meaning as in some Hindu scriptures, in that, "*gu* means 'darkness,' *ru* means light; thus a *guru* is one who delivers those who accept his teaching and discipline from darkness to enlightenment, from *samsara*, the road of rebirths, to *moksha*, spiritual realization and release."[19]

In Sikhism, the term *guru* is also understood as "God"; *sabad* the "voice of God"; *nam* the "name of God"; "the person who mediates and manifests the revelation of God to human beings"; and "the message or the scripture," which is called the *Guru Granth Sahib*. *Guru* is the dispeller of darkness. *Guru* is the God-conscious guide, the enlightened preceptor and an invaluable link between human beings and God. *Guru* is the object of utmost veneration, yet a *guru* is not to be worshiped as God. At the same time, one cannot reach God or attain salvation without the *guru*. While at

---

18. The *Mul Mantra*:
    Lord God is one, Absolute and Supreme;
    Peer has He none, in His Cosmic Scheme.
    Transcendent He is, yet Immanent too.
    Truth Eternal is His Name True.
    Sole Creator – He pervades all Creation;
    He knows no fear; is at enmity with no one.
    Timeless and formless – not incarnate is He;
    Self-existent – Being He is of His Own Being.
    Guru's grace alone may us unto Him attain,
    (That too if the Lord's Will does so ordain.)
Gurdip Singh Randhawa, *Guru Nanak's Japu Ji: Text, Translation & Study*, 4th ed. (Amritsar: Guru Nanak Dev University, 1996), 93.

19. Cole, *The Guru*, 2. (Italics added.)

times, the human *guru* and the divine *guru* are both considered to be the same, Sikhs are also warned against considering the human *gurus* as God.[20]

Human *gurus* attain the status of a *guru* through the revelation they receive from God, through the "voice" or "Word," that is the *sabad*. The identity of *guru* is not in the person but in the message that he brings from God. Since it was through the "word" or the "voice of God" that God revealed himself, the "Word" and *guru* became synonymous. While Nanak affirms that he reveals what he hears, for him "the *Sat Guru* meant the inner voice, the mystical movement of God in the depths of one's being" . . . *Guru* is trans-historical in nature, an abstract *guru* within one's soul, "the voice of God mystically uttered within."[21] Interpreting a certain passage, McLeod concludes, "The *Guru* accordingly is God; the *Guru* is the voice of God; and the *Guru* is the Word, the Truth of God. Guru Nanak uses the term in all three senses."[22] The *Guru Granth Sahib*, the embodied word, thus came to be venerated as the *guru*.[23] The Sikhs believe that every word in the *Guru Granth Sahib* is the word of God. It is the living *guru*. A Sikh worship place can be called a *gurudwara* only when the *Guru Granth Sahib* is installed in it. The Sikh religious assembly has religious sanction only when it is conducted in the presence of the *Guru Granth Sahib*.

Nam

Nam is translated as "name" in English. But in English, the word "name" does not express the full meaning of *nam* as a conceptual category. It is another main concept in Sikhism. It signifies the essential and functional qualities of God. The ultimate goal of the Sikh is to realize the *nam* in this life and to live by it. The realization of *nam* is achieved through meditation and devotion to it. This discipline is called *nam simaran* or "remembrance"

---

20. Pritam Singh Gill, *Trinity in Sikhism* (Jullunder: New Academic, 1973), 181.

21. Sunita Puri, *Advent of Sikh Religion: A Socio-Political Perspective* (New Delhi: Munshiram Manoharlal Publishers, 1993), 9.

22. McLeod, *Guru Nanak*, 199.

23. In the *gurudwara*, the Guru Granth Sahib should be opened daily. When it is opened, it should be laid under a canopy in a clean and tidy place. It is kept on a cot, or stool or a lectern, and covered with a cloth. Cushions are used to support it while it is opened, and is covered with a mantle when it is not read. It is fanned continuously while it is opened. When they enter the *gurudwara* they bow before the Granth Sahib touching the floor with their forehead. All Sikhs including men should cover their head in front of the open Granth Sahib.

or "recitation of the name of God." It is not a mere ritual, but a conscious practice in which one's ego is purged and becomes aware of the presence of God, gets attuned to his will and is transformed. As Guru Nanak put it:

> Why shoutest thou God's name like mad, for he who hath attained God hath hid him in the heart." According to Guru Amardas: "Everyone uttereth the Name of God, but utterance is not realisation. It is only when God abideth in the mind, by the Guru's grace, that one gathereth the fruit."[24]

In Sikhism the essence of God is *Sati Nam*, "all that God is."[25] *Nam* is also considered the "indwelling power" and not a merely a "word." It dwells within every human being, but is not always discerned.[26] When this power within is merged with the *nam*, one becomes conscious of God.

The Sikh Gurus use the terms *nam* and "word" synonymously. Both *nam* and "word" refer to the "revelation" of God. The third *guru* called the Sikhs to "recognize the true Word as the True Name" and he stated that "the *guru's* Word is nectar sweet; daily recite the name of God." The contents of the *Granth* are also described as the *nam*.[27] For Guru Nanak the *sabad* or Word is identified with the *nam*: "All things and wisdoms become manifested through the *Nama* and though one may wear many sectarian garbs yet one is strayed from the path without name – the *sabad*."[28] *Nam* indwells every person. Being present within a person, the *nam* may be understood as referring to one's conscience.

The "name" reminds of one's status as a spiritual being and relationship to God. It is nothing but living in the presence of God. *Nam japa* is

---

24. Gopal Singh, *The Religion of the Sikhs*, (New York: Asia Publishing, 1971), 55.

25. Shobarani Basu, "Some Religious Concepts in Hinduism and Sikhism: Guru and Sabda," in *Perspectives on Guru Nanak: Seminar Papers*, ed. Harbans Singh (Patiala: Punjabi University, 1975), 133.

26. Jodh Singh, *Gurmati Niranay*, chs. 1, 2, 6 and 8, passim, in *Textual Sources for the Study of Sikhism,* trans and ed. McLeod (Totowa, NJ: Barnes & Noble, 1984), 140.

27. Teja Singh, *Asa di Var da bhav prakasani tika*, (Amritsar), 24–28, in *Textual Sources*, 141.

28. Jodh Singh, "Guru Nanak's Concept of Sabad as Guru," *Studies in Sikhism and Comparative Religion* 1, no. 1 (October 1982): 74.

meaningless, if it does not affect ones conduct.[29] Thus, meditation on God's name leads to good actions and God consciousness whereby a believer becomes God-oriented and God-controlled in all that she or he does and is.

Hukam (Divine Will or Divine Order)

Hukam is also one of the foundational principles in Sikhism. The goal of human life is to understand *hukam*. *Hukam* as a concept is interpreted as the "Divine Law," "Divine Ordinance," and "Divine Will." Terms like *raza* and *bhana,* which refer to divine pleasure, are also used as synonyms of *hukam*. *Hukam* is associated with the activity of God and the human response. "Philosophically *hukam* is the apprehension of that mystery which underlines all existence, and which can express itself only in the action of submission and resignation."[30] Everything that exists does so because of the *hukam*. It is the principle of all life. The creation is the outcome of the will of God. No one can live beyond the will of God. It is a principle beyond human description, though to a certain extent, it may be comprehensible. Understanding this principle leads to the destruction of self-centered pride and alienation from God. With God, *hukam* is a constant principle, whereas with human beings it is something to be recognized – something to which human beings must submit. It is the vital principle that creates, sustains and regulates the universe.[31]

Hukam is the controlling authority of the supreme being who is true and as such it is also true. The *guru*'s command was to recognize this divine order and to submit to it.[32] This concept is also closely linked to the concept of the "voice of God" and its role in salvation or the realization of God.[33]

Understanding *hukam* is not an intellectual exercise, but a spiritual accomplishment. The internal comprehension is possible only through the grace of God and to those who submit their will to the will of God. Those

---

29. R. K. Tripathi, "Teachings of Guru Nanak Dev," in *Sikh Gurus and the Indian Spiritual Thought,* ed. Taran Singh (Patiala: Publication Bureau, Punjabi University, 1981), 232–233.

30. Cited by Wazir Singh, *The Sikh Vision: Problems of Philosophy and Faith* (New Delhi: Ess Publications, 1992), 34.

31. McLeod, *Guru Nanak,* 201.

32. Dalbir Singh Dhillon, *Sikhism Origin and Development* (New Delhi: Atlantic, 1988), 228.

33. McLeod, *Guru Nanak,* 203.

who live their lives in conformity with the *hukam* attain union with God. Human beings have the freedom to choose, however, whether or not to live in accordance with the *hukam*. Disobedience leads to *karma*.

Sangat

When the assemblies of Sikh devotees are gathered together in the presence of the *Guru Granth,* they are called the *sangat*. The term *satsangat* is used to denote the fellowship of seekers of truth. It is not necessary that the congregation gathers only in a *gurudwara*. The holy congregation gathers to sing praises for God and to listen to the exposition of the Sikh Scriptures. They also narrate stories from Sikh history. At times, social and political matters related to the community are discussed. The congregational worship is considered essential for the spiritual edification of the community. It is a place where devotees are nurtured in service for the community. They believe that true religious discipline matures in the company of the devoted. According to Guru Nanak, "*Satsangat* is the *guru*'s own school where one practices godlike qualities" (A.G.1316); "God resides in the *sangat*. He who comprehends the *guru*'s word realizes the Truth." (A.G.1314). As members of the *sangat* every Sikh is known as a *bhai* or brother. The term signifies the brotherhood of the Sikhs.[34]

Similar Concepts

The concepts or teachings of Bakht Singh bear many similarities or parallels with those that are found in Sikhism. Similarly, the practices he followed exhibit this clearly as well. It appears that Bakht Singh may have been a spontaneous synthesizer of Sikh and Christian teachings, a supporter of what might be viewed a responsible form of contextuality or even syncretism.[35] Even if this is the case, it must be remembered that Bakht Singh's theology emanates first and foremost from his own divine encounter and experiences with Jesus Christ. Bakht Singh had a good knowledge of the existing systems in Christianity. He inherited a specific form of spirituality; at the same time, he had a direct experience of God and an understanding

---

34. K. Jagjit Singh, "Sangat," in *Encyclopaedia of Sikhism* vol. 4, 41–43.

35. See Walter J. Hollenweger, *Pentecostalism Origins and Developments Worldwide* (Peabody, MA: Hendrickson, 1997), 132–141.

of Scriptures. Bakht Singh did not, however, simply replicate any of the traditional Christian theological concepts or the Sikh concepts, but he attempted to understand the Christian faith in terms that were consistent with his time and his Indian context. Bakht Singh fashioned cultural forms that made sense in Indian culture. Familiarity with foreign forms sensitized him to inappropriateness of these for India. His encounter with Jesus Christ was decisive but he had to work out his discipleship. In other words, Bakht Singh redefined and reinterpreted concepts that are common to both Sikhism and Christianity to create his Christian mold and shape the practices accordingly.

The Name of Jesus

Bakht Singh's first encounter with Jesus Christ was in a Christian service on a ship, while sailing from England to Canada. Since he did not want to kneel down during the time of prayer, he wanted to leave the service. But he realized that he was caught between two people who were kneeling. Moreover, he thought that he should show courtesy to the place as he did when he went to a mosque or a temple, and so decided to stay in place out of respect. Bakht Singh remembered it in the following account:

> So breaking my national pride, intellectual pride and religious pride I knelt down. . . . When I knelt down I felt a great change coming in me. My whole body was trembling. I could feel divine power entering into me and lifting me. The first change I noticed in myself was that a great joy was flooding my soul. The second change was that I was repeating the name of Jesus. I began to say "Oh, Lord Jesus, blessed be thy Name, blessed be thy Name." The name Jesus became very sweet to me, whereas before I used to despise the very name, and during conversations I had made fun of it.[36]

Bakht Singh went on to state that after this encounter (his conversion happened eighteen months after this experience), the name of Jesus was sweet to him and he lost the desire for things like smoking and drinking

---

36. Singh, *His Loving Hands,* 13–14.

in which he had previously indulged.[37] It was probably natural for Bakht Singh to be attracted initially to the name of Jesus, because reciting the name was the first spiritual lesson that Sikhs learned from childhood. He seems to have responded unconsciously to the name of Jesus, in the same manner that he has learned to respond to the *nam* within his Sikh tradition. The language that he used to describe the sweetness that the name of Jesus took on at that time is quite similar to the way in which Sikhism describes God, "Infinite, Unseen, unseizable is the Name, but sweetest of the sweet" (Maru M.1).[38]

In his teaching on baptism, Bakht Singh explained that at the time of baptism or in baptism a believer declares that

> The Lord Jesus Christ came into the world to invite sinners into His everlasting Kingdom, and by believing on the blessed name we can enter in . . . It is heavenly name, it is the only name by which men can be saved. There is no other name. That must be declared in baptism.[39]

In one sense, Bakht Singh's emphasis on declaring the "name of Jesus" at baptism may seem out of place, for it is already implied in that act. But the reason for proclaiming the name of Jesus became significant for Bakht Singh because he had finally discovered the name for the God that he had sought to worship in his earlier faith. He could name the God he worshiped. As a result of this discovery, the name of Jesus was especially prominent in his writings that date from his earliest Christian period.

The Word of God

Bakht Singh grew up in a tradition in which when one spoke of the "word of God" it was the same as saying "God," as well as "the revelation of God." It was also a belief in which "the word of God" was viewed as the ultimate spiritual authority over human beings. It might be the case that as a Christian, Bakht Singh sought some kind of confirmation that what he was reading in the Christian Scriptures was equivalent to his understanding

---

37. Ibid., 16.
38. Gopal Singh, *Religion of the Sikhs*, 57.
39. Manuscript of the message on baptism given in 1950, 11.

of the word of God in the Sikh Scriptures. He claimed that he was convinced from the first time he began to read the Bible, that it was the word of God. He attributed his experience of salvation to the specific way in which God's word seemed to address him with the words, "Verily I say unto You" in John 3:3. These words convicted him that he was a sinner and that he needed salvation.[40] Moreover, he testified that after his conversion phrases like "God said" and "God spoke" that he read in the Bible, helped him to believe that each verse in the Bible is God's specific Word and that those phrases had given him a new love for the word of God.[41] Bakht Singh needed this confirmation, because anything less than what he had believed in his previous religious ideology would have contradicted his faith.

The deep attachment that Bakht Singh held to the word of God had to do with the way he had understood the concept of the Word that was deeply ingrained in him. It seemed to surface whenever he referred to himself as being a sinner and to the fact that God had cleansed him. He often alluded to the fact that in 1919 he had torn a Bible into pieces. He considered this to be one of the vilest acts that he had ever committed in order to demonstrate his "hatred for it and the Christians."[42] Given that year he did this was 1919, one can understand Bakht Singh's reaction towards the Christians.[43] We do not have much information regarding his active participation in the national movement, but he did tell of an incident that happened during his college days. Because of Gandhi's call for non-cooperation, the students of Lahore College boycotted the visit of the Prince of Wales: "We all refused to go to any party given at that time."[44] In light of

---

40. Singh, *His Loving Hands*, 17.

41. Singh, *Unsearchable Greatness*, 37.

42. Singh, *My Chosen*, 23.

43. In Amritsar, Punjab, the British government imposed a curfew in the wake of the protest of people to the Rowlatt Act, which gave extraordinary powers to the Viceroy to quell sedition. On 13 April 1919, on the Sikh New Year's day, people from different parts of Punjab gathered in a garden to celebrate the Baisakhi or Vaisakhi festival, not knowing that a curfew had been imposed. General Reginald Dyer, the Brigadier of the British army, ordered fire to disperse the crowd. The garden had only one entrance and many people were massacred. The incident was popularly known as Jallianwalla Bagh Massacre. It resulted in feelings of deep anguish and hatred towards the British and Christianity, the religion of the British. "Vaisakhi," *Wikipedia* (article online); available from http://en.wikipedia.org/wiki/Vaisakhi.

44. Singh, *My Chosen*, 59.

these incidents, it is possible to interpret Bakht Singh's reaction towards the Bible and Christians in purely nationalistic terms. The way he viewed the tearing of the Bible after he became a Christian, however, is significant:

> I tore the Bible in 1919 and I used to make fun of the Name of the Lord Jesus. Like the soldier, I had pierced my Lord's side in my blindness, and yet He gave His blood to cleanse me, to purify and wash me. The very same Word became my living bread and my drink. The very same Book which I tore in pieces in my blindness has become my companion and my friend for the past 60 years.[45]

These words express not only the attitude of Bakht Singh towards the Scriptures, but also his attitude towards the "physical book" the Bible. It appears that for him tearing the "physical book" came close to tearing the physical body of Jesus. He confessed, "I was a man who was worthy to be burnt to ashes, because my hands had torn the Bible. I was a blasphemer against the Bible and the name of the Lord Jesus Christ, and made fun of Christians and yet He saved even me."[46] His understanding of the *Guru Granth Sahib* as the embodiment of the word of God, literally, *guru* meaning God, may have contributed to Bakht Singh's strong sense of hurting the physical body of Christ when he tore the Bible. His consciousness of guilt and the sense of being worthy of punishment show what the Book meant to him.

Another feature that comes out glaringly in his confession is his view that in destroying the Bible, he had in some way blasphemed the name of Jesus. He considered the Book in some way to be synonymous with the person of Jesus; Jesus was represented by his name. Bakht Singh maintained that "the full Bible (the word of God) in our own languages" was given by God. Koshy described that Bakht Singh accepted the "Bible as the infallible, inerrant, inspired word of God from Genesis to Revelation. In this respect he was a biblical fundamentalist."[47] One of the founding

---

45. Bakht Singh, "Living Waters," *Hebron Messenger* (4 February 1990): 4.
46. Bakht Singh, *Behold I Will Do a New Thing*, 4th ed. (Hyderabad: Hebron, 1994), 10.
47. Koshy, *Brother Bakht Singh of India*, 411.

members of the Assemblies explained that Bakht Singh taught that the Bible "is the apostles doctrine." That was why Bakht Singh was very particular that everybody should have their own Bible and they should carry it wherever they went. He said that "when we carry the Bible we carry the Lord Jesus Christ."[48]

Owen Cole has observed that when Christians affirm that it is the spirit and not the letter of the Bible that is important, they tend to treat the Bible in an extremely casual manner compared to the care with which the Jews, Muslims and the Sikhs treat the copies of their scriptures.[49] Bakht Singh seems to agree with this. He claimed that in the early days of his ministry in Karachi, a man had challenged him to show one good Christian in Karachi and he would become a Christian. He noted that this challenge forced him to ask God to reveal what he was supposed to do. God allegedly told him to go to all parts of India and require everyone who bears his name to possess a full Bible, whether they were literate or illiterate[50] and to teach them how to use the Bible.[51] As a result, he began to teach people that the Bible is no ordinary book, but that it should be used reverentially and they

---

48. Devadoss, *They Continued Steadfastly*, 7.

49. Cole, *The Guru*, 91.

50. Testimonies abound as to how God used the Bible in the lives of illiterate people. Some even testify that they learned to read on their own after possessing the Bible. An article in the Christian and Missionary Alliance magazine describes how an illiterate person heard Bakht Singh in 1941, bought a Bible with four days of his wages and how it helped him to reach the Hindus, who read the Bible for him and sustained him in his faith. When some of the Hindus persecuted him, he testified, "For through it all God's Word has been my comfort and strength. He has never left me nor forsaken me, and I have learned to trust Him and to draw strength from His promises day by day. How I praise Him and thank Him for His precious Word! How thankful I am that I obeyed Him and bought a Bible! God's Word to me now is my most treasured possession." Gerald L. Carner, "The Testimony of an Illiterate," Nargaon, East Khandesh, India," *The Alliance Weekly: A Journal of Christian Life and Mission* 78, no. 16 (17 April 1943): 249; available from www.cmalliance.org/resources/archives.

51. When I was traveling in a train in India during my winter trip in 2006, I stretched my legs and kept them on the opposite seat as no one was sitting there. My feet were near to a bag. A woman, to whom the bag belonged, noticed that my feet were near her bag. She came and asked me to remove my feet, for she kept her Bible in the bag. When I inquired, I found that she belonged to the Bakht Singh Assembly. In India, feet and footwear are considered unholy. Regarding the usage of the Bible in the subaltern communities, see Sathianathan Clarke, "Viewing the Bible through the Eyes and Ears of the Subalterns in India" (article online); available from www.brill.nl.

should expect God to speak from it.[52] He emphasized meditating on the Word and taught that it should be read while on one's knees. He explained, "By reading the Bible slowly and systematically upon our knees we receive many blessings . . . Then by quiet meditation upon the Word, many hidden mysteries will be revealed."[53]

Bakht Singh was concerned that when he visited Madras in 1937 some leading congregations were preaching against the verbal inspiration of the Scriptures, the virgin birth, the Second Coming, the Atonement and other things.[54] While it seems that Bakht Singh was heavily influenced by his pre-Christian thought forms, it should also be noticed that Bakht Singh tried to correct existing Christian beliefs that undermined the place and value of the Scriptures. If the Scriptures lost their significance and reverence, he maintained, it meant that the message was lost. Thus, he sought to inculcate the same reverence for the Bible that he had learned regarding his Sikh Scriptures as a child. As a result, the members of the Assemblies usually carry their Bibles to all of their meetings.

The prominence that Bakht Singh gave to the Bible during his ministry is unparalleled in the Indian church. He exhorted, "The Lord Jesus Christ is the Word . . . Let us give the Word unquestioning obedience." He further explained, "He became flesh so that the words of life might reign in you, and that is the reason why, when you are born again, you have a new appetite for the Bible."[55] For him, being a Christian meant coming under the control of the Word. Thus, he preached that in baptism, one declares that one will be governed and controlled by the Word:

> The Word of God will be my guide everyday. What this Book says I will obey. What this Book says I will abide by. What this Book says I will submit my head to it. Because it is God's Word I will never resist the Word of God What joy it is! Nobody can change the Book.[56]

---

52. Singh, *Return*, 68–69.
53. Singh, *Unsearchable Greatness*, 37.
54. Bakht Singh, "The Work Is Great," *Hebron Messenger, Special Issue (Part II) for Silver Jubilee of Jehovah-Shammah* (24 July 1966): 5.
55. Singh, *God's Dwelling Place*, 128.
56. Manuscript of the message on baptism given in 1950, 12.

Bakht Singh always claimed the authority of the Bible over the church and over all that he said and did. It seems clear that he continued the frame of mind towards Scriptures that he had learned as a Sikh, for he found no contradiction to his Christian faith in taking that stance. It should, therefore, comes as no surprise that Bakht Singh's Assemblies would also be centered upon the word of God. For them, like him, it was not just the physical book that was important. His followers treasured it as the word of God and became known for their ability to recite portions of the Scriptures because they had been taught to do so from their earliest childhood.

Voice of God

Themes that were familiar to him from his Sikh days also received frequent mention in Bakht Singh's teachings as a Christian. This, of course, does not mean that he was simply syncretistic, but rather he was drawn to the themes that he viewed as common in both religions, themes that seemed to be missing among many Christians of his day. Although he drew upon terminology that he had learned in his Sikh tradition, it also communicated an emphatic quality that was derived from his biblical understanding as a Christian. Bakht Singh was thoroughly familiar with the negative aspects of contemporary Christianity, and he sought to challenge those aspects in light of his own spiritual understanding and faith journey. Thus, Bakht Singh's theology was deeply informed by his own experiences.

Listening to the voice of God and doing his will were not familiar doctrines to many Christians in India at that time. Bakht Singh perceived that the absence of that teaching was one of the problems of the church. In other words, he underscored the need for experiential faith, defined by a life that was guided by God that was totally dependent upon God in every area of life. As a result, the concept of listening to the "voice of God" became one of Singh's main teachings. This idea, for him, was grounded in his experience when he first encountered Jesus and heard the voice of God saying: "This is my body broken for you, this is my blood shed for the remission of your sins."[57]

Unlike the Sikh understanding in which the "voice of God" is understood to be synonymous with the *guru* and his word, Bakht Singh maintained

---

57. Singh, *His Loving Hands*, 18.

that the "voice of God" could be heard – even aurally at times – through God's word, through the conscience (the inner voice), and through other people. However, he taught that God's voice can be heard only in the human spirit. For him, the prerequisite for listening to the "voice of God" was to have the light of God. In other words, one must repent (Matt 3:2) and have a born-again experience (John 10:27), experience the presence of God, and unquestioningly believe that every word in the Bible is the true word of God and obey it in order to hear the "voice of God." He went on to note that one realizes the presence of God through praising and worshiping God, and in this way one was prepared to listen to God's voice. He claimed to listen to God's voice every day.

Bakht Singh taught the tripartite anthropology that human beings are made up of body, soul and spirit. Conscience, intuition and worship are the faculties of the spirit, and through these one listens to or hears God's voice.[58] One person interviewed, mentioned that when he asked Bakht Singh how he listened to God's voice and how one is convinced that it was God's voice, he was told to follow his inner conscience.[59] In keeping with this line of thought, Bakht Singh wrote, "The Lord does speak thus through His messengers. You will know in your conscience that the words spoken by somebody were not ordinary words."[60]

Although he seemed to have come close to the Sikh concept of the inner voice as the *Sat Guru* or the abstract *guru* or the mystical voice of God uttered within, he was categorical in his belief that God is not abstract but "God is a person" and could be known "more intimately than we know anybody else."[61] The relational aspect of spirituality was much more deeply ingrained in Bakht Singh than were the dogmatic and intellectual aspects of the faith. Thus listening to the "voice of God" had practical implications for doing what God wanted a person to do and it could be known by finding God's will.

---

58. Bakht Singh, *The Voice of the Lord* (Hyderabad: Hebron, 1970), 16.
59. R. Earnest Dhanaraj, interview by author, Vellore, 12 December 2007.
60. Singh, *Voice*, 40.
61. Ibid., 10.

God's Will

Bakht Singh's understanding of God's will formed the crux of his spirituality. It is impossible to imagine that Bakht Singh was untouched by the ambiguity of the Sikh doctrine of God's will or *hukam*. It was probably the case that what he failed to realize in his Sikh experience, was attained in his encounter with Christ. It was a new discovery which gave meaning to the intended purpose or goal of the life for which he had been trained from his childhood. For him, finding the "will of God" was the essence and the identity marker of one's relationship with Christ. He wrote:

> If anyone questions me in India or anywhere, "What is your highest privilege as a Christian?" My answer is, "The privilege of finding and doing God's will." What a joy it is when God does speak to me saying: "This is the way." . . . Whatever may happen, I know my safety is in doing God's will.[62]

Bakht Singh's interpretation of the fullness of the Holy Spirit was unique. He claimed that the sign of the filling of the Holy Spirit was the ability to find God's will. As he puts it:

> If anyone claims to have the fullness of the Holy Ghost they have got to prove that they are able to find God's will at every step, and in every detail great or small . . . That is my test of the fullness of the Spirit of God. His will! His will! . . . Matt 26:39 . . . We are given the filling of the Holy Spirit to be led by Him and to walk in God's perfect path.[63]

He was strongly convinced that finding God's will was the most important thing that could happen in the life of a believer. For him, the life of Jesus was defined by doing the will of the Father, and it could never be any different for a believer (John 4:34; 5:30; 6:38; 7:17). The outward expression of the Holy Spirit was to lead and to teach God's perfect will in one's life.[64] Bakht Singh affirmed this idea by drawing upon several experiences in his own life.

---

62. Bakht Singh, *The Holy Spirit: His Work and Significance* (Hyderabad: Hebron, 2001), 122.

63. Singh, *Holy Spirit,* 57.

64. Ibid., 120–121.

While teaching on Ephesians 5:17, "Wherefore be ye not unwise, but understanding what the will of the Lord is," Singh explained how he realized the need to find God's will in his own life. One day when he was in Canada, the woman of the family with whom he stayed overheard his conversation with someone in which he immediately accepted an invitation to preach. She asked him if he should first find God's will before taking up any assignment.[65] Bakht Singh then told how her comment had affected him:

> I went to the seaside by some rocks and sat there the whole day, praying, "Lord, teach me to find Your will, I will follow You all the way," and the Lord taught me . . . So I gave God a promise – "Lord I am not going anywhere till You speak with me, I won't spend my money till You give me permission." I do not do anything until He speaks and God helps.[66]

His messages were full of examples of how God spoke to him in decisions as small as going to a barber shop. For Bakht Singh, every activity in life, however insignificant, fell under the purview of God. To him, it meant living under the total control of the Holy Spirit. There was no dichotomy between the secular and the sacred. Everything was of God and for God. In Sikhism, the concept of God's will leans towards fatalism and resignation. For Bakht Singh, it was different. It covered all of life's decisions and activities, and was the sign of constant communion with God.

Similar Practices

Worship

There are many similarities between the Christian and Sikh faiths. Both of them are monotheistic. Both believe in the congregational and private personal worship of God. Both teach the ethic of loving one's neighbor. Christians and Sikhs are people of a Book. What the *sangat* is for Sikhs, the church is for Christians. Sambhi is of the opinion that "the Sikh form of congregational worship is not much different from some church services."

---

65. Ibid., 121.
66. Singh, *Holy Spirit*, 122.

According to him, the Quakers and the nonconformists come nearest to the Sikh ideal.[67]

The central object of worship in the *gurudwara* is the *Guru Granth Sahib*. It is placed on a low cot and is usually draped in neat silken cloth. Before entering the *gurudwara*, one has to take off his or her shoes and cover one's head. They go on their knees before the holy book and make obeisance by rubbing their forehead on the ground, thus paying respect to the *guru*.[68]

The pattern of worship consists of two main items: the reading of the holy hymns with an explication or exposition given by some learned man or woman, followed by singing some passages from the holy *Granth*. The former element is called the *Katha*, and the latter is the *kirtan*. At the end of their meeting, the congregation stands with folded hands. One of them recites the *Ardas* or Sikh prayer, a set form which invokes the divine grace. They sit down and read a passage at random from the *Guru Granth Sahib*, which is considered to be an "order" or "word" of the *guru* for the day. Then *Karah Parshad*, a sweet pudding,[69] is distributed. Services are conducted every morning and evening. Attached to the *gurudwara* is a free kitchen called *langar*. Free food is served throughout the day, every day. All the faithful sit together and eat.[70]

Before entering the Assembly, the congregation leaves their footwear outside the worship place. A separate place is allotted for the footwear, where volunteers watch over it. Usually as soon as they enter, they kneel where they will sit, and after they have offered a personal prayer on their knees, they settle in their place. The congregation sits on mats or carpets that have been spread on the floor of the prayer hall. Bible verses are written on the walls or hung as banners in and around the prayer hall. Indian

---

67. Piara Singh Sambhi, "Living in a Multi-Cultural Society: A Sikh Looks at the Christian Church," *The Expository Times* 88 (1977): 292–293.

68. After leaving the sandals at the stands, the devotees wash their feet before entering the sanctuary. Some of them fall prostrate before the Granth Sahib. They are not to turn their back toward the Granth Sahib. They walk back reverentially and take their seats on the floor. Men and women sit separately and they are free to leave the *gurudwara* whenever they want. The author visited the *gurudwara* Bangla Sahib in New Delhi.

69. Parshad or Prasad means a gift of God to the devotees. Karah is an iron bowl. Sweet pudding prepared in an iron bowl.

70. Gill, *Trinity in Sikhism*, 228–229.

musical instruments are used. The order of service is generally divided into three parts: worship, the "Table worship" and the message.

Usually, the service lasts two to three hours. After the service the congregation joins together for a love feast.

Though it may not be categorically assumed that Bakht Singh imitated the Sikh pattern or order, the similarities between them are remarkable. The faithful among the Sikhs as well as in Bakht Singh's Assemblies engage in reverential acts upon entering the place of worship. They leave their footwear outside, kneel and pray as soon as they enter, and cover their head, although it is the women who do this in the Assemblies.[71] Thus the practices found in Bakht Singh's Assemblies find more parallels within Sikh worship than are found in the patterns practiced by the mainline churches in India.

Shoe stand, *Gurudwara* Bangla Sahib, Delhi

---

71. Women are expected to cover their head. In Indian context, the scarf is a part of the women's dress, so it is comparatively easy to cover their head. Girls who wear different or modern style of clothing carry a scarf with them to the church and cover their head with it during the service.

Shoe stand, Hermon Compound (Hebron) Hyderabad

Architecture

The architecture of the *gurudwaras* differed from place to place. Some are magnificent buildings, while the older structures were plain flat roofed buildings. The walls are inscribed with verses from the *Guru Granth Sahib*.[72] Statues and candles are not used in the *gurudwaras*.

The architecture of the Bakht Singh Assemblies is clearly Indian and does not follow the architectural pattern found in the western churches. The architecture of the Assemblies is similar to that found in the early *gurudwaras*. They are plain or ordinary buildings with a large hall for use in worship. No symbols are kept in the Assembly, although the walls are inscribed or decorated with verses taken from the Bible. Today most of the independent churches follow a similar architectural pattern including Bible verses on their walls.

---

72. W. Owen Cole, and Piara Singh Sambhi, *The Sikhs: Their Religious Beliefs and Practices*, 2nd rev. ed. (Brighton: Sussex Academic, 1998).

Walls inscribed with Scripture in *gurudwara* Bangla Sahib, Delhi

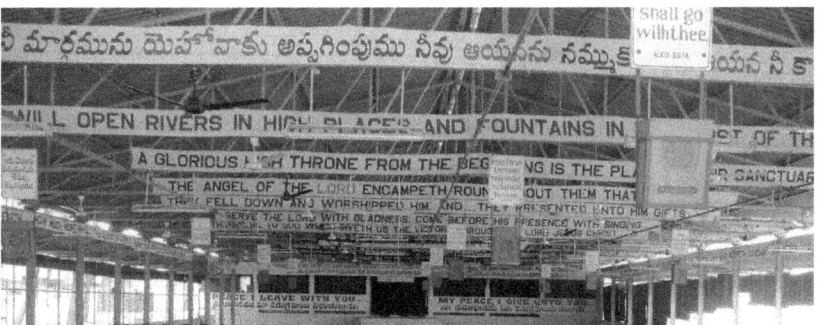

Hermon, Hyderabad

Music and Musical Instruments

It is customary for Sikhs to assemble for congregational worship early in the morning or in the evening. Singing of *kirtan* to the accompaniment of the drum, harmonium and other instruments is an important part of worship. Harmonium and (*chimta*)[73] are used in the Sikh *gurudwaras*.[74] The Sikhs follow the Hindustani genre of music.

In Bakht Singh's Assemblies the harmonium and *chimta* are also used in the congregational worship. The playing of guitars in youth meetings was not allowed until the 1980s, and in some urban Assemblies they are now allowing the guitar in the main worship service. The *chimta* is not a South

---

73. Chimta is an instrument that has a pair of steel tongs with rows of brass discs fixed along their length.

74. Cole and Sambhi, *Sikhs*, 51.

Indian musical instrument. In South India the main musical genre is the classical Carnatic music, which is normally not a congregational form, but one used by trained soloists. The Christian *Bhakti* poets of Andhra have transformed it into the congregational music form by introducing certain adaptations while maintaining the lyrical structures.[75] The Assemblies adopted the Hindustani musical genre, however, which was more convenient for congregational singing.[76] Some of their songs were set to popular musical styles with simple colloquial language which does not incorporate the poetic style of hymns.

Greetings

VahiGuru is part of the Sikh salutation. When the term *VahiGuru* first came into use, it meant "praise to the *guru*."[77] Later, according to the code of conduct adopted by the Sikhs, when Sikhs meet, they greet each other by saying "*VahiGuru ji ka Khalsa, VahiGuru ji ki fateh*"[78] (Hail the *khalsa* who belongs to the Lord God, hail the Lord God to whom belongs the victory). For the Sikhs, this greeting is not only a salutation; it is an affirmation of their faith.[79]

The members of the Assemblies greet one another with "Praise the Lord." They usually address each other as brother and sister. Since this is again a unique characteristic of the Assemblies, the influence of Sikhism should probably not be minimized. Sathkeerthi Rao mentions that men hugging each other as part of the greeting was introduced by Bakht Singh in the Assemblies. While this was a common practice in North Indian culture, among South Indian Christians it is not a common practice, and in most cases only members belonging to the Assemblies practice it.[80]

---

75. Raj, *Christian Folk Religion*, 158.
76. Earnest Dhanaraj, interview by author, Vellore, 11 December 2007.
77. McLeod, *Exploring Sikhism*, 89.
78. McLeod, *Textual Sources*, 81.
79. Gurbachan Singh Talib, "VahiGuru ji ka Khalsa VahiGuru ji ki Fatheh," in *Encyclopaedia of Sikhism* vol. 4, 401.
80. Sathkeerthi Rao, interview by author, Pasadena, 25 September 2008.

Promises

The final act of the Sikh congregational worship is "to take a command" which is called the "*vak lao.*" This practice involves randomly opening the Sikh scriptures and reading the first hymn on the left hand page as the command for the day.[81] In some *gurudwaras* the command is written on the bulletin board for those who were not present during congregational worship.[82]

Bakht Singh used to give a verse or verses from the Bible (usually only the Bible reference) for those who had asked for his prayer. At the end of his correspondence and in his editorial letter in the *Hebron Messenger* he mentioned two or three Bible references. Giving promise cards on the 31st of December to individual members and also giving general promises to the Assemblies for the year has become part of the ongoing practices of the Assemblies. Although one cannot attribute a direct correspondence between these practices introduced by Bakht Singh and the *vak lao* that is practiced in Sikhism, this was one of the practices begun in the Assemblies from the beginning that has since been adopted by other churches and denominations in India.

Begging

Guru Nanak considered begging to be degrading and he denounced the religious leaders among both Hindu *gurus* and Muslim *Pirs* who lived by means of begging for alms.

> Those who call themselves Gurus and pirs but go about begging for alms;
> Never fall at their feet to show them reverence.
> They who eat what they earn through their own labour and give some of what they have in charity;
> Nanak says: they alone know the true way of life (M1, Var Sarang, 1(22), AG 1254).[83]

---

81. Balwant Singh Dhillon, "Guru Granth Sahib as Eternal Guru," in *Guru Granth Sahib and Its Context*, ed. J. S. Neki (New Delhi: Bhai Vir Singh Sahitya Sadan, 2007), 98.

82. Gurudwara Bangla Sahib, Delhi.

83. Pashaura Singh, "Early Markers of Sikh Identity: A Focus on the Works of First Five Gurus," in *Sikh Identity: Continuity and Change*, eds. Pashaura Singh and N. Gerald Barrier (New Delhi: Manohar, 1999), 74.

The *khalsa* were also charged neither to beg for charity, nor to covet property or money offered in the name of God.[84] Discussing the vocation and social functions of the Sikhs, J. P. Singh Oberoi observes that "the only thing he [a Sikh] is asked to abjure is the degrading practice of sporting the begging bowl."[85] The Sikhs believe that when they pray to God, they should not beg for some rewards or for the removal of their miseries, because God knows even without telling anything.[86]

Similarly, Bakht Singh strongly condemned those in ministry, who openly asked for money. He called them beggars, and he questioned, "Can such people truly say that they are sent from God? O ye beggars, ye beggars! God wants to make you princes; not earthly princes, but God's princes. . . . God can give much more than anyone can ask or think."[87] He claimed that when he received God's call for ministry, God told him never to make any suggestion or tell any man about his needs.[88] Faith living is one of the strong features of the Assemblies and it was demonstrated quite clearly in the life of Bakht Singh and in the lives of "God's servants."[89]

Bakht Singh's messages are replete with illustrations of how God supplied his needs without his ever mentioning about the need. He considered any mention or a hint of a personal need in congregational prayer as asking, a practice that he did not encourage. Believers in the Assemblies

---

84. Thomas Kadankavil, "Sikhism: A Sacrament of Steel," *Journal of Dharma* 14, no. 3 (July–September 1989): 298–306.

85. J. P. Singh Uberoi, "The Five Symbols of Sikhism," in *Sikhism*, eds. Fauja Singh, et.al. (Patiala: Punjabi University, 1969), 136.

86. Darshan Singh, *Indian Bhakti Tradition and Sikh Gurus* (Chandigarh: Punjab Publishers, 1968), 158.

87. Singh, *My Chosen*, 34.

88. Singh, *His Loving Hands*, 51–52.

89. In the early Eighties, my parents rented their house to a "God's servant" in that town. I observed from close quarters how most of the time God used to provide for their needs in the last minute in a miraculous way. Until the congregation found a place to worship, they used to conduct their worship services in the verandah (portico attached to the exterior of the building) of my parent's house. In fact, that was how I became interested in the Assemblies even though I come from a mainline church background. Though I appreciated their faith living, later when I sensed that God wanted me to be in full-time ministry, the thing that kept me from immediately obeying God was the fear of living by faith. Out of curiosity to see their convocations, I attended a convocation one day. The only session I attended was the youth meeting during that convocation. Paradoxically, it was here that I was convinced that I had to take a step of faith.

continue this practice as a manifestation of their faith in their day-to-day lives. Although Bakht Singh attributed this to one of the specific commands that he claimed to have received from God at the time of his call, it cannot simply be discounted that it may also reflect his pre-Christian mindset.

The Importance of Family and Sharing

Guru Nanak insisted that one should live on the basis of his or her honest labors. He discouraged the ascetic life. He was a strong advocate of family. He emphasized the importance of being a householder while leading a spiritual life. He demonstrated this during his stay in Kartarpur. He wanted his followers to lead a normal life as a householder, recognizing one's duties to the family and society to which they belonged. According to his teaching, "To run away from the responsibilities of a householder is the highest of ingratitude. Of all the *dharmas*, the *dharma* of a householder is the highest. One attains salvation, the state of bliss, in one's own home."[90] Insisting on family relationships Guru Nanak advocated moderation and a healthy detachment. The concept of an earnest living was not confined to the family. It was to be extended to the rest of the society. The earnest means was usually enjoined through the practice of sharing with others and serving others. Thus, for Guru Nanak, "Truth is higher than everything but higher than the truth is truthful living."[91]

Bakht Singh, too, always taught the importance of family life. Although he was not against celibacy if one wanted to remain single for God, almost all of the "God's servants" were married and then they were given in charge of an Assembly. The members of the church were exhorted to be honest and to live out their faith in their work places. He never dichotomized the secular from the sacred in the life of the individual believer.

The Tithe

It was Guru Arjun who introduced the practice of tithing in Sikhism. The Sikhs were exhorted to devote one tenth of their income in the name of the *guru* for the welfare of the community. This practice is called the *daswandh*. It could be given either in cash or kind. It is said, "Earn your livelihood and

---

90. Puri, *Advent*, 65.
91. Ibid.

put a tenth part of it in the mouths of Sikhs." The money was used for the maintenance of the *langar* and the *gurudwara* administration.[92]

Bakht Singh also insisted on the importance of tithing in the Assemblies. Monthly tithing has since become the culture of the Assemblies. One of the people that I interviewed commented that Bakht Singh was the first person to have taught the Christian congregations in Andhra Pradesh about giving generously. He noted that Bakht Singh "taught from Malachi and created history in the whole matter of giving."[93] Though one cannot attribute this practice in the Assemblies to a Sikh antecedent, it is clear that Bakht Singh practiced and taught the concept of tithing and giving to his congregations. From the beginning, the Assemblies were self-supporting and were never dependent on foreign funds, unlike the common practice found both in the mainline churches and in many other independent congregations in India.[94]

Guru ka Langar and Love Feast

Guru ka langar is a common kitchen that is operated in the name of the *guru*. The *langar*,[95] or free community kitchen, is considered to be one of the earliest institutions in Sikhism. It was established by Guru Nanak. Guru Amar Das, the third *guru*, made it an expression of the notion of equality in a practical way. Every Sikh *gurudwara* has a *langar* attached to it: "The Sikh Gurus combined worship and bread. A Sikh Temple is the 'Temple of worship and Prayer,' and the *langar* attached to it is the 'Temple of Bread.'"[96] Following the congregational prayer at the end of worship, all Sikhs sit together for a common meal. *Sangat* and *pangat* go together (i.e. eating together and meeting together go together). The term *pangat* refers to a row. People sitting together in a row and sharing a common meal

---

92. Singh, *Sikh Vision*, 112–113.
93. Sathkeerthi Rao, interview by author, Hyderabad, 14 November 2007.
94. Rao, "Bakht Singh Movement," 153.
95. Langars were a common feature of the Muslim *Sufi* tradition in the 12th & 13th centuries. Even today some of the *Sufi* centers have them. This is a North Indian tradition, which is not familiar in South India. See Parkash Singh, "Guru Ka Langar," in *Encyclopaedia*, vol. 2, 207.
96. Parkash Singh, *Community Kitchen of the Sikhs* (Amritsar: Singh Brothers, 1994), 23.

without any distinctions is an act of piety for the Sikhs.[97] The *langar* is kept open day and night. Every Sikh takes part in the functioning of the *langar* either through some physical work such as sweeping, cooking, washing dishes, or by contributing money to it. Women and children join in the preparation and serving of the meal. It is considered to be the place where brotherhood, service and equality are taught.[98]

Men and women volunteering in the *langar* at *Gurudwara*, Bangla Sahib, Delhi

---

97. Singh, "Guru Ka Langar," 209.
98. Dalbir Singh Dhillon, "The Institutions of Guru (Guruship), Gurudwara, Sangat and Langar," in *Guru Nanak: Ideals and Institutions*, eds. H. S. Soch & Madanjit Kaur (Amritsar: Guru Nanak Dev University, 1998), 217.

Men and women volunteering in the *langar* at *Gurudwara*, Bangla Sahib, Delhi

Men and women volunteering in the convocation at Kalimpong, 2005

Men and women volunteering in the convocation at Kalimpong, 2005

Bakht Singh introduced the practice of the "love feast" into the Assemblies. The "love feast" follows the Sunday service in the Assemblies. At this time, the congregation sits together for a common meal, which is served by volunteers. Bakht Singh mentioned that from the beginning the Assemblies had decided to give hospitality to whoever visited them for fellowship, so they were always open for fellowship at all times (Isa 56:7, 8).[99] In his account of the beginnings of the Assemblies, Rajamani commented, "Many new converts, too, took at the outset this public step of sitting down together to eat a communal meal. Thus they overcame their former caste or social distinction."[100] The physical work in the Assemblies such as cooking, cleaning and serving is done by the members of the congregation. All the faithful, irrespective of their status, are expected to take part in this activity as part of the training in service, brotherhood, and humility.

Most of the work for the construction of the *gurudwaras* was done by the Sikh volunteers as part of their religious practice. This practice is called "Karseva." Similarly in the Assemblies, the congregation

---

99. *Hebron Messenger* (24 July 1990): 6.
100. Rajamani, *Monsoon Daybreak* (London: Open Books, 1971), 91.

encourages volunteers to engage in the physical work necessary to construct new Assembly buildings.[101]

Festival Processions

Sikh festivals are called *Gurpurb*. The birthdays of Guru Nanak and Guru Gobind Singh, and the martyrdom of the fifth *guru*, Guru Arjan, are the three important anniversaries that are celebrated as the main festivals by all Sikhs. During these festivals, special assemblies were held in the *gurudwaras* and discourses were given on the lives and teachings of the *gurus*. As they chant the holy hymns, Sikhs carry the *Guru Granth Sahib*, in procession through the village or through the city.[102] This practice of carrying the *Granth* in procession around the neighborhood is called *Nagar kirtan* or *Jalous*.[103] Posters were also erected to announce the festival.[104] Both men and women can lead the singing as they go in the procession. Older men and

---

101. Earnest Dhanaraj, interview by author, Vellore, 11 December 2007.
102. Harmandar Singh, "Gurpurb," in *Encyclopaedia of Sikhism* vol. 2, 195.
103. W. Owen Cole and Piara Singh Sambhi, *Christianity and Sikhism: A Comparative Study* (New York: St Martin's Press, 1993), 133.
104. Cole and Sambhi, *Sikhs*, 138.

women, who cannot walk long distances, join the procession at the rear end in vehicles.

One of the conspicuous practices of the Assemblies was going out in processions through the streets of the city or a town. During the time of the holy convocation, all the participants of the convocation go in procession through the streets. Each participant carries his or her own Bible. They sing songs, shout slogans, carry banners of cloth with verses from the Bible written or stitched, and all stop at the corners of the streets to preach the gospel. Following the preaching they kneel on the road for prayer. Since Bakht Singh believed that one should offer prayer while kneeling down, the practice was followed irrespective of the place where the prayer was offered. It was also considered as a witness to the Lord. One of the persons interviewed, noticed that the apparent difference between the two processions was that, while women can lead the singing in the Sikh processions, it was not allowed in the Assembly processions.[105] For a congregation to go out in processions through the village or city was a rare practice in the denominational churches. Since it was mostly the Assemblies who follow this practice among the Christians, it may well be assumed that Bakht Singh had the Sikh processions in mind when he introduced them in the Assemblies.

Ritualism

Guru Nanak vehemently condemned the rituals and the religious practices of his day. He was equally critical of the Brahminical superiority and emptiness as well as the individual *Sadhus* and *Jogies*, a type of Hindu mendicants of his time, who did not live up to their calling. He attacked their superficiality, externalism and hypocrisy. Nanak taught:

> If they happen to know the nature of God, they will realize that all rites and beliefs are futile. (AG 470)
>
> Rituals and ceremonies are chains of the mind. (AG 635)
>
> Cursed be the ritual that makes us to forget the Loved One. (590)[106]

---

105. David Jayakumar, interview by author, Pasadena, 24 August 2009.
106. Cole and Sambhi, *Sikhs*, 41.

Ahluwalia has observed: "Guru Nanak made a concentrated attack on the value-conserving potency and absolutizing tendency of ritual. He deliberately de-sacralized what was held ritualistically sacred, adding that what is considered profane (and hence subject to purificatory rites) may not be so at all."[107]

Bakht Singh's rhetoric was also highly critical about the existing structures found in the institutions of the historic denominational churches and their dominance over the people. He viewed them as forms of "bondage," "slavery" and "control." He wrote, "The church of Christ cannot be bound by earthly man-made laws; constitutions are often made for the sake of the authority they give, an authority like that of the Brahmins over the Hindus. Christians who want power over their fellow-Christians might truly be called 'Christian Brahmins.'"[108] As a result the Assemblies do not recite the creed and the Lord's Prayer. Bakht Singh did not approve of these practices because,

> We are not told in any part of the Bible to repeat these passages. *We are not under any commandment but we have come under God's grace.* Our Lord has taught us that when the Spirit of grace comes into us, we automatically love and serve God and love our neighbour and fulfill the law, not by merely repeating the Ten Commandments, the Lord's prayer or the Apostles Creed.[109]

Bakht Singh did discourage women from wearing jewelry and celebrating marriages in a traditional manner. There is no exchange of rings in wedding ceremony of the Assemblies, only the recitation of the vows. Bakht Singh discouraged some of the common cultural practices in marriages, funerals and some everyday practices. He claimed that they merely followed the traditions, and viewed them as idolatrous. He emphasized the need to live by the Spirit rather than by tradition and law. He believed that there would be no freedom of the Spirit when one followed the tradition and

---

107. Jasbir Singh Ahluwalia, *The Sovereignty of the Sikh Doctrine: Sikhism in the Perspective of Modern Thought* (New Delhi: Bahri Publications, 1983), 76.

108. Singh, *God's Dwelling Place*, 113.

109. Bakht Singh, *True Liberty* (Hyderabad: Hebron, 1994), 16–17.

rituals. So he exhorted, "But where there are rites, ceremonies, and rituals, it means the devil has robbed people of their liberty and their joy. . . . Do not go back into bondage and be a slave to any formality but live in the Spirit."[110]

Bakht Singh never explicitly claimed to have followed the Sikh religious terminology or religiosity. The close parallels that are discussed above, however, cannot simply be ignored. The beginning of Bakht Singh's Christian journey started while he was yet a Sikh. It came in a personal encounter with the Bible when he was a Sikh apart from any previous Christian background of which we know. It seems apparent that his Sikh tradition informed his reading even of the Bible. At the same time, he seems to have been fully aware of what was happening within the Christian faith that he had adopted.

Bakht Singh's understanding of the word of God, especially his reaction to having once torn a Bible to pieces, informs his understanding of the *Guru Granth Sahib* as the embodiment of the *guru*. His emphasis on the word of God, the need of having a personal experience with God, and a life that is controlled and led by the voice and will of God, gave a unique standing to the Assemblies in India. Bakht Singh brought the authority of God and of the Bible into the Assemblies as an alternative to the boards and constitutions that dominated the people in the denominational churches.

Moreover, along with the Scriptures, Bakht Singh often alluded to his experiences as reference for his teachings. Alongside the Scriptures, he generally supported an understanding of the voice of God and finding God's will with an incident in his life. His prior Sikh religiosity had a definite bearing on his understanding of these. Since finding the will of God or listening to the voice of God was not a major doctrine found in any of the denominational churches, it may be assumed that Bakht Singh's emphasis on this principle stems from his understanding of the purpose and goal in the life of a Sikh, that is, to find and live by the will of God. In that sense, since he had realized his purpose in life through Christ, that experience naturally became one of his main teachings in the Assemblies.

---

110. Ibid., 18.

Most of the practices in the denominational churches, which the Indian Christians recognized as offensive to the Indian religious worldview and mindset, were addressed by Bakht Singh in a practical way. In the form of worship, the pulpit-centered worship and orientation of the denominational churches were countered by a free time of individual worship, although preaching remained a strong anchor in life together. He introduced practices such as sitting on mats, leaving footwear outside the place of worship, singing songs set to Indian tunes, using Indian musical instruments, and constructing the place of worship according to Indian architectural patterns. Still, tithing, sitting on the floor, using Indian musical instruments and lyrics were common in most of the denominational churches.

The significance of Bakht Singh's Sikh heritage is probably characterized by some of the practices that were not common in any other church tradition in India. Chief among those was the "love feast" as a regular event following the Sunday service. Even today, other than the Assemblies, few churches follow this practice. Needless to say, it was a Sikh practice which Bakht Singh emulated, though he renamed it in keeping with a practice found in New Testament church. In the Christian community, where common greetings were exchanged mostly in the western style,[111] his introduction of a religious greeting, "Praise the Lord," reveals an affirmation of the spiritual relationship between one another as well as removing the secular-sacred bifurcation in one's life. It also establishes an affinity within the community that is defined by a relationship oriented towards God and each other.

Not disclosing their financial needs and living by faith was another characteristic that defied the traditional methods of fund raising and depending upon the West for the sustenance of the churches. For the Sikh, begging or even disclosing one's needs to others is associated with the honor and sovereignty of God. It amounts to belittling the all-powerful God

---

111. Usually Indians greet their elders by saying "*Namaste*" that is, by offering a greeting equivalent to "good morning." Among the Christians (in cities and towns), however, it is common to greet one's elders with "good morning." In West Bengal, the Assemblies practice the traditional culture. Usually people who are nearby greet an elder or "God's servant" saying "praise the Lord " in their native tongue, by folding their hands together and bowing their head before them. The elder keeps his hand on the head of the one who greets him as a sign of blessing and a form of acceptance of the salutation.

who knows the needs of every one. So the *gurus* warned, "Disgraceful is the life of those who sell the name of God."[112] Bakht Singh's understanding of living by faith was not associated so much with the faith of the person as to the sovereignty and all-sufficiency of God in whom he believed. In that sense, Bakht Singh exalted and replaced God into a system, that otherwise depended on the charity of the West or the generosity of the rich. It created a culture of mutual responsibility within the limited means of the congregations, and at the same time it gave autonomy to the local churches to function in a self-sufficient way. Bakht Singh's Sikh background must have only reinforced his faith and dependency on God as he experienced God's provision in his own life as a Christian.

Bakht Singh presented Christianity to Indians in an "Indian cup" by redeeming it from the "alien" fold. But it appears the cup that Bakht Singh chose was the one from which he also drank, and that was the cup of Sikhism. While some of the concepts and practices discussed signify the external similarities of the teachings and practices in the Assemblies, the interior nature of Bakht Singh's spirituality and theology could be traced to the *Bhakti* tradition which formed the spiritual ethos of North India, and especially Sikhism.

---

112. Kadankavil, "Sikhism," 305.

CHAPTER 6

The *Bhakti* Theology of Bakht Singh

Bakht Singh's teachings and writings are so steeped in the Bible that it is sometimes difficult to perceive that there existed a sophisticated worldview behind the reading and interpretation of it. Roger Hedlund defines the theology of Bakht Singh as "decidedly biblicist and Christ-centered . . . Here is a theology Christocentric in content, strongly devotional in character."[1] Having identified Singh with the evangelical tradition in India, Robin Boyd did not find any difference between the Indian evangelical writings and the western evangelical literature "except perhaps for illustrations drawn from Indian life, like those which lend vividness to the writings of the famous Sikh convert evangelist, Brother Bakht Singh."[2] The closer resemblance of Singh's theology with the Brethren or Baptist conceals the Indian character which has been hidden within his theology.

Interpreting the biblical message in Hindu terms (or local idiom) was considered generally to be one of the criteria for doing Indian theology.[3] Bakht Singh's messages, however, lacked Indian (or local idiom), Hindu or Sikh terminology.[4] Moreover, Bakht Singh never appeared to have inter-

---

1. Hedlund, Quest, 177.
2. Boyd, An Introduction, 216.
3. Ibid., 217.
4. The medium of communication for Bakht Singh was generally English, except when he ministered in North India, especially Punjab. Speaking in English must have limited his possibility to use the local idiom. One of the interviewees, Sathkeerti Rao, disclosed that he heard Bakht Singh saying, "I wanted to counteract the ministry of Stanley Jones." According to him, Bakht Singh did not like Stanley Jones' approach of preaching using Hindu Scriptures so he "developed distaste for what Jones was doing and Hinduism . . . He wanted to outdo Jones." However, the researcher could not trace any further evidence or information regarding this.

acted with the "theological community," nor did he encourage seminary or theological college education. The questions must therefore be asked: How does one understand the theology of Bakht Singh? What makes him a theologian or an Indian theologian, and why does it make him so? Reading Bakht Singh from his spiritual orientation and upbringing reveals that his theology or his theologizing was aided by the tradition of *Bhakti* and that he personified, practiced, and preached *Bhakti* through the Scriptures. Does it mean that his theology could be called *Bhakti* theology and consequently the movement a Christian *Bhakti* movement?

Sources of Authority: Pramanas

In order to understand the theology of Bakht Singh, it is essential to establish the sources of authority that he followed. One of the questions raised by Indian Christian theologians in their quest to understand Christianity in the Indian thought forms was: "What is the basis of theology?" or "What are the sources of authority that must be used to formulate an Indian theology?" The question arose because of the dominance of western dogmatic theology and the importance attributed to historic church traditions by the West, in the doing of theology.

Indian spirituality, which is based largely on the concept of "experience" or *anubhava*, sought to discover whether a direct experience of Christ apart from the mediation of Scriptures and traditions was possible. Indian theologians wondered whether it was possible for such an experience to become the basis of their knowledge about Jesus because, "the emphasis on experience seems to permeate the entire system of thinking in Hinduism."[5] These questions led A. J. Appasamy, an Indian theologian, to establish the sources of authority for Christian theology in India. Based upon his study on the traditional standards of Hinduism he chose three final sources of authority – *Sruti*, *Yukti*, and *Anubhava*. *Sruti* literally means "hearing" or "that which is heard by the sages," derivatively also carrying the meaning of "revelation"; *Yukti* means "argument," "inference" or "reason," that is, the

---

5. Martin Alphonse, *The Gospel for the Hindus: A Study in Contextual Communication* (Chennai: Mission Educational Books, 2003), 253.

beliefs derived from the Scriptures should be tested by reason; and it is the *anubhava* or "personal experience" that proves these beliefs.[6]

For Appasamy reason was second only to the Scriptures. For Bakht Singh, it was not reason that was second to Scriptures, it was "experience" that held the second position.

The Scriptures

The Scriptures or the Bible, formed the supreme and ultimate authority for Bakht Singh. The priority given to the sources of authority is understood to be of fundamental importance in doing theology. Questions raised by Indians who believed that all too often Scripture had been placed in a subordinate position to the dogmas of the church in the denominational churches became a significant difficulty that Indian theologians struggled to answer. *Sruti* or Scripture had a significant place in their belief system. Appasamy asserted that the Bible "is the foremost *Pramana*, the highest court of appeal for everyone."[7] One of the major emphases in Bakht Singh's teaching was the place that he gave to the word of God in the life and work of a believer and the church.[8] He maintained that every word in the Bible must be understood as the word of God. His main critique against the seminaries, or theological colleges, and the denominational churches of his day, was that, from his perspective, they failed to give primary place to the Bible in their preaching and teaching. He was categorical in this criticism when he wrote:

> I don't encourage them to go to modern Bible colleges because they have so much emphasis placed upon that which was not necessary. They give Bible training secondary place and other subjects first place. I believe the Bible colleges produce speakers and orators and teachers but not men of God, not men living by faith on the Word of God.[9]

---

6. Boyd, *An Introduction*, 136–137.

7. T. Dayanandan Francis, *The Christian Bhakti of A. J. Appasamy: A Collection of His Writings* (Madras: Christian Literature Service, 1992), 57.

8. Manuscript of Bakht Singh's message on baptism given in 1950, 12.

9. Bakht Singh, interview by T. E. Koshy, notes 1970.

His primary criticism against the denominational churches was that they gave more importance or priority to customs, traditions and constitutions than they gave to the word of God. He charged, "You are very bothered about the blue book;[10] but you are not in the least concerned about God's Book!"[11] For him, the lack of spiritual growth in the life of believers and the churches was because the churches and the leaders were preoccupied with following human traditions and practices that in his mind had replaced the role of the Scripture. As a result, he taught, "Unless we honour God's word fully we have no right to claim our share in His fullness. We lose our share of fullness by ignoring the word of God."[12] As we have already noted in previous chapters, Scripture was the ultimate authority in the life and teachings of Bakht Singh. For this reason, he offered biblical texts (though some might call them "proof texts") for everything that he taught and practiced.

Experience

The second source of authority for Bakht Singh was experience. While he understood much about God from his reading of Scriptures, it is the case that his personal encounter with God, his experience of God, contributed much to the basis of his knowledge about God. He was uncompromising in his teaching about the need for everyone to have a personal experience of Jesus Christ as Savior and Lord. None of his messages, as well as his editorials in his magazine, would end without some mention of the need of being born again. He spoke and wrote to them, "We should make sure that we have a definite, personal, living experience of the living Lord Jesus Christ."[13] Thus it was the continuous experience of Christ in the life of a person that helped to form the basis of his theology. It had to be measured by what Scripture stated, but it provided meaning to the teachings of Scripture.

For those who are considered to be formal Indian theologians, experience played a role as well. Robin Boyd has argued for instance that, "The Indian tradition lays great stress on 'realisation,' and this is true not only of

---

10. Refers to academic exercise book.
11. Singh, *Return*, 70.
12. Singh, *Fullness of God,* 10.
13. Singh, *Strong Foundation*, 3.

Bhakti marga but also of *jnana marga*, for a man is not regarded as entitled to speak of religious matters unless he himself can speak of his personal experience of unity with God."[14] As a result, Indian Christian theologians like Chenchiah and Sadhu Sundar Singh have given a prominent place to experience as a valued source of authority. Like Bakht Singh, Sadhu Sundar Singh clarified that his experience and visions were always based upon Scripture and they never contradicted it. He also announced that "a revelation which I have received in ecstasy is worth more to me than all the traditional church teaching."[15] P. Chenchiah observed, "The courage to think through the challenges of Christianity without the doctrines and the dogmas . . . may be the new gift of the spirit of the time to Indian Christians."[16] Chenchiah's desire seemed to have been fulfilled in Bakht Singh's approach. Doctrines and dogmas of the church do not appear in the latter's thought. He held both the Scriptures and experience as the *pramanas* or the sources of authority for his theology, but in the end, it was Scripture that had the final say.

Hermeneutics

Scripture and then experience form the hermeneutical key for Bakht Singh. Unlike the traditional biblical interpretation in which semiotics and the historical context of the text play an important role in the interpretation of the Bible, Singh seemed to have adopted his own method of interpretation that depended upon the need of the congregation, a method that was more familiar to traditional Indian religious practice.

Bakht Singh regarded the Bible as its own best interpreter. He believed, "The Bible is the best commentary we have."[17] He seldom used either classical theological language or Indian religious terms in his messages. Instead, his messages were replete with biblical language and terminology, and at

---

14. R. H. S. Boyd, *Khristadvaita: A Theology for India* (Madras: Christian Literature Society, 1977), 24.

15. Cited by Boyd, *An Introduction*, 228.

16. Cited by T. V. Philip, "Chakkarai and the Indian Church," in *Society and Religion Essays in Honour of M. M. Thomas*, ed. Richard W. Taylor (Madras: Christian Literature Society, 1976), 154.

17. Singh, *God's Dwelling Place*, 20.

times without any explanation of what specific terms meant. Mostly, his messages were filled with Bible verses, strung one after another in succession. These verses were typically interpreted literally in his messages, without considering the meaning they might have held in their original historical context. Probably this method was appealing to the people because, as Frits Staal observes, in the Indian religious tradition, "The words have to be handed down in exactly the same form in which they have been heard. There is no tradition for the preservation of meaning. A concern regarded as a mere individualistic pastime."[18] Bakht Singh believed that the apostles studied and preached the Bible in its totality. For him, "The apostles travailed upon their knees for God's message, and spoke, as God's mouthpieces, the whole counsel of God – the full Bible. They were not concerned only with a few favourite passages, but with the whole Scripture."[19]

Bakht Singh used Old Testament illustrations to expound on the concepts of the New Testament and vice versa. The reason that he gave for this practice was that, "whatever happened in the Old Testament was a shadow of that which is now happening in our period in the New Testament."[20] Thus, Bakht Singh was willing to think of types and shadows, and was equally at home employing allegorical interpretation in many cases. He drew from Old Testament symbols, names of places, and the names and experiences of Old Testament people to interpret the meaning or teach many concepts that he found in the New Testament. For example, he gave some meaning or interpretation to every item found in the tabernacle in order to teach something about the nature of the church.[21] For him, being a Christian meant coming under the control of the Word.

Some of Bakht Singh's messages consisted simply of a narration of the Bible story with direct application to the daily life of the believer. This form that he generally adopted was to narrate the experiences of the characters

---

18. Frits Staal, "The Concept of Scripture in Indian Tradition," in *Sikh Studies: Comparative Perspectives on Changing Tradition*, eds. Mark Juergensmeyer & N. Gerald Barrier (Berkley, CA: Berkley Religious Studies Series GTU, 1979),122.

19. Singh, *God's Dwelling Place*, 116.

20. Singh, *Fullness*, 8.

21. See Singh, *God's Dwelling Place*.

in the Bible story,²² which could then become examples to the believers. In fact, the narration of experiences through storytelling was a common method employed by Indian Christians. Storytelling that comes directly from the Scriptures is one of the most popular forms of religious communication to be found in India. As Subhash Anand has observed regarding the Indian use of narrative:

> (The narrator) narrates the myth with such unction that the audience listens attentively. He also makes the life-situation of his audience part of the myth, and while narrating it makes them to see what the myth is trying to convey to them. Thus the myth is fluid. It liberates religion from the concepts of a bygone era, concepts that do not make much sense to the contemporary audience. It enables the devotee to integrate the present needs into his reflection.²³

In addition to the Scriptures, Bakht Singh employed experience as the source of authority for his theology. As already noted, the concept of experience is important in the Indian understanding of faith and the practice of religion. Accordingly, Bakht Singh tried to explain his theology through illustrations from "lived experiences." He usually supplemented his biblical teaching with illustrations taken either from his own life experience, or from the experiences of day-to-day life with which his followers could identify. As already mentioned, Boyd saw that the teachings of Bakht Singh were filled with vivid "illustrations drawn from Indian life."²⁴ Llewellyn observed that, "Similes, metaphors, illustrations from village and city life in their own sweet Punjabi language bring the message to their hearts."²⁵ However, it was not a method that was unique to Bakht Singh; rather, "Images drawn from quotidian life have been common in Indian religious

---

22. See Singh, *David Recovered All: High Way to Victory; Walk before Me*, 29th reprint (Hyderabad: Hebron, 2005).

23. Subhash Anand, "The Liberative Potential of Popular Religious Traditions," in *Re-Visioning India's Religious Traditions: Essays in Honour of Eric Lott*, eds. David C. Scott and Israel Selvanayagam (Delhi: ISPCK, 1996), 101.

24. Boyd, *An Introduction*, 216.

25. Llewellyn, "Bakht Singh of India," 84.

discourses, and particularly in *Bhakti*."²⁶ This was true in the life of Sadhu Sundar Singh as well.

Sundar Singh considered the "Witness of Anubhava" as providing the hermeneutical principle for Christian preaching.²⁷ K. Subba Rao, a mystic and an independent preacher and theologian, also made experience a primary tool to be used to interpret Christ. He said:

> "I am only a devotee of Jesus Christ" he began, not a Bible scholar or theologian. I can preach only about Christ my Lord and Friend, who made the supreme sacrifice on the cross for me, a sinner and for you all . . . I have no doctrine but the Gospel of Lord Jesus. I don't like arguments which only confuse our thinking. They can never find conquest over experience.²⁸

In the Assemblies, time is allotted for believers to share their personal testimonies. It appears to be the case that it is the experiences of the people that teach and help one to understand the inner meaning of the biblical text rather than the teaching of dogmas or concepts. Martin Alphonse has remarked that, "Nothing could have been more profound and vital to a Hindu heart than to hear a spiritual teacher emphasizing his personal experience as the basis and proof of one's spirituality."²⁹ In other words, personal experiences and listening to the experiences of others helps one to learn certain spiritual truths. According to Appasamy, what the Indian church and Indian theology needed was the realization that experience should precede theology rather than theology preceding experience. According to him, "Theology, being an intellectual statement of such living experience, would then possess a power and genuineness all its own."³⁰ Echoing a similar position, Bakht Singh maintained that, "It is not theory that qualifies,

---

26. Sumit Sarkar, *Writing Social History* (New Delhi: Oxford University Press, 2000), 289.

27. P. Surya Prakash, "The Contribution of Sadhu Sundar Singh: Preacher and Theologian," *Bangalore Theological Forum* 31, no. 1 (July 1999): 110.

28. C. Daniel Airan, *Kalgara Subba Rao: The Mystic of Munipalle* (Vijayawada: M/s N. Kutumba Rao & Co., n.d.), 48.

29. Alphonse, *Gospel for the Hindus*, 264.

30. A. J. Appasamy, *Christianity as Bhakti Marga*, 3rd ed. (Madras: Christian Literature Society, 1991), 4–5.

but the experience that is gained by coming out triumphantly through the tests that God sets for us," that proves the genuineness of a believer.[31] Reddimala Samuel observes that, "Every member of the [Bakht Singh] movement claims to have had this [born again] great experience either through a vision or a voice. The experience of Christ has sometimes been described as receiving light in darkness."[32]

Since experience formed a source of authority for Bakht Singh's theology, it points to the fact that it is normally associated with the *Bhakti* tradition within Indian religious life. But, what is *Bhakti* and how does it correspond to the theology of Bakht Singh?

Bhakti

Bhakti is one of the three *margas*[33] or paths within Hinduism that lead one to realize God or to attain salvation. Over time, *Bhakti* evolved from an intensely interior mystical spirituality to a personal devotion and love of God that was available to and attainable by everyone, irrespective of caste, gender, creed or status. In other words, while it originated from a classical notion, it eventually evolved into a popular spirituality and a common religious ethos within Indian society. By incorporating *Bhakti* into his understanding and practice of Christianity, Bakht Singh was able to develop what may be termed a Christian *Bhakti* theology of his own which subsequently shaped the Assemblies into a kind of Christian *Bhakti* movement.

The Meaning of *Bhakti*

The word *Bhakti*[34] takes on different connotations depending on the context. Used within both secular and religious contexts, the term *Bhakti*

---

31. Singh, *God's Dwelling Place*, 110.

32. Reddimala Samuel, "A Study of Bakht Singh Movement, Its Origins and Growth especially in Andhra Pradesh," BD thesis (The United Theological College, Bangalore, 1971), 18.

33. The *Karma Marga* and *Jnana Marga* are the other two paths. The first is reaching God through works and the second through knowledge.

34. The term *Bhakti* is derived from the Sanskrit word *bhaj*. *Bhaj* is used to express love. ". . . *bhaj* can have many meanings: to enjoy, possess, enjoy carnally, embrace; to favour, prefer, choose, elect; to honour, worship, adore, revere, esteem; to be attached to, to court; to be devoted to, be loyal . . . *Bhaj* in religious usage would convey the meaning of

generally implies a personal relationship or devotion. Even though *Bhakti* could be generally translated as love or affection, Dhavamony noted:

> As a religious technical term, *Bhakti* is the most difficult word to translate. The word, in fact, though stable enough in its essential meaning, assumes different doctrinal and affective connotations. The best rendering of the word *Bhakti* to our mind, is "godward love in utter self-surrender." Nonetheless, "loving devotion" often seems to fit the context.[35]

In *Bhakti*, this love is thought to be reciprocal. As the devotee surrenders to God, God through his grace offers salvation to the devotee. Taken as a religious concept, *Bhakti* has its roots in the *Vedas*.[36] The meaning in the *Vedas*, however, was related to ritual practices, and not to worship or love towards God.[37] In the *Svetasvatara Upanishad* the term *Bhakti* was understood as "an attitude of devotion and surrender to God."[38] It was in the *Bhagavad-Gita* that *Bhakti* was employed to denote the "love of God," "God's love of human beings," and "one's personal relationship to a personal God."[39]

While *Bhakti* as a religious concept was found in the *Vedas* and *Upanishads*, it was in *Bhagavata-purana*[40] that *Bhakti* as a "path" or "means to attain God or salvation" was strongly advocated. Moreover, it presented *Bhakti* as a way open to all castes, genders and ages.[41] This is considered to be the textbook of the *Bhakti* school. In the *Vedas* and *Upanishads* salvation could be attained or is available only to the first three castes in the caste hierarchy. The Sudras, that is, the fourth in the order of castes, and

---

choosing God as one's part, of worshipping, adoring, loving God." Mariasusai Dhavamony, *Love of God according to Saiva Siddhanta* (Oxford: Clarendon Press, 1971), 13–14.

35. Davamony, *Love of God*, 22.

36. Vedas, Upanishads and Bhagavad-Gita are classical Hindu religious texts.

37. Dhavmony, *Love of God*, 47–56.

38. Aiyadurai J. Appasamy, *The Theology of Hindu Bhakti* (Madras: Christian Literature Society, 1970), 21.

39. Dhavmony, *Love of God*, 77–83.

40. *Puranas* are another class of Hindu sacred writings. *Baghavata Purana* is one of the popular *Puranas*.

41. Subhash Anand, *The Way of Love: The Bhagavata Doctrine of Bhakti* (New Delhi: Munshiram Manoharlal Publishers, 1996), 105.

women were neither allowed to read the sacred texts, nor were they eligible for salvation.

In the classical texts (*Vedas, Upanishads* and *Gita*) *Bhakti* as "devotion" and "love of God" came to be associated more with mysticism and personal interior religion. This understanding of *Bhakti* was mostly followed by the Vaishnava Sects.[42] *Bhakti*, to a large extent, came to be identified with Vaishnavism and Ramanuja. With the emphasis of *Bhakti* in the *Puranas*[43] it was branded as a lower form of spirituality and hence, as the religion of the masses. Commenting on the difference of meaning given to the term *Bhakti* in the *Gita* as over against the *Puranas*, Ghurye has observed:

> As against this, the "*Bhakti*" complex of the *Gita*, which is strong both on thinking and considering . . . on enlightening and knowing . . . remains both a moral and intellectual endeavour, though securing ecstatic delight to the worshippers, who are participants in the common enterprise of God-seeking. The late "*Bhakti*" complex even when it is pure and strictly within the moral bounds tends to become amoral and almost non-intellectual rising into a purely ecstatic exercise.[44]

This observation by Ghurye reflects the attitude of the religious elitists and intellectuals towards the *Puranas* and the common folk. Ironically, even though *Bhakti* occupies a central place in Hinduism today, both the western and the Indian scholars have neglected to a large extent the study of *Bhakti*, treating it simply as a practice of and for the lower classes.[45] Hindu elitists and the followers of Vedic religion "refuse to find any kinship with devotion, with the worship of humanized divinity."[46] In fact,

---

42. The Vaishnavites worship Vishu as their personal deity. Ramanuja was the main proponent of Bhakti in a systematic and philosophical manner.

43. Plural is used here because, although the names are not mentioned, other Puranas also deal with *Bhakti*. Subhash Anand introduces, "The Puranas have been called 'the scriptures of the common man,' even of 'the religiously disfranchised people.'" . . . the Puranas are the property of all the castes, and also of the outcastes. They can be studied not only by men, but also by women." Anand, *Way of Love*, 1.

44. Govind S. Ghurye, *Foundations of Culture: Religious Consciousness* (Bombay: Popular Prakashan, 1965), 278.

45. Davamony, *Love of God*, 2.

46. Jayant Lele, "The *Bhakti* Movement in India: A Critical Introduction," in *Tradition and Modernity in Bhakti Movements*, ed. Jayant Lele (Leiden: E. J. Brill, 1981), 2.

Bhakti was explicitly a revolt against the elitist form of religion, and it was developed explicitly to meet the needs of "the Indian masses . . . that little tradition with which *Bhakti* becomes associated is a way of life. It is a living tradition. They merely listen to it while the intellectuals merely suspect it."[47] Thus, *Bhakti* became a religion of the heart and made its way into the social and ethical realms of Indian religious culture. *Bhakti* became a living tradition through the *Bhakti* movements during the medieval period in India.

Bhakti Movements

The two major traditions in *Bhakti* are *Nirguna Bhakti* and *Saguna Bhakti*. *Nirgun*, which means "without attributes," refers to a divine being viewed mostly as unmanifest and non-anthropomorphic. Worship of this Being or Brahman is called *Nirguna Bhakti*. *Sagun* means "with attributes." *Saguna Bhakti* is the worship of the divine being with anthropomorphic manifestations, a deity, or a personal God.[48] In *Nirguna Bhakti* the devotee and deity become one. Submerged, "Here both 'I' and 'Thou' exist and function within the devotee in the act of devotion." In other words, it believes in the oneness of the two. In *Saguna Bhakti* the devotee and deity remain consciously separate beings, and they function in that consciousness.[49]

Saguna Bhakti is mostly popular in South India, while the *nirguna* is currently more popular in North India. The *Bhakti* movements have their roots in South India. Between the sixth and the eighth centuries AD, with the rise of the *Vishnava* and *Shaiva* poets in the Tamil South, there was a revival within Hinduism. The *Vishnavas*, who worshiped *Vishnu* as their personal deity, were called *Alvars*; whereas the *Shaivites*, who worshiped Shiva, were called *Nayanars*. They popularized the concept of *Bhakti* through their singing of hymns in their local language. Some of these poets belonged to the Sudra castes.[50] This movement slowly declined until the arrival of Ramanuja in the twelfth century. Ramanuja popularized the

---

47. Ibid., 15.

48. David N. Lorenzen, "Introduction: The Historical Vicissitudes of Bhakti Religion," in *Bhakti Religion in North India: Community Identity & Political Action*, ed. David N. Lorenzen (Albany, NY: State University of New York Press, 1995), 1.

49. Krishna Sharma, *Bhakti and the Bhakti Movement: A New Perspective* (New Delhi: Munshiram Manoharlal Publishers, 1987), 44.

50. Appasamy, *Hindu Bhakti*, 28–30.

worship of *Vishnu* as a personal God and love or *Bhakti* as the pathway to reach God. He systematized the concept of *Bhakti* in Hinduism and he continued Hindu orthodoxy by approving the caste system. However, he also upheld the idea of moving the non-Brahmin into prominence within orthodoxy. As a result the followers of Ramanuja spread the *Bhakti* movement across India.[51]

Between the thirteenth and seventeenth centuries the *Bhakti* movements in India brought about a great transformation in religion. Ramananda (c. 1400–1470), the fifth in succession to Ramanuja, radicalized the *Bhakti* tradition by breaking away from his caste. Through his influence, the movement spread in all directions and took various forms. Because of the influence of Ramanuja and his disciples, temples began to be opened in Andhra for the *Sudras*, and in one case for the outcastes.[52] John E. Clough mentions that the first convert of the mass movements was a disciple of Ramanuja.[53] R. R. Sundara Rao maintains that the *Bhakti* movement was in full swing by the time Christianity made its presence felt in Andhra, and in its time influenced Christians.[54]

Bhakti became a religion of both the elite and the common people. The *Bhakti* saints of each region had their own emphasis with the underlying unity of *Bhakti* or a direct loving relationship with God as their common core. All of them had a concept of sin, a common recognition of the need for cleansing or forgiveness and grace, and a hope of salvation or liberation,

---

51. Kenneth W. Jones, *Socio-Religious Reform Movements in British India* (Cambridge: Cambridge University Press, 1989), 11.

52. B. S. L. Hanumantha Rao, *Religion in Andhra* (Guntur: Tripura Sundari, 1973), 258.

53. Yerraguntla Periah, the first Madiga convert and the leader of the mass movements in Ongole, was initially a disciple in the Ramanuja sect. Later he joined Bandikatla Veeramma, a Sudra caste woman, who was an initiated disciple of Yogi Potuluri Veera Brahmham. The disciples of Veera Brahmham are called Raja Yogis. Veeramma initiated Periah into this sect. Thus he became a leader of standing in the Madiga community. "He had a *guru*-staff in his hand, which he never discarded, not even after he became a Christian Preacher." John E. Clough, *Social Christianity in the Orient* (Philadelphia, PA: American Baptist Publication Society, 1915), 92–94; Clough also describes, "The hardest case of the kind on the Ongole field was that of Gumbadi family. There were four brothers, all Mala priests, belonging to the Ramanuja sect." One of the brothers a priest of Vishnu could read and also practiced Raja Yoga and secret nature worship. Clough, *Social Christianity*, 180.

54. R. R. Sundara Rao, *Bhakti Theology in the Telugu Hymnal* (Bangalore: CISRS, 1983), 1.

although the meaning differed depending on the school of thought. For most of them to know God personally and to be in communion with him became the essence of salvation. The "knowledge of God comes by a firsthand personal experience, and not from philosophical comprehension of God."[55] Their mode of worship and teaching was usually by means of songs (*kirtans* or *bhajans*), in the local, vernacular languages. Karine Schomer summarizes these changes in the following manner:

> The devotional transformation of medieval Hinduism known as *Bhakti* movement was a phenomenon of crucial importance in the history of Indian religion. Starting from Tamil South in the seventh century, gradually spreading northward through Karnataka and Maharashtra, and sweeping over North India and Bengal from the fifteenth century onward, the impulse toward a personal devotional faith profoundly changed both quality and the structures of religious life.[56]

Love or devotion as *Bhakti* became widely recognized as the "soul of all religious, ethical, philosophical, and aesthetic quests." Thus, *Bhakti* "had its roots in the bedrock of Indian culture and was probably always, and still is, pan-Indian."[57] Ainslie T. Embree opines:

> There was thus no school of thought that failed to attach a very high value for devotion. . . . Among devotees there was no caste, no distinction of high or low, except that those who lacked devotion were considered the lowliest. Such a view naturally gave God's grace, called forth by true and intense devotion, an overriding power over the fate that beset one as a result of one's own actions.[58]

---

55. Alphonse, *Gospel for the Hindus*, 88

56. Karine Schomer, "Introduction: The Sant Tradition in Perspective," in *The Sants: Studies in the Devotional Tradition of India*, eds. Karine Schomer and W. H. McLeod (Berkley: Berkley Religious Studies Series / Delhi: Motilal Banarsidass, 1987), 1.

57. Greg M. Bailey and I. Kesarcodi-Watson, eds., *Bhakti Studies* (New Delhi: Sterling Publishers, 1992), 7.

58. Ainslie T. Embree, *Sources of Indian Tradition. Volume One: From Beginning to 1800*, 2nd ed. (New York: Columbia University Press, 1988), 323.

In South India *Bhakti* came to be identified more with mysticism, later on as it developed further, other elements of *Yoga*[59] and *Tantra*[60] were introduced into *Bhakti*. While some of the *Bhakti* saints integrated *Bhakti* within Hindu orthodoxy by opening up religion to both women and Sudras, others rejected the external forms of worship, including idol worship, temple rituals, priestly hierarchy and caste structures. Sant Kabir (c. 1398–1448), the popular North Indian *Bhakti* saint and a disciple of Ramananda, and Guru Nanak (1469–1539), the founder of Sikhism, took the *Bhakti* movement to new heights.

Kabir belonged to the *sant*[61] tradition of North India. In a way, it was he who synthesized the *Bhakti, Yoga, Tantra, Sufi*[62] and *Nath* traditions.[63] Kabir "combined within it a classical tradition based on an intellectual conception of *Bhakti* (especially as found in *Bhagavad-Gita*) as well as elements of essentially 'protest' religiosity."[64] Moving on to the North, *Bhakti* became a mass movement. Thus, it is said that in North India, all Sikhs and almost all Hindus may be called followers of the *Bhakti* tradition. Ainslie T. Embree observes:

> Although it is possible to interpret the *Bhakti* tradition as the religion of the poor masses, and as a protest against the dominance of priests and rulers, *Bhakti* should not be seen as a religion of the downtrodden and oppressed. Devotional religion in India, as elsewhere, has been practiced by all sorts and conditions of men and women. Indeed, it has helped to bind

---

59. A system or discipline to reach God by having control over the senses.

60. Involves the esoteric practices of meditation, mysticism, rituals and magic. The Nath tradition belongs to this school of Shaivism.

61. Sants are the poet-saints belonging to both *saguna* and nirguna schools. The designation is mostly applied to the nirguna saints of the Hindi speaking areas of Punjab and Rajasthan and the *saguna* saints of Maharahstra. Sant, Saint, *Sadhu, Bhagat* or *Bhakta* are used as synonyms.

62. Muslim Mystics or Mysticism in Islam.

63. See McLeod, *Guru Nanak*; Schomer and McLeod, eds. *The Sants*.

64. Vijay Mishra, "Kabir and the Bhakti Tradition," in *The Sants: Studies in the Devotional Tradition of India*, eds. Karine Schomer and W. H. McLeod (Berkley: Berkley Religious Studies Series / Delhi: Motilal Banarsidass, 1987), 187.

together the many diverse elements of the Indian subcontinent into a functioning society."[65]

Guru Nanak's teachings had close links with the *Bhakti* tradition, which, in its different forms, dominated Indian religious thought for centuries. Both Nanak and Kabir advocated the *nirguna* form of *Bhakti*, and condemned both ritual and caste. They emphasized an approach to God through love, recognized a *guru*'s role in one's spiritual life, and upheld the importance of a householder's life.[66] Some view Sikhism and *Bhakti* as synonymous, while others consider Sikhism on its own. The relation between Sikhism and *Bhakti*, however, reveals that Bakht Singh had been exposed to the teaching of the *Bhakti* form of Sikhism. The ways and approaches that he had adapted to propagate his ideas and to communicate the Christian faith and life, seem to demonstrate that the *Bhakti* approach to religious understanding continued to manifest itself even in his Christian expression.

Sikhism and *Bhakti*

Historians differ in their understanding of the relationship between Sikhism and *Bhakti* and the *Bhakti* movements. While some view Sikhism as a culmination of *Bhakti* and various *Bhakti* movements in medieval India, others do not agree that Sikhism has anything to do with *Bhakti* except that it happened to be a contemporary of the *Bhakti* movements.[67] The majority of historians, however, adhere to the former view in which Sikhism is identified with *Bhakti* and the *Bhakti* movements. According to Daljeet Singh, "Sikhism and Sikh *bhakti* are synonymous terms."[68] The statement reveals the significance of *Bhakti* in Sikhism. Sunita Puri has observed that:

> Guru Nanak elevated the medieval *bhakti marga* to the zenith of sublimity and made it a practical way of life for his disciples by giving it an authoritative tone. The devotion directed to the

---

65. Embree, *Sources of Indian Tradition*, 344.
66. Anil Chandra Banerjee, *Guru Nanak and His Times* (Patiala: Punjabhi University, 1971), 57–60.
67. See S. Kapur Singh, "Guru Nanak: His Place in History," in *Sikh Gurus and the Indian Spiritual Thought*, ed. Taran Singh (Patiala: Punjab University, 1981).
68. Daljeet Singh, "The Essentials of Sikh Bhakti and Hindu Bhakti," *Dialogue and Alliance* 5, no. 3 (Fall 1991): 21.

supreme Lord is the vital response required of all those who have perceived the presence of God suffused throughout His creation and in whom has been awakened a longing for union with Him.[69]

Sikh *Bhakti* resembles the Hindu form of *Bhakti* with certain corollaries added to it. Their disciplines are similar in many ways, especially in terms of the characteristics of *Bhakti*. The *gurus* did not accept the ninefold[70] path or the nine types of *Bhakti* practiced by the *saguna* tradition. They comment:

> The Bhagtas worship in nine ways;
> The Pandits shout veds;
> [. . .]
> All say that they have found God;
> But it is only the saints whom God Uniteth with Himself.
> All the above mentioned efforts
> I abandon, and seek God's protection;
> Nanak, I fall at *guru*'s feet.[71]

Although the *gurus* did not accept these nine types of *Bhakti*, there was a strong emphasis on the disciplines known as *Sravana, Manana* and *Nidhiyasana*. While these disciplines were part of the ninefold path, for the Sikhs these characteristics come under a separate discipline or a separate means of realization of God. *Sravana* means "study" and "listening to the Scriptures" under a qualified *guru*. It involves the aspects of *guru*, faith, congregation, prayer, singing and abiding in his *hukam* and *Raza* (Will). In other words, the total form of the Sikh worship could be summarized as *Sravana*. *Manana* denotes a constant reflection upon what has been learned

---

69. Puri, *Advent*, 53.

70. According to the *Bhagavata-Purana* there are nine forms or expressions of *Bhakti*: *Sravana* (hearing the stories and the praises of the Lord); *Kirtana* (singing of His glories); *Smarana* (remembrance of His name and presence); *Padasevana* (service at the feet of God); *Archana* (worship of God); *Vandana* (salutation and loving adoration); *Dasya* (cultivating the Bhava of a servant with God); *Sakhya* (friendship with the Lord); and *Atmanivedana* (complete surrender of the self). The nine modes of *Bhakti* are the ways in which a devotee attains the supreme ideal of life. A devotee can take up any of these paths and reach the highest state.

71. Cited by Singh, *Indian Bhakti Tradition*, 84.

from the worship. *Nidhiyasana* implies "a meditation that leads to the realization of the unity of all things in God."[72] Guru Nanak instructed, "Let us, by singing, reflecting and having emotional attachment with Him, shed the miseries of others and take them to the Home of Happiness."[73] It appears that the *gurus* were not critical about the features of *Bhakti*, for they too followed a similar discipline. But they were critical of the way the *bhaktas* practiced the nine types of *Bhakti*.

The Sikh Gurus emphasized not only the interior religion through the path of *Bhakti*, but also the importance of its expression in the external life. Their emphasis was on *Bhava Bhakti or Prema Bhakti*, that is, *Bhakti* expressed through an emotional attachment – a motiveless attachment to God, or *Bhakti* expressed through love. For the *gurus*, God is love and he should be reached through love. Since it is a loving attachment, devotees express their love, or worship God, as Father, Mother, Brother, Friend and Husband.

> "O Nanak, father and mother is great Hari,
> We are His children, Hari feeds us."
> "Thou art my friend, Thou art my dear.
> Thou art my lover, with Thee is my love.
> Thou art my honour, Thou art my wealth.
> Without Thee, I cannot live for a while."[74]

All the *bhavas* operate at this level of expression, while the final aim is a motiveless attachment to God. Thus, there is only one *bhava*, that is, *Bhakti bhava*. This love is to be shared with the community. For the *gurus*, *Bhakti* is not to live a life of a recluse, but to be involved in the world while detached from it. By developing a sense of detachment from the world and attachment to God, the devotee develops ethical qualities in which the conduct of the devotee is transformed. This transformation happens when the devotee continuously and consciously strives to surrender the ego and abide in the will of God.[75] Thus, Sikh *Bhakti* could be summarized in the

---

72. Ibid., 144–145.
73. Ibid., 145.
74. Ibid., 89.
75. Singh, *Indian Bhakti Tradition*, summary of different chapters.

words of Daljeet Singh: "It is necessary to emphasize that in Sikh *Bhakti* the acceptance of total responsibility in all fields of life for the service of humanity is the inseparable counterpart of love for God," and "This religious system may therefore be called 'activity *bhakti*,' since the goal is to carry out the will of God."[76] This suggests the question: What kind of *Bhakti* did Bakht Singh follow and how did he Christianize it?

The *Bhakti* Theology of Bakht Singh

Bhakti in Christianity was not a new concept, that is, one introduced by Bakht Singh. Many Indian Christians had long expressed their faith in the form of *Bhakti* or in the *Bhakti* tradition.[77] Robin Boyd notes that the western theologians, Rudolf Otto and Ninian Smart, believed that "*bhakti marga* provides the closest Indian approach to the 'shape' of Christian reality."[78] Narayan Vaman Tilak and A. J. Appasamy are the well-known Christian *Bhakti* saint and scholar respectively in Indian Christianity. Tilak was nurtured in the Hindu *Bhakti* tradition of Maharashtra. His *Bhakti* or devotion was communicated like that of the other *Bhakti* saints through lyrics and poetry. Tilak drew upon the *Bhakti* idioms of the Hindu *Bhakti* saints and consciously employed them in order to relate Christianity and the *Bhakti* tradition.[79] While for Tilak it was an experiential journey in devotion, for Appasamy it was more of a scholarly endeavor intended to communicate the gospel to the Hindus in an Indian way. Appasamy, who was influenced by the *Bhakti* tradition of the South, tried to interpret Christianity (John's Gospel) in the light of the teachings of Ramanuja. He equated *Bhakti* and mysticism, and like Ramanuja, he advocated an interiorized spirituality of intense personal devotion and experience of the mystical union with Christ. Appasamy's interiorized spirituality is defined more by intellectual meditation accompanied by love. He leaned, however,

---

76. Singh, "Essentials of Sikh Bhakti," 25–28.

77. One of the latest groups that adopted *Bhakti* as their spirituality in India is the "Christ Bhaktas" from Chennai (i.e. Madras). For them everything related to their relationship with Christ, their spirituality, liturgy and ecclesiology is *Bhakti*. See Jonas Adelin Jorgensen, *Jesus Imandars and Christ Bhaktas: Two Case Studies of Interreligious Hermeneutics and Identity in Global Christianity* (Frankfurt: Peter Lang, 2008).

78. Boyd, *Latin Captivity*, 96.

79. Boyd, *An Introduction*, 114–117.

towards the classical interpretation of *Bhakti* and seemed to agree with the notion that the *Bhakti* in the *Puranas* was a lower form of religion.[80]

While Appasamy represents the classical *Bhakti* tradition of South India, P. Solomon Raj identified *Bhakti* as part of the folk religion in Andhra Pradesh. The founder of Bible Mission, Fr. Devadas composed several *Bhakti* hymns for the common people. He wrote them on themes that they encountered in their daily life. This *Bhakti* disposition became part of the Andhra Christian culture, both in the great tradition and the little tradition.[81]

Bakht Singh grew up within the *Bhakti* tradition and Sikh culture of North India. His spirituality clearly reveals that he belonged to this tradition and his understanding of Christianity resembles it. Not only did Bakht Singh belong to this culture in general, but it also appears that there was a *Bhakti* streak within his family. His mother was a devout follower of Guru Nanak. In an interview, Shrichand Chhabra,[82] the younger brother of Bakht Singh, mentioned that the family visited both the Hindu temple and the Sikh *gurudwara*, and the children were taught to treat these places as the "house of God without question, or without argument." Explaining his brother's spirituality he said, "To him (Bakht Singh) Jesus had become a dearly beloved." He described a conversation with his brother in which he questioned him about hurting the family because of his Christian religion. To that Bakht Singh is said to have replied, "You do not understand, because you are not in love."[83]

This background informs the religious or spiritual roots of Bakht Singh, and consequently, his approach to his faith. Since I do not know the Punjabi language, I have relied upon the English text of his messages. This may not allow us to see everything that he said that corresponds with *Bhakti* terminology, but it is sufficient to demonstrate the fact that he has

---

80. Appasamy, *Christianity as Bhakti*, 24–27.

81. Raj, *Christian Folk-Religion*, 158–159; See also Chilkuri Vasantharao, *Jathara: A Festival of Christian Witness* (Hyderabad: Liturgy and Literature Committee, CSI Diocese of Medak, 1997).

82. Srichand Chhabra is a devout Hindu and is the Patron-in-Chief of Mata ka Mandir, New Delhi.

83. "Tu ne Ishq me nai tha" I remember he used the word Ishq." The word Ishq means love. Shrichand Chhabra, interview by author, tape recording, Delhi, 29 November 2007.

used the *Bhakti* terminology.[84] The language of his spirituality appears to be entirely biblical because of the hermeneutical methodology he followed. The common expression of *Bhakti* comes in the form of poetry or songs. Bakht Singh was neither a poet nor a singer. He was a teacher and a preacher. Thus, his articulation of *Bhakti* came through his preaching, teaching and living. A closer examination of his writings (sermons) and lifestyle uncovers the *Bhakti* thought pattern and language in his teaching, theology and consequently, in the movement itself.

The Spiritual Experience of Bakht Singh

Though the North Indian tradition of *Bhakti* adheres mostly to the *nirguna* stream, Bakht Singh deviates from it by accepting the *Saguna Bhakti* of a personal God. This doctrine also goes against the teachings of Sikhism, which does not believe in incarnation. Bakht Singh's personal encounter with Christ formed the crux of his *Bhakti*. His encounter and his spirituality may be compared to that of Sadhu Sundar Singh. Visions and intense ecstatic experiences distinguished Sundar Singh's spirituality, whereas the voice of God and its corollary, the will of God, dominated Bakht Singh's life. Both of these experiences were mystical, but the modes of mysticism by which they were manifested seem to differ. It could be that Sundar Singh could be compared to a Hindu mystic, while the Bakht Singh could be compared to a Sikh mystic, with Christ as their divine object. Constant communion with God through prayer defined their religious experiences. Both of them were seekers of the truth. It was a direct encounter with Christ that sets the foundation of their Christian lives.

About his experience Bakht Singh wrote:

> Matthew 28:20 "Lo I am with you always." These words are meant for all who would like to have the experience of His abiding presence. Even though I did not have such an experience myself before my conversion, I knew one thing; that there was a living and true Friend who could be with us always. In

---

84. Eleanore Llewellyn described the preaching of Bakht Singh in the early days of his ministry in North India as, "Similes, metaphors, illustrations from village and city life in their own sweet Punjabi language bring the message to their hearts." Llewellyn, "Bakht Singh of India," 84.

the Sikh religion I had to recite a prayer every morning at bath time. As soon as I poured water upon my head these words came spontaneously out of my mouth. "O God! Thou art true; Thou hast been true from the beginning and Thou shalt be true. No man can know Thee, though he meditates for centuries and gather the whole world's knowledge. O God! I have no virtue in me. I only depend upon thy grace. Show me the Friend and the Satguru (the Teacher of the Truth) who can help me and lead me." I had repeated these words for many years with a longing to meet that Living Friend. I used to go to some lonely place, forest or riverside, hoping that there I might meet an old man with a long white beard, who would say with a loving voice, "Come on my child, I will be your Friend." This prayer which I repeated daily in my blindness gave me a longing to see that living Friend. In the end I began to blaspheme against the Holy Bible and tore a copy of it into pieces. I did this to show my hatred towards Christianity. Also I became a slave to many vices. Even though I did all this, nevertheless, God Himself sought and found me, even a sinner like me, and forgave my sins. For the past thirty-three years He has been my Friend with whom I can talk freely, and on whom I can depend for help."[85]

This account indicates that Bakht Singh already had a strong religious formation and a deep, life-long desire to know God in a personal way; the culmination of this formation and desire was his encounter with Jesus. He maintained that his walk with God started by listening to the "voice of God." He testified, "I heard the voice of God one day clearly, on the 16th of December 1929, saying: 'My son, thy sins be forgiven thee.' That is how I began my walk with God." On another occasion he wrote:

> I said, "O God speak to me. I want to hear Thy Voice. I have no ambition for any other experience. The longing of my soul is that you should speak to me and show me thy way day by day." I believed like a child. Even though it may take some

---

85. Singh, *Looking unto Jesus*, 8.

time to learn the lesson that God must speak, the fact remains that when He becomes real He does speak. A day came when I began to hear His Voice every day.[86]

The prayer, "Lord I only want Thee. I have no other desire now; . . . Give me the privilege and honour to be with Thee and Thee alone," he maintained, "changed everything in his life and gave great satisfaction."[87] In spite of what appears to have been his intentional avoidance of the use of local idiom and his intentional usage of biblical terminology, Bakht Singh's expressions betray his moorings in the *Bhakti* tradition. Coming from the background of Sikh spirituality as he did, where both individual and congregational worship form the main features of the religion, Bakht Singh practiced and preached the importance of prayer, worship and meditation.

Bakht Singh's Expression of *Bhakti*

Along with the importance of the personal experience of God and of the Scriptures in the life of a believer, Bakht Singh introduced free worship into the Assemblies. While today this might not mean much, at the time that he did it, this would certainly have distinguished his Assemblies from the denominational churches around them. The entire Sunday worship service that includes the breaking of bread or Table worship (holy communion) and messages is viewed as one single unit of worship. The worship service was followed by a love feast, where all sat together and partook in a common meal. Bakht Singh taught:

> As we learn to thank God for the privilege of suffering for his sake, we find our joy multiplying in proportion to our gratitude. When we live in God's presence, we find our joy becoming full (Ps 16:11). So we have to find time to wait upon the Lord, read God's Word, meditate, worship and pray. Then our joy will become full.[88]

The order of *Bhakti* that Bakht Singh upheld was nearly parallel to the Sikh *Bhakti* order. Listening to the Scriptures, reflecting and meditating

---

86. Singh, *Voice*, 19.
87. Singh, *True Salt*, 51.
88. Singh, *Fullness of God*, 4.

on what has been learned from Scriptures, form the main discipline of the Sikh *Bhakti*. According to Darshan Singh, *Sravana* includes in itself the following means for the attainment of *Bhakti*: the *guru*, faith, congregation, prayer, study of holy verses (scriptures), singing (*kirtan*) the praises of the Lord, and abiding in his *hukam* (divine order) and *Raza* (will).[89] In other words, it denotes the total worship in Sikhism. *Kirtan*, the continuous singing of the Scriptures or praises of God, is the main form through which the Scriptures are heard by the congregation with a short homily in the morning and evening service. The participation of the individual in the worship or praise of God as such is minimal in the Sikh worship. Sikh worship revolves around the *Guru Granth* and follows a "liturgical" or written form of prayers and praise. Bakht Singh redefined it into his own form of worship, for use in the Assemblies.

Worship (*Aradhana*)

Bakht Singh was avowedly against the liturgical worship, that was the common worship expression of the denominational churches. One of the unique features of the Assemblies was their "free" time of individual worship. *Kirtana* (singing of his glories), *Smarana* (remembrance of his name and presence), *Padasevana* (service at the feet of God), *Archana* (worship of God), and *Vandana* (salutation and loving adoration) were the elements of *Bhakti*, and they belong to the personal and corporate nature of worship. Though these are common features of any worship, it is the importance and emphasis on worship that made the Assemblies distinct from other Christian bodies. The term used for Sunday services in Telugu, the vernacular spoken in the state of Andhra Pradesh, is *Aradhana*, meaning worship. Colin Blair has observed that, "In contrast to the heavily westernized churches his [Bakht Singh] assemblies have about them an almost Sikh atmosphere. Overtones of *Bhakti* are evident in the long meetings, much singing and praying that compose them."[90]

During their worship service, Bakht Singh insisted that all worshipers should kneel during prayer and worship. The length of the time given to

---

89. Singh, *Indian Bhakti Tradition*, 145–146.

90. Colin Blair, "Communicating to Hindus and Muslims in India," ThM Thesis (Fuller Theological Seminary, 1983), 54.

the Sunday worship is unstipulated, though the starting time for the service was a common feature among the Assemblies. The practice of sitting long hours in order to hear religious discourse was a common phenomenon found among various Indian religions. In fact, it can be said that Indian religiosity is not bound by time and space. The imposition of time limitations and a formally routinized liturgical worship format practiced by the historic denominational churches was not only alien to the Indian religious culture, but could also have been a suffocating experience to be endured. In a way, the long hours of worship gave the people the option to come in whenever or to whichever part of the service they wanted to attend. The free time of worship and the long hours or messages that Bakht Singh brought to the Assemblies must have helped his people to reconnect with a religious culture from which they had become uprooted.

Singing has a particularly significant place in all programs of the Assemblies. They have a separate hymnal of their own. In Andhra Pradesh, most of the denominational churches have a common hymn book called *Andhra Kraistava Keerthanalu*. It contains translated hymns and Telugu lyrics tuned to the classical *Karnatic* music, an Indian musical genre. The language used in most of the lyrics found in this hymnal is Sanskritic and classical poetic Telugu. It is difficult, even for a person who is literate, to understand that type of Telugu. James Muttickal identifies certain shifts that happened because of the *Bhakti* movements in India. For example, "Poetry comes out of palaces to the streets," and the religious language shifts from "Sanskrit to Vernacular."[91] In a similar manner, the songs that are sung within the Assemblies have been composed using simple tunes and in colloquial idiom by members of these congregations.

Bakht Singh worked as an itinerant evangelist among the "sweeper" community in Punjab. Some of them had been born again. They began to gather for Bible study at 4 a.m. before they went to work.

> They would kneel by the baskets and brooms and sing Punjabi songs. When they went to work they kept on singing while they swept the roads... The first couple of songs were

---

91. James Muttickal, "Mystic Poets of *Bhakti* Movement," in *Journal of Dharma* 29, no. 3 (July–September 2004): 341.

composed by these Punjabi sweepers... These songs were both devotional and inspirational. Bakht Singh began preaching in the open air twice a day in different parts of Karachi with the help of these "singing saints."[92]

Later, Moses Dawn became one of the main composers for Assemblies music. He composed several songs based upon the Scriptures and the messages of Bakht Singh. Koshy observed, "What Sankey was to D. L. Moody, Moses Dawn was to Bakht Singh."[93] Regardless of the language in which a song was originally composed, it was soon translated into all of the languages used in the worship life of the Assemblies, while keeping the same tune. Here again the movement corresponds to the pattern employed by the *Bhakti* saints.

According to Bakht Singh, "Worship means 'worth-ship.' It is to be able to say in a broken language: 'What is my Lord to me? What will I give back to Him in return?'"[94] Worship is the first step towards spiritual growth and the lack of it can lead to spiritual barrenness. Roger Hedlund has observed in the experience of Bakht Singh, "God's work in depth was not through extraordinary gifts of outward signs and miracles so much as through private praise and adoration."[95] For Bakht Singh devotion and true worship went together. As he put it:

> There is plenty of Bible knowledge and teaching in many countries, but very little devotion. People can sing and pray, but they cannot give the Lord true worship... Humble worship and devotion should be real in our hearts, so both physically and spiritually we must bow down. We must be humble, devoted and full of the worship which leads to growth both in family and in the church.[96]

---

92. Koshy, *Brother Bakht Singh of India*, 125.
93. Ibid., 183.
94. Singh, *Return*, 54.
95. Hedlund, *Quest*, 177.
96. Bakht Singh, *Bethany* (Hyderabad: Hebron, Reprint, 2002), 31–32.

Worship involves not only praising God, but offering or surrendering oneself to God. While teaching on the anointing of Jesus by a woman at Bethany (Mark 14:1–9), Bakht Singh explained:

> She wanted to anoint the body of the Lord Jesus as a King would be anointed, so she brought the most precious ointment to Him saying by faith, "Lord, I am prepared to pour out all for Thee. Now you demand anything from me, and I am prepared to give it to you." That is true worship . . . Just as she broke the box, and poured out every drop of it, so we have to be broken completely, and poured out. True worship comes when we are truly broken and humbled, "we will say I will give all I have."[97]

Since the giving of an offering was considered part of one's worship in the Assemblies, Bakht Singh believed and taught that those who knew how to worship God also knew how to give and to testify to God's glories. In the Assemblies at the time of offering, those who have not given themselves to God or do not have the born-again experience are exhorted not to participate in the giving of an offering.

Bakht Singh not only stressed the significance of corporate worship, but he also zealously practiced and promoted the need for personal devotion. He emphasized the importance of the individual believer within the larger congregational life. Maintaining a consistent personal relationship with Christ was one of the main teachings of Bakht Singh and the Assemblies. This personal relationship could be recognized through ones' discernment of the "will of God" and the "voice of God."

The "Voice of God" and the "Will of God"

The most intriguing features of Bakht Singh's spirituality, especially those aspects of his own personal experiences, were listening to the "voice of God," and finding and obeying the "will of God." Bakht Singh told a number of incidents from his life in which he claimed to have heard the "voice of God." The "voice of God" gave him direction. At times it told him to

---

97. Ibid., 56–58.

go to a certain place or not to go there, to meet with certain people, or to speak specific words, and the like. Bakht Singh claimed:

> If anybody asks me: "What is your highest privilege as a Christian?" I would reply that knowing and doing God's will is my highest privilege. Those who know God's will and are doing it, find it through God's Word, His messengers and other circumstances.[98]

He went on to explain that:

> When we can truly say with all our heart: "Thy will be done," *then* that joy will be our strength to do His will. Outwardly we may have to endure something of the pain, the sorrow, the burden of Gethsemane, but our hearts will be strong in the strength that comes with doing the will of God.[99]

Similarly he made it clear that, "This is the primary condition for hearing the voice of God: You must be willing to go and do what God tells you to do without argument."[100]

And again he wrote:

> It is only as you are in the will of God that you can hear the Voice of God speak to you again and again. The Voice of God comes as confirmation. Do you want to hear the Voice of God clearly? Then learn to find and do God's will every day even in the smallest matter.[101]

At various times during his ministry, Bakht Singh referred to several occasions from his own experience in which he claimed he heard the "voice of God" in an unusual manner.[102]

While it may be difficult to understand and at times it may have seemed ambiguous when Bakht Singh spoke about the concept on "God's will" and listening to the "voice of God," what he seems to have been trying to

---

98. Singh, *Voice*, 94.
99. Singh, *Joy of the Lord*, 6.
100. Singh, *Voice*, 49.
101. Ibid., 44.
102. See Singh, *Voice*.

convey was that one should be clear of God's will in specific incidents and decisions that believers confront throughout their lives. This, however, required a redefinition of terms, for it is not the way of Sikhism.

As we have already noted, in Sikhism the ultimate goal is for the devotee to follow or surrender to the *hukam*.[103]

> Through His Will He creates all the Forms of things,
> But what the form of His Will is, who can express?
> All life is shaped by His ordering.

The *guru*'s command was to recognize the divine order and to submit to it.[104] It is written: "Submit to the *Hukam*, walk in its way."[105] This concept is also closely linked to the concept of the "voice of God" and its role in the salvation or realization of God. According to McLeod, "When one meets the True *Guru* and understands the *hukam* one attains to Truth. Salvation is not wrought through one's own efforts. Nanak, such a claim would bring destruction, (not salvation)."[106] In Sikhism, then, it is the Cosmic Order that is to be realized or perceived by devotees, an order to which they must submit in order to attain union with the transcendent being.[107]

In Bakht Singh's theology finding "God's will" involves the believers ability to know the mind of a personal God and his working in one's own life and in the world, and then following his guidance through out one's life. Although it appears upon close examination that Bakht Singh's theology is Sikh in its origin, he reinterpreted the concepts specifically to give it a Christian meaning. Bakht Singh acknowledges that he learned to find God's will while he lived in Canada with the Haywards.[108]

In both Bakht Singh's theology and Sikh *Bhakti* there is a strong sense of the sovereignty of God and the need for utter submission to it by the believer. Surrendering one's "self" to God and being united with him is the goal of all *Bhakti*. This understanding was very much evident in the following words by Bakht Singh:

---

103. Refer to the previous chapter for a detailed description of *hukam*.
104. Dhillon, "Institutions of Guru, 228.
105. McLeod, *Guru Nanak*, 200.
106. Ibid., 203.
107. Puri, *Advent*, 55.
108. See ch. 5, p. 125, n 65 and 66.

I thank God at last I yielded in April 1932. I said to Him, "Today I yield my life to Thee. I give you everything and I make no reservation. You can send me anywhere, and keep me anywhere, for any length of time. Lord I give myself to Thee."[109]

The concept of self-surrender (*atmanivedana*) is common to all *Bhakti* traditions. In the Telugu hymnal used within the historic denominational churches, this aspect of *Bhakti* is very much present in the lyrics written by the *bhaktas*. The same concept is understood as *prapatti* (self-surrender) in the Vaishanava tradition where it is said to be based upon the last word of the *Bhagavad-Gita*.[110] Bakht Singh's *Bhakti* was defined by an intimate, continuous relationship with a Sovereign God, who speaks, and who should be obeyed. Thus he wrote, "God does speak, and if you believe in God, you must listen when He speaks. He is not something abstract. He is a person. We can know Him, hear Him, be led of Him, and know Him more intimately than we know anybody else."[111] Since it is a relationship with a person to which Bakht Singh refers, *Bhakti* is intended to be expressed through the attitudes and feelings of the devotee.

Bhavas (Feelings, Attitudes, Sentiments, Moods)

Bhakti consists of various *bhavas*, that is feelings or emotions of the devotee to the deity. Although it is clearly a way of thinking that calls for a mystical understanding, *Bhava Bhakti* may be found concealed within the biblical language that Bakht Singh used and in the common imagery that he employed to explain it. His understanding of one's relationship with God could be explained according to the *Bhakti* concept of *bhavas*. Echoing similar sentiments of *Bhava Bhakti* in Sikhism, Bakht Singh explains different aspects of the love of God. For him, first and foremost in the love of God was God's love as a Savior (Gal 2:20); then God's love as Father (Heb 12:6, 10), Mother (Isa 66:13); Brother (Matt 12:48–50); Friend (John 15:15; Isa 41:8); Bridegroom (Rev 19:7; 21:2) and King (Rev 1:5; Eph 6:12).[112]

---

109. Singh, *Voice*, 61.
110. Rao, *Bhakti Theology*, 73.
111. Singh, *Voice*, 10.
112. Singh, *Holy Spirit*, 83–89.

The sentiment of *Santa bhava* is clearly expressed in Bakht Singh's exposition of the "Joy of the Lord" in a believer's life. In this state of *Bhakti* the devotee is in the presence of God, enjoying him fully. As a result of the contemplation and meditation, the devotee reaches a joyful state, while peace and joy rule the devotee's heart.[113] Appasamy has also noted that, "One of the striking characteristics of *Bhakti* experience is its joy."[114] Explaining the Scripture, "In thy presence is fullness of joy; at thy right hand there are pleasures for evermore" (Ps 16:11 KJV) Bakht Singh wrote:

> Joy multiplies as we live in the presence of God, and it is only there that *full joy* is found. . . . Our prayer is that you may learn this secret of dwelling in the presence of the living and loving God, for this is His intention and purpose for His people (Ps 37:4).

He went on to add that,

> The joy which we receive at new birth, and which multiplies as we live in the Lord's presence, becomes stronger when we find our delight in the Lord and entirely forget our other desires, whether for eating or drinking, or promotion or name, or even for expert Bible knowledge. If we delight ourselves in the Lord, how much more will be given us in the joy of the Lord than these things can ever bring![115]

A similar concept of passionless devotion is also found in the Sikh *Bhakti*. According to Guru Nanak a person attains *Bhakti* when he or she becomes unconscious of everything else and desires God with all his or her power.

> "Nanak is hungry for God, and careth for naught besides.
> I ask for God, I ask for nothing else."[116]

The attitude of *Sakhya*, in which the devotee considers God to be a friend, unfolds in Bakht Singh's words:

---

113. Rao, *Bhakti Theology*, 34–36.
114. Appasamy, *Hindu Bhakti*, 130.
115. Singh, *Joy of the Lord*, 3–4.
116. Banerjee, *Guru Nanak*, 171.

> The love of God was seeking for fellowship and companionship – for friends to be with Him forever – and so that love found expression by being poured out on the cross. When you are born again, God pours that same love upon you and rejoices over you . . . even as Eve was given to Adam to be a companion, a friend, a partner, and to satisfy his innermost longings and share with him what he could not enjoy with the birds, trees or animals.[117]

> The Lord wants us to enjoy His friendship and to share His secrets just as two friends who are very close to each other are able to share each other's secrets . . . If day by day we spend our quiet time prayerfully we find the Lord Jesus Christ speaking to us from His Word, and showing us many secret things, which were hidden from the wise and the prudent. But to gain friendship our response to him must be a true one.[118]

For Bakht Singh, one of the signs of being cleansed by Jesus' blood comes in the believers' ability to feel or sense or experience God's presence and communion as one would experience a friend.[119]

The Assemblies of Bakht Singh are known for their attitude of service, especially as it is lived out within their congregational life. In a clear parallel, the attitude of *Dasya bhava* which describes the devotee as a slave or servant to God as master is manifested in the congregational and community life in Sikhism. The *langar* and the *Karseva* in the *Gurudwara* are clear examples of their service orientation.

Even before Bakht Singh established the Assemblies, while he was still an itinerant preacher in Punjab he practiced what he called the "love feast" in a place called Martinpur. As a result of his ministry in Martinpur, a revival broke out and two groups, which had previously been in conflict with one another, came together and partook in this "love feast." Eleanore H. Llewellyn has captured the incident in the words of Bakht Singh, "What a feast we had! . . . No wedding feast had ever compared with it. Such love,

---

117. Singh, *Joy of the Lord*, 52.
118. Singh, *Walk before Me*, 12.
119. Singh, *Unsearchable Greatness*, 32.

such rejoicing, such desire to share! And after the feast we heard the refrain, 'We must tell others.'"[120] Though to a certain extent the Assemblies are insular, the Assemblies are known for their service and care for each other within their community.

Just as it is in *Bhakti*, the supreme state of relationship for Bakht Singh came in the *Madhurya bhava*. This is the highest form of *Bhakti*. At this stage the devotee regards the Lord as his or her lover. The lover and the beloved become one.[121] To a great extent, the words of Bakht Singh's brother that, "To him (Bakht Singh) Jesus had become a dearly beloved," echoes this same sentiment. In expounding Isaiah 62:4, "The Lord delighteth in thee," and Isaiah 62:5, "As the bridegroom rejoiceth over the bride, so shall thy God rejoice over thee," Bakht Singh claimed:

> [It was this state to which] the ultimate goal towards which these experiences of the joy of the Lord are leading us. The above verse indicates at once that the object of all his dealings with us is fellowship with himself. That goal towards which He is drawing us on step by step, so that we cannot draw back, is the highest joy of perfect oneness and union with our Lord.[122]

He went on to explain:

> What a husband and wife can give to each other cannot be given by mother or brother or sister, or in any other relationship. In a way that is equally unique, there can be a deep mystical union between man and God that even angels in heaven cannot experience, because they cannot receive the divine love which He gives to man. That is the marvel of redemption.[123]

The notion of union between God and human beings is common in all strands of *Bhakti* and that is the object of all devotion. While the disciplines differ, the end result is the same. In *Saguna Bhakti*, especially in the Vaishnava *Bhakti*, the aspect of emotional element in terms of ecstasies is present. The devotees go into trances as they worship a personal deity

---

120. Llewellyn, "Bakht Singh of India," 82.
121. Rao, *Bhakti Theology*, 39–55.
122. Singh, *Joy of the Lord*, 48.
123. Ibid., 51.

through the use of idols and rituals.[124] By way of contrast, Bakht Singh was strongly against the emotional manifestation of *Bhakti*. The Assemblies were known for their emotional restraint. They do not even clap during the Sunday service.

Thus far, Bakht Singh's concept of *Bhakti* appears to be sort of an interior religion. This conclusion is far from true, however, for not only did he practice and teach *Bhakti* like the *Bhakti* "saints," through his devotion he also contested the existing structures of religion and, in a sense, paved the way for a *Bhakti* movement within Christianity.

The Indian Christian *Bhakti* Movement

Bakht Singh's critique of the existing state of Christianity in India, with its practices, customs, and its continued observance of caste discrimination, resonates with the rhetoric of the *Bhakti* "saints." Accordingly, Bakht Singh also viewed the church structures and constitutions in place within the historic denominational churches as forms of "bondage," "slavery," and "control." As I have noted earlier, he argued:

> (T)he Church of Christ cannot be bound by earthly man-made laws; constitutions are often made for the sake of the authority they give, an authority like that of the Brahmins over the Hindus. Christians who want power over their fellow-Christians might truly be called "Christian Brahmins."[125]

He further contended:

> Some people are trying to bind Christians together by man-made constitutions. No church constitution – not even the constitution of the Church of South India – and no man-made constitution whatever can truly bind together the Church of God. It is the inward flow of abundant life in the heart of the believer which binds us, and nothing else can.[126]

---

124. Appasamy, *Christianity as Bhakti*, 24. In fact, one of the reasons that Bhakti was considered a popular and lower form of spirituality was the association of Bhakti to ecstatic manifestations.

125. Singh, *God's Dwelling Place*, 113.

126. Ibid., 112.

He did not accept the dogmatic teachings of the denominational churches. In the Assemblies, the creeds and the Lord's Prayer are not recited. For the followers of Bakht Singh, a formal liturgy and creeds are human-made practices, and it is worthless to recite them without understanding and appropriating their meaning. Formal liturgies and written creeds were also understood as restricting the freedom of each believer to engage in the spontaneous expression of devotion or worship of God. As Bakht Singh summed it up, "There is no need now for anyone to go to an earthly High Priest. Man can speak to God Himself through the Lord Jesus Christ, the High Priest, and get an answer and hear the voice of God daily."[127]

Indian *Bhakti* movements usually questioned the hegemony of the priestly classes, dogmatism and ritualism. The path of *Bhakti* offered a liberating alternative from the oppressive Brahminical priesthood and ruling classes. People who were deprived of direct access to God because of their caste, were now free to worship God directly. In the language of Kabir and Nanak, protest represented the idiom of *Bhakti*. They questioned the relevance and authenticity of the ritualistic Brahminical religion.

Kabir derided this system of religion by noting that:

> If union with God be obtained by going about naked,
> All deer of the forest be saved.
> They who bathe in the evening and the morning,
> Are like frogs in the water.
> While dwelling in the womb man hath no family or caste;
> All men have sprung from the seed of Brahm.
> *God* cannot be obtained *even* by *offering* one's
> Weight in gold;
> But I have purchased Him with my soul.[128]

Nanak registered the same concern when he noted:

> There are many dogmas, there are many systems,
> There are many scriptural revelations,
> Many modes to fetter the mind:
> But the saint seeks for release through Truth;

---

127. Singh, *Voice*, 47.
128. Cited by Banerjee, *Guru Nanak*, 58.

> Truth is higher than all these, and higher
> Still is the life lived in Truth.[129]

The *Bhakti* movement, though largely associated with the medieval period in India, had its beginnings with the Alvar "saints" of the South. It spread across the subcontinent, taking different shapes and forms according to the regions and communities with which it came into contact. It has been observed that it finally blossomed "into the satyagraha movement across the whole country under Gandhi."[130] It became "an idiom not only of selflessness but also anti-structure."[131] R. N. Vyas observed:

> Despite the differences of dresses, colours, languages and climates and creeds, India has a rare unity. This unity is the creation of devotion. [Bhakti] Devotion has melted the distinctions into a throbbing unity of mind and has effected an integration of hearts because of which a mighty current of unity runs through the apparent diversity in India.[132]

One may notice a similar impact of Bakht Singh's movement on Indian Christianity, although perhaps not in as sweeping a manner. Countering the worship pattern of the denominational churches, Bakht Singh adopted local patterns of congregational worship and tried to demolish the caste, language and regional barriers that existed in the denominational churches. He rejected the notion of tradition that came with the western missionaries and attempted to give an alternate paradigm, with biblical principles and devotion as normative for the life and worship of Christian community. As P. Solomon Raj testifies about the Assemblies:

> These groups and fellowships have provided a different kind of religious experience to people, a kind which was not commonly found in the "mission compound" Christianity, and

---

129. Ibid.
130. Rohini Mokashi-Punekar, *Bhakti as Protest* (article online), 1; available from http://www.arts.ualberta.ca/cms/punekar.pdf.
131. Amiya P. Sen, "Bhakti Paradigms, Syncretism and Social Restructuring in Kaliyuga: A Reappraisal of Some Aspects of Bengali Religious Culture," *Studies in History* 14, no. 1 (1998): 91.
132. R. N. Vyas, *Melody of Bhakti and Enlightenment* (New Delhi: Cosmo, 1983), 164.

some Christians from mainline churches, while keeping their membership in their respective churches, have joined these prayer groups and ashrams and house-churches, for special fellowship and prayer.[133]

By refusing to keep track of formal membership list, to legislate a constitution, or recognize a structural hierarchy, Bakht Singh tried to introduce an egalitarian, democratic and anti-hierarchical ethos into the notion of a church. In an imposed system of time- and rule-bound worship patterns of the denominational churches, he offered the freedom to worship individually and collectively in a manner familiar to Indian religiosity. He introduced the priesthood of all believers in a tangible way and emphasized that every member in the congregation had a role to play in the fellowship. By rejecting formal theological education for those in ministry, he in fact redeemed the church from an elitist clerical paradigm to a lay leadership and ministry.

Writing on the lifestyle of the indigenous pastors that he met, Bishop Victor Premasagar of the Church of South India comments:

> The dedication of the indigenous pastors, their prayer life, personal piety, humility, their availability at all times and utter dependence on God, are very much appreciated by their members . . . As the pastors of the mainline churches are not able to pay pastoral visits to the homes of their members, these members invite the indigenous pastors to visit them and pray with them.[134]

In allowing the literate members of the Assemblies to preach and to lead in the Assemblies of mixed educated groups, even when they were not theologically qualified or formally educated, Bakht Singh affirmed the value of *Bhakti* and the spiritual life of the individual as being more important than formal education in a religious or Christian witness. In other words, he asserted that *Bhakti* was the only way to claim devotional equality with,

---

133. Raj, *Christian Folk Religion*, 5.
134. P. Victor Premasagar, "Are Indigenous Churches a Silent Protest against the So-Called Mainline Churches?" in *The New Wine Skins*, ed. P. Solomon Raj (Chennai: ISPCK/MIIS, 2003), 165–166.

or primacy over, seminary educated pastors and teachers. In a way, this move gave dignity and worth to many believers who were otherwise uncared for and overlooked, and helped them to own their religiosity and their fellowship. In other words, Bakht Singh made Christianity an Indian religion of the believers.

Ravindra Raj Singh has observed, "One of the functions of *Bhakti* has always been to existentialize metaphysical insights, to translate into the lived world experience an abstract relationship. Holiness is to be recognized as realizable, as evident in the person of the *guru*."[135] Bakht Singh strongly condemned hypocrisy or church-oriented Christianity. For him, faith should be reflected in the day-to-day events of life. He challenged his congregations:

> On Sunday mornings you may pray beautifully, sing cheerful songs and look good and pious for about one hour. But when you go home, do you practice what you have seen and heard? Do you carry with you the light of God into your business and into your shop? . . . Can people see the marks of money and ambition? . . . Yes! but what can they see from the lives of many of you? Beedies, cigars, cigarettes, worldly saris, and arms full of bangles up to the elbow. Can people see from such lives that you are Christians?[136]

Bakht Singh vigorously advocated the practice of holiness in the day-to-day life of the individuals. In fact, believers were taught to separate themselves from the world and from non-believers.[137] On the other hand, Bakht Singh did not separate the secular from the sacred when it came to the life of the believer. He exhorted, "Wherever believers may be, in schools, in workshops, in hospitals or anywhere else, they must shine as lights. Our lives must show forth the virtues of our Lord Jesus Christ."[138] Sirajul Isalm has remarked that the discipline of *Bhakti* taught people to "live a life

---

135. Ravindra Raj Singh, "The Pivotal Role of *Bhakti* in Indian World Views," *Diogenes* 156 (Winter 1991): 70.

136. Singh, *God's Dwelling Place*, 67.

137. See Bakht Singh, *The Overcomers' Secret* (Hyderabad: Hebron, 1981).

138. Singh, *Fullness of God*, 21.

above narrow individualism and preserved the moral and human values."[139] Bakht Singh taught that spirituality and ethics go together. In other words, one's spirituality should be manifested in the day-to-day life of the believer.

Bakht Singh always emphasized the equality of all believers. He proclaimed that at the "Lord's Table all believers are equal . . . Every man-made difference is broken, and we have a bond which keeps His children together."[140] As a practical demonstration of equality, the love feast is practiced. In the Assemblies, caste barriers were also overcome to a large extent. Most of the full-time workers and Assembly members married across caste, language and regional barriers. By making only the experience of being born again as the criterion for membership in the Assemblies, Singh dispensed with the ritualistic nature of denominational Christianity. In fact, Bakht Singh appealed to a common notion of devotion and experience, the religious norm of Indian spirituality. By doing this he addressed all communities or religions on their own ground. Interestingly, a significant number of Bakht Singh Assemblies are in the Southern (Andhra Pradesh, Tamil Nadu), Eastern (West Bengal,) and Western (Gujarat) parts of the country. And each of these States has a history of strong *Bhakti* movements.

In addition to the alien cultural roots of the form of Christianity that had been introduced into India, the spirituality of this form of Christianity was also alien. Adhering to doctrines and submitting to the control of an institutional structure did not, in any way, relieve Christians in India from the hierarchical structure and hegemony in Hinduism that they were supposed to have discarded. In fact, by the time Bakht Singh established his Assemblies in 1941, the social, religious and political mindset in India was geared towards seeking freedom and independent identity in every sphere. While the Christian elite sought answers to this within the structures through the introduction of indigenous forms of worship and theology, average church-goers or the common folk sought a form of spirituality with which they were familiar.

Into this context came Bakht Singh, who introduced the notion of devotion or *Bhakti* that was a common religious ethos in Indian society. He

---

139. Md. Sirajul Islam, *Sufism and Bhakti: A Comparative Study* (Washington DC: Council for Research in Values and Philosophy, 2004), 226.

140. Singh, *God's Dwelling Place*, 121.

did this first of all, by treating the Scriptures and experience as *pramanas* over against a set of doctrines. By this means he opened up a new, as well as an accepted, avenue of spirituality to Indian Christianity. Unlike the Indian Christian theologians who deliberated on developing a theology that was Indian, Bakht Singh interiorized the *Bhakti* disposition so that *Bhakti* became one with his nature and flowed out of him in its Christian form. However, it did not become essential for Singh to use the local idiom in order to communicate *Bhakti*. Rather, he imparted *Bhakti* by articulating it in biblical terms.

Bakht Singh's theology revolved around the concept of a relationship to a personal God. By advocating a spirituality of consistent, continuous relationship with this personal God through meditation on the Scriptures, prayer, as well as on individual and corporate worship, Singh brought Christianity into the mainstream understanding of *Bhakti*. In a way, he synthesized the mystical and practical aspects of *Bhakti*. The importance of listening to the "voice of God" and surrendering to "God's will" both individually and corporately, not only affirmed the relationship of the devotee to God, but also undercut the legitimacy of the clergy class. At the same time, by enhancing the role of the individual in the congregation, individual and corporate *Bhakti* became significant. Devotion and submission to God implied being faithful in every sphere of life and this inculcated in the believer a spirit of active *Bhakti*.

Bakht Singh not only verbally condemned the caste system and the dogmatic and hierarchical nature of the denominational churches, he also took the practical step of introducing an alternate church model. By redefining the Christian message through the lens of *Bhakti*, in essence he Christianized *Bhakti*. In the hands of Bakht Singh, *Bhakti* became a Christian idiom. Thus, he can be called the genuine Indian Christian *Bhakti* theologian, whose theology flowed out of his experience and practice. By using biblical terminology and colloquial language to teach and practice *Bhakti*, Bakht Singh demonstrated that it was possible to do Indian Christian theology without using Hindu or Sikh terminology. In this way, he confirmed that following Christ is not just an intellectual exercise, rather it is a constant and consistent combination of experience and its expression in life. As he understood it, theology comes out of experience. Thus he established that "theology is not a matter of making correct propositions; it is a matter of coming into contact with the living God, and, on the basis of that direct experience (*pratyaksa anubhava*), describing God in a way that truly approximates to his inner reality as that is revealed in Christ."[141] What distinguishes Bakht Singh from the rest of the Indian Christian theologians is that he was able to give shape to the phenomenon called *Bhakti* in the form of the Assemblies.

How then did the Assemblies distinguish themselves from other churches? What was the impact of Bakht Singh and the Assemblies on Christianity in India? It is to these questions that we turn now.

---

141. Boyd, *Khristadvaita*, 45.

CHAPTER 7

Religious Culture of the Assemblies and Its Impact on Christianity in India

The Assemblies of Bakht Singh developed a separate or distinct identity of their own within the larger Christian community in India. By requiring all who claimed to be a Christian to have undergone in a decisive and fundamental way the experience of being born again, the Assemblies developed a unique sense of self-confidence that they are the true church, the true believers in Christ. To a large extent, with this kind of self-awareness, they insulated themselves from the outside world as a community of believers belonging to God. While others were able to recognize the members of the Assemblies by their particular form of piety, their approach to piety led many members of the Assemblies to maintain a "holier than thou" attitude towards other Christians.[1] Although Bakht Singh was opposed to humanly devised customs and practices, in the process of gaining a unique identity, the Assemblies developed a distinct subculture within the broader Christian community. Certain unique practices of the Assemblies became the identity markers of the Assemblies, although later on some of them were adopted by other churches.

---

1. The members of the Assemblies were called "bhaktulu" in Telugu, which means "holy people," by the members of the denominational churches. This was used more as a derisive term.

Special Features
The Role of "Promises" from Scripture

One of the distinctive practices of the Assemblies has been the practice of giving "promises" from the Bible. After praying for individuals Bakht Singh usually gave a Bible reference as a promise for them.[2] In every letter to which he dictated a reply, he added three or four Scripture references at the end, according to the need of the person with whom he was corresponding. The editorial letter in the *Hebron Messenger*, written by Bakht Singh, always carried three or four references at the end as promises. Daniel Smith recalls that, "Many times I have seen him, without once referring to his Bible, quote two thousand verses for batches of letters and these fairly spring forth from his well-stocked memory and also range over almost every chapter of the blessed Book."[3] Though the observation may well be overstated, it does convey the importance that Bakht Singh gave to the word of God as well as the consistency of his practice of giving promises from Scripture to those with whom he interacted.

One of the more important services in the Assemblies is the "Watch Night Service" held each year on the 31st of December. The congregation gathers together at 9 p.m. and the service may last until 4 or 5 in the morning. The special feature of the service is that each individual receives a promise for the upcoming year on a promise card. Three promises are given for the entire Assembly for the upcoming year. For example, the promises that were given for 1964 included Jeremiah 33:3, Ephesians 3:20, and Isaiah 65:24.

Usually, the promises are explained in the sermon preached during the Watchnight Service. The Assemblies receive the promises ahead of time so that all the Assemblies have the same promises in hand. These promises provide the text on which someone preaches, and the Assemblies claim these promises for the year. All three of the promises are also printed and sold on "motto cards" to be used as reminders throughout the year. Bakht Singh explained that the service was a time for rededication, and for many

---

2. This practice still continues today. When I attended the convocation in Kalimpong, I traveled back home with one of the leaders of Hebron. As we were parting at the airport, he gave a Bible reference to me as a promise.

3. Smith, *Bakht Singh of India*, 72.

it has also proven to be a time and place for them to respond to the call for salvation. He taught the Assemblies that during the year when difficult times and situations arose, if they claimed these promises with faith they might be helped to overcome their trials or needs.[4] This practice attracted many outsiders to attend the service in the hope that they would find out what God would provide for them throughout the upcoming year. This practice became a source of strength and a blessing for many. At the same time, it has become a ritual, even a way to determine one's future or luck for the year, especially for those who attended the service only for that purpose. In recent years, some of the denominational churches began this practice of giving promise cards in their services as well.[5]

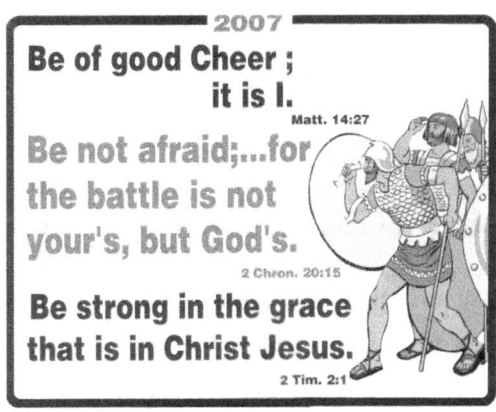

Motto Card for the year 2007

Importance of Scripture Memorization

Another dimension that this practice of giving promises has played is that it has firmly established the point that the word of God is the direct source of authority in the life of the believer. It has furthered the practice of the Assemblies of memorizing passages from the Scriptures. In fact, one of the significant features of Assembly believers is their knowledge of the Bible and their ability to orally recite the text. Bakht Singh could quote hundreds

---

4. Bakht Singh, "Letter of Praise and Prayer," *Hebron Messenger* (10 January 1982): 2.
5. For example, Church of South India, Kurnool, Andhra Evangelical Lutheran Church, Guntur.

of biblical texts without once looking at the Bible. Most of "God's servants" as well as the regular members are known for this practice. One of the ways that they were taught this discipline was through songs that are based upon portions of the Scripture. Kinnear recounted the process this way, "All the songs were based on the Scriptures and usually based on convocation messages, composed around expository messages, and the Scriptures were kept in view in the song so that they can memorize them."[6]

Although Bakht Singh emphasized the importance of the written word of God in the life of the individual believer and the congregation, he did not make Christianity a religion only of the literate or the elite. By requiring the congregation both of the literate and the illiterate alike to learn or memorize the biblical text by heart, he brought the word of God to the common folk and made them feel at home with it. Within the context of the textual authority of the Scriptures, Bakht Singh valorized orality and made the Bible become not only a Word that is read, but one that is also heard, keeping in tune with the understanding or place of *sruti* or hearing in the Indian religious culture.

The Development of an Identifiable Subculture

Certain practices by the members, especially with respect to their lifestyle or outward appearance, became typical among the members of the Assemblies. In the Assemblies, the members address each other as "brother" and "sister." They greet one another with the greeting, "Praise the Lord." This sort of addressing and greetings were not common features found in the denominational churches, although some interdenominational organizations and independent churches follow the same pattern.

When members go into the neighborhood or on the streets to engage in various acts of evangelism, they carry long, cloth shoulder bags in which they place their Bible, song book, as well as tracts and portions of the Gospels. In a way these bags function as identity markers for members of the Assemblies, markers that identify them as belonging to the Assemblies. Assembly preachers usually dress in white for preaching. Women who have dedicated themselves to full-time ministry, prefer to wear white sarees

---

6. Koshy, *Brother Bakht Singh of India*, 411.

when they engage in public evangelism.⁷ Koshy has pointed out that in the early days of the ministry, "white sarees came to be known as 'Bakht Singh sarees,' and often sold out as they were in great demand all over Madras."⁸

Bakht Singh was highly critical of the external appearance of those he saw as nominal Christians. Advocating a simple lifestyle and personal holiness, he condemned certain practices that were culturally Indian. Women were encouraged not to wear ornaments on themselves and flowers in their hair.⁹ Bakht Singh taught that beauty lies in obeying God and not in adorning jewels and being fashionable. He taught that believers should live a life of separation, distinct from the lifestyle of worldly people.¹⁰ Consequently, they developed a distinct style in their appearance, and their women could be recognized by their appearance as belonging to the Assemblies.

Although even today the effects of such pronouncements may be seen among the wives of "God's servants" and those who have dedicated themselves for full-time ministry, they are not common among ordinary congregation members. The lack of jewelry and ornamentation among women is another identity marker of Assembly members, although it is also a common practice among some Pentecostal groups.

Living a life of separation from the world is also expressed in different ways. For example, Clement comments that, "Going to theaters and drinking and smoking are not acceptable; . . . No silly talk of any kind is tolerated . . . Men must not wear women's clothing and vice versa."¹¹

Openness to All People

Unlike some independent congregations which aim to reach a particular community, language or caste, the Assemblies of Bakht Singh were open to all groups of people. Amrithraj Nelson has observed that they are basically multi-ethnic churches.¹² Susheel Rao has also commented that in the

---

7. Kuchipudi Clement, "Bakht Singh," in *A Dictionary of Asian Christianity*, ed. Scott W. Sunquist (Grand Rapids, MI: Eerdmans, 2001), 54.

8. Koshy, *Brother Bakht Singh of India*, 194.

9. Wearing flowers in the hair by women was a common cultural practice for all religions. Only widows are not allowed to wear flowers.

10. Singh, *Holy Spirit*, 167–168.

11. Clement, "Bakht Singh," 54.

12. Amirtharaj Nelson, *A New Day in Madras: A Study of Protestant Churches in Madras* (Pasadena, CA: William Carey Library, 1975), 128.

Assemblies, "The gospel is addressed to all classes of people. No special effort is made to reach the Dalits or the oppressed classes in the society."[13]

Since most of the people who joined the Assemblies in the beginning originally belonged to the denominational churches, the Assemblies were considered to be proselytizers or "Sheep Stealers." Later on, as the movement expanded, the growth in the Assemblies was considered to have come largely through the evangelization of non-Christians.[14] James A. Bergquist and P. Kambar Manickam observed:

> [That] so-called "sectarian" church groups are everywhere active is clear enough. Mostly they are confined to areas where established churches are the strongest, an indication that the independent movement in India is more characteristically domesticated phenomenon than an indigenous Christian movement exploding into Hindu and Muslim society.[15]

While this observation may be true enough for other groups, Berquist and Manickam went on to observe that it must be qualified specially "with respect to the Subba Rao and Bakht Singh movements."

Usually in the urban congregations the messages are preached in English with translation into one or two local languages. In the convocations songs are sung in different languages simultaneously. Thus, the Assemblies represent the heterogeneous nature of the Indian community.

Holy Convocations

One of the predominant features of the Assemblies is the annual event of holy convocation. The convocations gained prominence because of the large number of people that attend these meetings not only from the whole of India, but also from other countries. As a result, they represent various ethnic, language and culture groups. The order and discipline required to conduct these meetings, in light of the numbers of people being served, is phenomenal. Hundreds of people are served food simultaneously. At the same time all participants begin eating after a chorus is sung and the slogan

---

13. P. A. Susheel Rao, "Bakht Singh Movement," 153.
14. Nelson, *New Day in Madras*, 270.
15. Bergquist Manickam, *Crisis of Dependency*, 65.

"*Bholo Khudavan Yesu Masih ki*" (Shout, Hail to the Lord Jesus), with the response "Jai" is chanted two or three times.[16] Thousands of people are accommodated on a single campus by constructing temporary booths. Daniel Smith has provided a picturesque description of these convocations:

> At these times of "vacationing together," two or three thousand believers live as one big family. Streets of bamboo booths, with coconut leaves for roofing, are erected within the compound to house the multitudes . . . Each street of booths and also each booth has a Bible name. A sweet promise from the Word hangs at the entrance to each. Everywhere float banners with scripture verses of rare choice.
>
> There are teams for cooking, teams for serving (banana leaves for plates, rice scooped out of big vessels, curry ladled out of a bucket and tumblers of water), teams for sweeping, teams for drawing water from deep wells, teams for filling water pots in the booths, teams for preparing the mats for service, teams for hanging banners, teams for watching every part of the compound, teams for welcoming and helping visitors at the railway stations, and teams for praying (so that there is a cycle of prayer for the whole 24 hours of the day).[17]

The entire work is done voluntarily by members of the Assemblies. Members who are involved in secular jobs take leave from their work and get involved in the work for the convocation. Full-time workers who are in training in other Assemblies, who do not have major responsibilities in their local congregations, participate in the arrangements by staying in the premises at least a month before the convocation.[18] After announcing the date of the convocation, all the Assemblies allot a special period of time to pray for the convocations. From those who clean the vessels used to serve

---

16. David Jayakumar, interview by author, Pasadena, 24 August 2009. The slogan is in Urdu and was usually used in Hebron, while other Assemblies translated it into their local languages. It is not known whether the slogan was originally started by the North Indians or Bakht Singh simply introduced it because he knew the Urdu language and Hyderabad is a city dominated by Urdu speaking people.

17. Smith, *Bakht Singh of India*, 65–66.

18. Bro. Tendoop, interview by author, Kalimpong, 20 December 2005.

the crowds, to the preachers who deliver the sermons, every item is the subject of detailed prayer for more than three months.[19]

Bamboo booths at the convocation in Kalimpong, 2005

Bamboo booths at the convocation in Kalimpong, 2005

---

19. David Jayakumar, interview by author, Pasadena, 24 August 2009.

Roger Hedlund has noted that, "These gatherings served to awaken the realization that "every believer is called to serve." Whether serving as full-time Christian workers or employed in secular jobs, all believers are "a kingdom of priests and kings" called to serve."[20] As part of their witness to the community, those who attend the convocation go in a procession on the streets, singing and preaching the gospel. Since Bakht Singh believed that one should kneel when they pray irrespective of the place, when they offer prayer as part of the witness in the procession, the congregation kneels on the streets too. In India, except in the religious places of worship, it is very unusual that anyone would kneel in the public. To kneel on the street signifies the reverence and humility of the people to the God they worship and is also considered a witness. Clement comments, "This scene [kneeling on the road] was very impressive, especially during the convocation season when thousands of men, women, youth, and children would joyfully witness for Christ in public."[21] Because of the popularity of the convocations, Hindus and members of other churches also attend the meetings.

Going in a procession for open-air preaching, congregation kneels down on the road for prayer.

---

20. Hedlund, *Quest*, 155.
21. Clement, "Bakht Singh," 53.

Marriages

Bakht Singh may have been the first Indian to insist that a born-again believer should marry only a believer and that marrying an unbeliever went against the clear teaching of the Scripture. As a result, the congregations were known for arranging marriages only between believers. Most of the full-time workers who lived in the Assemblies were married by Bakht Singh after he sought the will of God for them. In other places, "God's servants" or the elders take the responsibility for doing so. In cases where the parents of the young people are unbelievers, the elders of the Assemblies or "God's servants" usually arrange marriages for the young people in their congregations. Although the consent of the parents is generally sought, sometimes their consent is given a minimum level of importance. This was one of the practices conducted by the Assemblies that led the denominational churches to criticize them. Since in Indian culture, it is generally the responsibility of the parents to arrange the marriages of their children, some unbelieving parents resented the role that Assembly leaders have taken in arranging marriages for their believing children. Their desire to have their children married in the way that they wanted it done was not honored.[22]

It must be acknowledged that through this system Bakht Singh revolutionized the system of marriage among Christians. By insisting that each person should know "God's will" when finding a life partner, and by insisting that a believer should only marry another believer, he addressed the age-old and strongly prevalent question of the role of dowry in Christian marriages. Even today, the dowry system is one of the "evils" that Christian churches and communities seem unashamedly to perpetuate. For the most part, Bakht Singh was able to contain this evil among members of the Assemblies, although it is found among some of them today.

Bakht Singh was also opposed to the extravagance of elaborate and pompous wedding celebrations, which are a common practice in South India. Instead, he advocated simple, cost effective weddings, thereby discarding all the cultural rituals that are associated with South Indian Christian marriages. His emphasis upon seeking the "will of God" helped people to cross all barriers of caste, region, language and education. It may

---

22. Conversational interviews with Christians, who belong to mainline denominations, about the practices in the Assemblies.

be the case that the largest number of inter-caste and cross-cultural marriages among Christians is to be found in these Assemblies.

Bakht Singh was strongly opposed to women adorning themselves with jewelry and wearing expensive clothes, or following any rituals during the wedding.[23] Tying "tali" or "mangalasutra," an ornament that is the symbol of marriage, and exchanging flower garlands between the bride and the bridegroom, form an important part of the wedding ceremony, both for the Hindus and Christians. The groom ties the "tali" around the bride's neck as a symbol of marriage union. This practice is followed by the Christians in the westernized weddings. Bakht Singh dispensed with these symbols as well as the practice of exchanging rings in the wedding. In the beginning, the only practice found in the Assembly weddings was the exchange of vows that were written by the Assembly. Later on, the practice of exchanging Bibles was introduced.

Prior to taking their vows, both bride and bridegroom individually pray aloud before the congregation. In order that the marriage be solemnized by Bakht Singh and "God's servants," some of the Assembly members go through the ceremony according to the practice of the Assembly. After the ceremony is over, some have followed the cultural traditions such as the tying of the tali and the exchange of flower garlands and rings, outside the premises of the Assembly. Although these practices are culturally accepted by all communities, Bakht Singh's opposition to them not only created a kind of subculture within the Assemblies, but also, at times it led to double standards among the members. These days, however, some local Assemblies allow some of the practices like adorning veil (western style) and exchanging rings.

In the elaborate list of promises made in the marriage vows, the bride takes an extra vow that the bridegroom does not take. It states, "*I promise to keep myself in subjection* to him and regard him as the head of the family in the Lord." By specifically inserting this clause in the vow, a hierarchy,

---

23. Dave Hunt narrates the process of Paul Gupta's (the founder of Hindustan Bible Institute) wedding plans. The bride's family was not happy at the proposal that Bakht Singh would solemnize the marriage because he insisted on simple weddings. "No costly sari for the bride, only a plain, white cotton suit for the groom, no jewelry, no pomp." See, Dave Hunt with update by John S. Gupta, *God of the Untouchables* (Honolulu, HI: Straight Street, 1999), 60.

rather than a concept of equality, is established. It also affirms the higher status of men over women.

Another vow that both the bride and the groom promise to each other is, "I promise to begin my day on my knees along with her/him, with the word of God. I promise to end my day on my knees along with her/him with the word of God." This is one of the promises with which some of the younger generation in the Assembly are not comfortable. While the idea of starting the day and ending the day praying together is ideal, making it a marriage vow before God is considered unwarranted and beyond the purview of the marriage vows. Some members felt that missing or skipping the prayer time together sometimes creates a feeling of guilt and is difficult to keep up the practice in a consistent manner. Imposing well meant practices on others can some times become demanding.

Funerals

Bakht Singh taught the congregations that the death of believers is only a promotion to glory, therefore, they are to praise God at the time of a believer's death rather than mourn for their dead. So the members are taught to refrain from the kind of severe mourning over their dead that takes place in surrounding cultures. Instead they carry their dead in a procession to the burial site while singing songs of praise and hope – a practice that is common among the denominational churches too.

Two of those that I interviewed in Kalimpong, North East India, told how the funeral processions of the Assemblies had an impact on the local people and were one of the important witnesses that led to new evangelistic opportunities that lead to conversions. This region of India is a Buddhist-dominated area. In this rural area the Buddhists, who cremate their dead, had to perform various religious rituals during and following the cremation. They engage in ancestral worship in which they invite the dead spirit, and they offer whatever the spirit requests. The fulfillment of those desires was to be undertaken by the family; many times, this leads an already impoverished family into debt and poverty. The Buddhists, who cannot comprehend "singing" upon the death of a loved one, often inquire about the reason for their singing. This simple act leads them into further contact with these Christians. In this way, they are attracted to the gospel of Jesus

Christ.[24] While members from the denominational churches usually bury their dead in black caskets, the members of the Assemblies cover the casket in white cloth to signify holiness. Sometimes, Scripture references or verses are stitched or written on the white background.

Evangelism

Bakht Singh developed a structured and organized method for evangelism and discipleship. He began his ministry as an independent itinerant evangelist. Evangelism, therefore, took primacy throughout his ministry. He believed that a believer should be prepared to preach the gospel "in season and out of season." Bakht Singh and the Assemblies were known to make use of every opportunity to preach the gospel, irrespective of the occasion. Clement observes, "He [Bakht Singh] would take advantage of every occasion – funerals, marriages, and cottage meetings – to share the gospel."[25]

Bakht Singh organized evangelistic rallies, which he called "Gospel Raids" or gospel campaigns. The term "Gospel Raids" was adopted from the Indian experience in the Second World War. In 1943, a Japanese plane dropped bombs on the harbor of Madras. Taking this as a cue Singh recalled, "This one raid was all that Madras suffered, but it gave us an idea – why not extend our conquests for the Lord by making "Gospel Raids" on the towns and villages surrounding Madras?"[26]

The general procedure used in these campaigns is that a team of congregation members along with the elders and "God's servants" go into a village or town and rent a place to stay. Once settled, they go around the streets singing gospel songs and preaching at public centers. They call this "open-air gospel" or "open-air preaching." They kneel down on the road for prayer. Both men and women distribute tracts and sell portions of the gospels. They also carry placards or banners of cloth on which Bible verses have been written. Men shout various Bible verses and slogans like "*Jai Yesu Masih Ki*" (Hail, Jesus Christ), loudly. People who are contacted on the streets are invited for a gospel meeting that night. The team stays several

---

24. Jaya, interview by author, Kalimpong, 19 December 2005, D. Wangdi Lepcha, interview by author, Kalimpong, 21 December 2005.
25. Clement, "Bakht Singh," 53.
26. Singh, *Write the Vision*, 15.

days in each place. If people respond to the gospel, some of the team members stay behind for the follow-up work, while the rest of the team moves on to another place.[27]

Some of their more popular evangelistic methods include open-air preaching and street processions. Open-air preaching was not a common practice in the 1940s. Solomon Raj wrote, "In those days it was not often that denominations joined together going in a procession through the city streets distributing leaflets and preaching and kneeling and praying on the street corners."[28] Moreover, allowing women to participate in the open air was a unique and radical move on the part of Bakht Singh. At times, those who participate in the open-air preaching faced opposition. People pelted them with stones, or threw mud and cow dung on them.[29] Occasionally, members of the historic denominational churches, who opposed such preaching, were also involved in such activities.

By involving the entire Assembly in the evangelistic work, Bakht Singh made evangelism part of the basic lifestyle of believers. He encouraged believers to proclaim the gospel personally in their work place and in their neighborhoods. Most of the members of the Assemblies are involved in doing personal evangelism with their colleagues in the work place, and this has resulted in the conversion of some non-Christians. The emphasis that the Assemblies give to lay ministry is recognized as a strength in the movement. It has contributed significantly to the growth of the Assemblies. Laymen who belong to the Assemblies often go directly from their workplace to the Assembly, in order to sell Gospel portions from house to house. These regular visitations lead to contacts and people are added to the Assemblies.[30] Solomon Raj observes, "Bakht Singh has certainly created bands of young laymen who in their spare time, would study the Bible and preach the word of God away from their secular jobs."[31]

---

27. Smith, *Bakht Singh of India*, 56–57.
28. Raj, *New Wine Skins*, 55.
29. Bakht Singh, "The Work Is Great," *Hebron Messenger (part II), Special Issue for Silver Jubilee of Jehovah-Shammah* (24 July 1966): 5.
30. Nelson, *New Day in Madras*, 46.
31. Raj, *New Wine Skins*, 55.

One of the ways that the movement has spread to different parts of India and outside the country has been through the migration of the members from one place to another. Members who hold a secular job have become instrumental in establishing groups of worshipers in their localities. When they are transferred to a different place where there is no Assembly, some of them begin to worship or start a small Bible study group in their own house with their family members. Slowly, they invite their neighbors or those who are interested in hearing the gospel to join them. As the group increases, they begin to conduct worship services on Sundays. Thus an Assembly comes into being.

One example of this may be found in the story of C. D. Benjamin, an engineer who was transferred to different places in India during the course of his career. Wherever he was transferred, he was instrumental in establishing an Assembly. The ministry further extended from the place where he was stationed to neighboring villages.[32] As a result, according to Koshy, C. D. Benjamin was instrumental in starting more than thirty Assemblies in various parts of India.[33]

Bakht Singh stressed the importance of the word of God not only in the life of each individual believer, but also in the gathered Assembly. He also stressed its importance as a method for communicating the gospel directly. As a result, writing Scripture verses on both sides of the walls of each Assembly, and the carrying of placards and banners with Bible verses written or printed on them, became new ways of engaging in evangelism. This is called "sign post evangelism." One of "God's servants" from Delhi took up a project of writing Bible verses on walls, trees and stones wherever it was allowed, along the entire road from Delhi to Kashmir.[34] The practice of writing Bible verses on walls is now followed by other independent and mainline churches.

In his discussion of the value of communicative art in the form of graffiti, of external wall painting, with texts and sometimes pictures as a form of people's art (also of political parties), Richard Taylor suggests that this art form should be practiced by Christians. He speculates that there are

---

32. Bakht Singh, "Editor's Letter," *Hebron Messenger* (9 July 1967): 2.
33. Koshy, *Brother Bakht Singh of India*, 441.
34. Sree Vani, interview by author, Delhi, 28 November 2007.

thousands of miles of Christian compound walls in India on which to experiment. Taylor notes, "The followers of Bakht Singh have made a good start in this direction. They call it 'sign post evangelism.' It is Bible verses all over outside walls – a little like Muslim monumental calligraphy, really. It is a real beginning in the taking of biblical graffiti seriously."[35]

Hebron, Hyderabad

In India, graffiti has long been a communicative method used by the political parties, but using it for religious purposes in public places was first popularized by Bakht Singh. Today one may find the same method being used by other religious groups to propagate religious teachings in the state of Andhra Pradesh.[36]

Nurturing of the Congregations

Bakht Singh gave as much importance to the nurturing of believers in the congregations as he did to evangelism. While working as an itinerant

---

35. Richard W. Taylor, "Communication through Art Forms," in *Christian Communication in India: Problems and Prospects*, ed. Mathai Zachariah (Delhi: ISPCK, 1981), 54.

36. In recent years, teachings from the Gita and other Hindu Gurus are written on the walls in public places in Andhra Pradesh. E.g. Kurnool.

evangelist for a number of years, Bakht Singh realized that the results from evangelistic ministry would not last long if the believers were not given proper teaching. He wrote:

> We became increasingly conscious of the danger of believers going astray through love of the world, through wrong doctrines and through lack of suitable spiritual food and fellowship in the churches where we left them. We had always thought that our responsibility ended with the revival meetings, Bible study and prayer-fellowship . . . we noticed that in spite of such follow-up work, there was no appreciable growth in the believers, and before long, large numbers would simply fade out of the picture altogether.[37]

With this knowledge and background in mind, Bakht Singh consciously organized programs throughout the week for the edification of believers. Though most churches have similar programs today, it was not a common practice at the time the Assemblies began. The program of a typical week was Wednesday Bible studies, Thursday brothers/sisters meetings, or cottage prayer, and Friday or Saturday prayer meeting or fasting prayers. Following the Sunday worship service, believers would go out for open-air preaching in the afternoon and attend evangelistic meetings in the late evening. In all of these meetings the congregation was taught to depend upon the word of God and to live a life of holiness, faith and witness. Special meetings were conducted periodically with speakers coming from other Assemblies or visitors from other countries.

Bakht Singh demonstrated the importance of prayer in his own life as well as in the life of the Assemblies. Describing the place of prayer in Bakht Singh's life, Daniel Smith wrote:

> Throughout the day every matter is brought before the Lord in prayer. No move is made and no journey undertaken without prayer. He never ventures outside without prayer, never enters or leaves a home without prayer, never receives or sends a visitor away without prayer . . . Twenty times a day you may

---

37. Singh, "A Prepared Place," 3.

hear the word, "Shall we pray," and this prayer is always on the knees.[38]

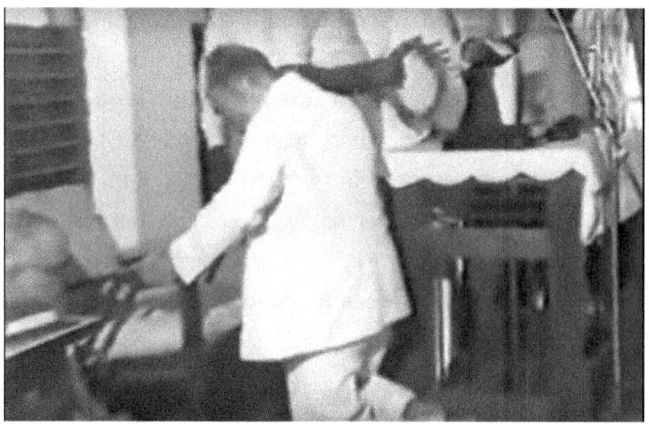

Bro. Bakht Singh kneeling down for prayer in his very old age

Weekday prayer meetings, second Saturday fasting prayers, and all-night prayer meetings, became the norm in the Assemblies. Bishop Victor Premsagar of the Church of South India commented on the difference between the denominational churches and the importance given to prayer in independent churches. He recounted an incident in one of the Church of South India (CSI) churches:

> One congregation complained to me that their pastor did not permit them to have all-night prayer in the church and he locked the church and went away. I asked him why he did that. His answer was "We do not have all-night prayer in the CSI, the Pentecostals and other fundamentalist groups practice it." . . . I told him that he had missed a good opportunity by not asking them to pray for himself and for me as well.[39]

---

38. Smith, *Bakht Singh of India*, 85. When I visited Hebron in January 2008, I had to wait to meet Bro. G. T. Benjamin, the elder of the Assembly because people kept coming and he was praying for them. During the interview, people waited outside for prayer. It was in the middle of the week and most of the visitors were from places outside the city. Prayer and seeking prayer from the godly is a common practice in Indian culture that was largely ignored by the mainline churches.

39. P. Victor Premasagar, "Silent Protest," 165.

Members are taught to have regular personal Bible study and prayer in regular quiet times early in the morning. Regular family prayers are also encouraged. Bakht Singh also insisted that both individuals and congregations kneel during their time of prayer.

The ministry in the Assemblies caters to all age groups. Apart from the Sunday School ministry for children, the Assemblies conduct Vacation Bible School for children during summer holidays. Parents are encouraged to teach the Bible and memory verses from the Bible to their children.[40] Immediately following the annual holy convocation, a youth camp is conducted every year. A Youth Supplement to the *Hebron Messenger* is published every month. Youth fellowships have also developed in certain Assemblies.

Keeping the doors of the Assembly open throughout the day, and allowing people to meet and receive counsel from "God's servant" or elders all through the day, are distinctive to Bakht Singh's Assemblies. People have access to "God's servants" whenever they are in need of it. Though it is not a common practice among the mainline churches where the doors of the church buildings are closed during the week days, the Hindu temples and the Sikh *gurudwaras* are open throughout the day. People may go to the temple or *gurudwara* any time they want to worship their god. By opening the doors of the Assemblies all through the day, Bakht Singh appealed to the familiar concept in Indian culture of visiting God at any time. When I visited Hebron in January 2008, I had to wait for a long time to meet Bro. G. T. Benjamin, the elder of the Assembly, because people kept coming and he was praying for them. It was a week day and most of the visitors were from places outside the city. Prayer and seeking prayer from the godly is a common practice in Indian culture that was largely ignored by the mainline churches.

Most of the Assembly buildings have been constructed for the purpose of worship, with living quarters for "God's servant" attached. At times, worship services are conducted in the living room of an elder's house. On

---

40. In a conversation with a family who have been members of the Assembly for a long time, the now grown-up members of the family recollected how in their childhood they were not served breakfast on Saturdays until they had memorized their Psalm for the week.

the one hand, this has worked out for the spiritual growth and betterment of the congregations, but on the other hand, it has had negative consequences on the families of "God's servants." "God's servants" have had limited time for their family and children.[41]

Assemblies as Centers of Training

Bakht Singh did not believe in seminary or theological college education. He believed that "a 'western style' Bible school is not what is required" within an Indian context.[42] Members who dedicated themselves to full-time ministry were trained by requiring them to live in the Assembly either in Hebron or in another central place with other believers, and then by sending them out for ministry in other places.

Those who were called to full-time ministry usually lived in the Assembly for training. Guests and some members who wished to be trained in the Assembly joined them temporarily. Morning and evening, they were expected to follow a strict personal discipline of quiet time and meditation on the word of God and personal prayer. Family prayer in the morning and evening was a regular feature, where books of the Bible were read in sequence. These were also considered to be teaching opportunities for the workers. As part of training, four days each week, 1 ½ hours of systematic Bible study was conducted by the senior "Gods' Servant" or visiting teachers.[43] Bible study gatherings were also arranged for systematic Bible teaching for newly born-again believers, youth and "God's servants." Periodic three-week Bible studies were held for "God's servants" in different places during the year.[44] "God's servants" from all over the country came together once a year for a time of Bible study and renewal. This was usually following the holy convocation in Hebron. Once a month, regional Bible studies for "God's servants" were held at different regional headquarters. Although foreigners were allowed to teach and participate in the Bible studies for

---

41. Information gathered from different interviewees.
42. G. G. Abbiss, "Training in Hebron," *India Church Growth Quarterly* 6, no. 1 (January–March 1984): 12.
43. Ibid.
44. "Editor's Letter," *Hebron Messenger* (30 March 1969): 2.

"God's servants," they were not allowed to attend elders meetings or meetings where ministry decisions were made.[45]

Bakht Singh emphasized that one's spirituality must be manifested in his or her lifestyle, that is, the way one lived. He took the lead here, by demonstrating a simple lifestyle based upon faith. In so doing, he advocated a lifestyle that was supposed to be a witness, one that was befitting of believers. He was often critical about believers who gave importance to materialism, and he promoted a modest lifestyle through his own life and teaching. Bakht Singh's integrity regarding money and his exemplary life were generally recognized and accepted by others. Susheel Rao summed it up well when he said, "That Brother Bakht Singh is a man of God, completely dedicated to God's service and is living by faith, cannot be denied and is seen clearly, in his lifestyle."[46]

Bakht Singh also expected full-time workers and the congregations to live a similar lifestyle. One of the first lessons full-time workers were expected to learn was to depend upon God for everything. They were taught to live by faith and not to reveal their needs to anyone. They were taught to share whatever they had and to live together whenever they were sent out in teams. Bakht Singh practiced this in his own life from the beginning of his ministry. Llewellyn testifies to this way of life when she writes:

> You ask him for special meetings in your city or village. He must have special guidance before he can accept. He must also have assurance that his present work is done before he can leave, even though some other request may have to be deferred. You are not sure whether you will have enough to bear the expense of the meetings. Let there be no fear. If it is God's will for him to come, the money will also be provided. The important thing is to be sure that the message for today is God's message for his people. He spends long hours in prayer.[47]

Bakht Singh taught that for "God's servants" and full-time workers to express their needs to others was a form of begging. It was not depending

---

45. Bro. Stephen, interview by author, Delhi, 21 November 2007.
46. Rao, "Bakht Singh Movement," 152.
47. Llewellyn, "Bakht Singh of India," 87.

on God. In the Assemblies, "God's servants" do not have fixed salaries. The congregation is supposed to care for them. Bakht Singh frequently exhorted "Gods' Servants" on depending upon God. He reminded them that, "If God's servants cannot live and demonstrate a life of faith, they cannot be examples to other believers. When God's servants become beggars, God's work suffers much. If they cannot live a life of faith, it is far better for them to quit."[48] During the training period when the full-time workers lived in Hebron, they were provided with food, but not with other essentials such as soap and toothpaste. For these essentials, they were required to exercise their faith in God. In that way, they were to learn to depend on God.[49]

Those who were dedicated to the ministry, and others who went for temporary training, were assigned duties depending on their abilities. They were trained to do all kinds of physical service, from janitorial work to cooking. Abbiss wrote:

> Practical work of different types takes a large proportion of the time for the young men. Those with necessary skills and aptitude work in the bookroom. This involves the keeping of accounts, maintaining stocks, buying and selling, along with overseeing the books, tracts, etc., through the press in different languages. Some will be assigned to the general office to attend to the various matters that arise during the day, such as purchase of rail tickets, attending to mail, etc., plus being available day and night to answer the telephone. The correspondence course work (in English, Telugu and Urdu) provides effective ministry for some, and there is also the job of keeping the compound neat and clean.[50]

Bakht Singh was a strict disciplinarian; he did not withhold punishment for the disobedient. Although there were a few instances where he slapped some men, the main punishment would be not involving them in any work. Within the Indian context of leadership, the practice of a *guru* slapping a disciple would not be considered offensive, but rather as part of

---

48. Bakht Singh, *Come Let Us Build*, 3rd ed. (Hyderabad: Hebron, 1994), 29.
49. Sis. Kalyani, interview by author, Hebron, 11 October 2007.
50. Abbiss, "Training in Hebron," 11.

the discipline within a family. Since men were supposed to lead a congregation he did not spare them any discipline.[51]

Bakht Singh was very particular in maintaining confidentiality. He allowed only a few members to handle his correspondence and he made it a point to reply to every letter personally though he did dictate his letters, which were then either typed or handwritten. All of the correspondence was burned periodically, in order to maintain confidentiality, because most of the correspondence was personal.[52]

Although Bakht Singh tried to involve his coworkers in the decision-making process, his word was final, as is the case with any Indian spiritual leader. He was never questioned by any of his coworkers. In a way, this practice led to negative consequences at times, for instance, in situations where he was kept in the dark about the actual happenings in particular Assemblies. It also led to the concentration of power in him. People looked up to him for everything and his word became "divine." One of the main criticisms against Bakht Singh was that he allowed people to make him an indispensable person in their lives.[53]

Women

On the one hand, Bakht Singh was quite conservative with regards to the role of women in the Assemblies and families. On the other hand, he was way ahead of his times when he involved them, along with men, in public processions leading up to the open-air gospel preaching. Bakht Singh involved women when they went on Gospel Raids to different parts of the country as early as the 1940s, at a time when women did not openly move with men. They participated in open-air preaching by distributing tracts and selling gospel portions along public roads. In the 1940s Indian culture, women did not move around freely on the streets. Yet, within that cultural context, Bakht Singh allowed women to participate in open-air processions. Although women were not allowed to preach in the Assemblies or in Gospel Raids, the fact that he allowed them to participate in the open-air

---

51. Sis. Kalyani, interview by author, Hebron, 11 October 2007.

52. Bro. Stephen, interview by author, Delhi, 21 November 2007.

53. This was a common observation made by the interviewees who belonged to the Assembly as well as by outsiders.

processions alongside men was an affirmation of his conviction that women were important in the work of ministry and all believers have a responsibility to preach the gospel.

Women were allowed to testify within the worship service, and to participate in the time of worship through individual praise and adoration. They were not allowed to address a combined gathering of women and men. They were also not allowed to become elders in the Assemblies. One of the marriage vows that the bride takes in the wedding ceremony is, "*I promise to keep myself in subjection* to him and regard him as the head of the family in the Lord." All these point to the fact that Bakht Singh and the Assemblies assign a secondary position to women both in the family and the Assembly. Although the concept may be justified biblically, it does raise serious questions regarding the issue of gender equality in family, church and society.

Women went out two-by-two for door-to-door evangelism and house visitation. Though the involvement of the women in the ministry was never highlighted, in reality women were, to a large extent, instrumental in the spread of the ministry. Rajamani narrates the fact that the retreats conducted for the sisters on public holidays resulted in a deep burden to pray for other parts of the State. This also led to contacts with people in other towns, and consequently to the spread of the ministry. Sisters would go out two-by-two visiting jails and slum dwellers. Through their ministry in "some areas they became spiritual leaders who were looked up to by many for guidance. In other cases the sick were brought for prayer, and God graciously answered."[54]

In 1942, some women and girls who were converted to Christianity were turned out of their homes. So there arose a need to accommodate them. A separate house was rented for the sisters to stay in, and they called it "Hephzibah." Two foreign missionary women, Miss Violet Green and Miss Grace Stalley, lived in Hephzibah and helped in the training of sisters in Bible study and evangelism.[55] In some of the Assemblies, women (believers) who were abandoned by their families were given shelter. They

---

54. Rajamani, *Monsoon Daybreak* (London: Open Books, 1971), 113.

55. Ibid., 95. Miss Stalley was with the Open Brethren in South India, and Miss Violet Green was with a strict Baptist Mission. They became acquainted with the work of

lived there, serving in the Assembly, and were cared for in their old age, too.[56] In fact, the role of women in Bakht Singh's movement needs further research. In Hebron, the headquarters of the movement, women who were dedicated for full-time ministry lived in separate quarters. Everyone was assigned tasks according to their gifts and qualifications. Some of them were in charge of the kitchen; others were involved in office work. All of them would go out for the purpose of ministry or they were involved in prayer.[57] Some of the sisters who were dedicated to the ministry were married to full-time workers. Those who were called to remain single continued to live in Hebron or other centers.

Impact of Bakht Singh on Christianity in India

In the initial stages of Bakht Singh's work, the historic denominational churches reacted negatively to it. When he had founded the Assembly, some of the pastors from the historic denominational churches in Madras confronted Bakht Singh to ask why he was conducting services on Sunday and administering second baptism. Bakht Singh gave answers directly from the Bible and he challenged them to show from the Bible that what they were doing was correct. The conversation ended with them setting a date for further discussion. This discussion never took place.[58] Since most of the people who initially became members of the Assemblies originally belonged to the denominational churches,[59] the Assemblies (and other inde-

---

Bakht Singh and voluntarily asked to be associated with it. A. J. Flack, Sidmouth, Devon, UK to (Bharathi, Pasadena, USA), 13 December 2006.

56. In the Assembly in Darjeeling, nearly twenty women who do not have any one to take care of them, live in the Assembly. The wife of the "God's servant" requested the team (I was in the team from the Kalimpong convocation that visited Darjeeling) to pray for one of the women who had cancer and had an appointment with the doctor the next day. The wife of the "God's servant" accompanies her to the hospital.

57. Mrs Sarala Joshi, interview by author, telephone, 23 October 2008; Mrs Dhanaraj, interview by author, Vellore, India, 12 December 2007; Sis. Kalyani, interview by author, Hebron, 11 October 2007.

58. Bakht Singh, "The Work Is Great," 8.

59. In Andhra Pradesh one of the strongest independent churches that the mainline churches had to contend with was the Bakht Singh Assemblies. P. Solomon Raj describes one of the motivating factors that made him conduct research on indigenous churches: "My quest into the problem of sectarian movements, as they were called, started in the year 1956, when I was first appointed as student's chaplain, after my ordination in a small town called

pendent churches) were viewed as "sheep stealers" and "splinter groups" by the older churches. Some churches in Andhra Pradesh went so far as to remove people from their employment, for example, as school teachers, because they had been baptized in the Assemblies for the second time.[60]

Other Churches

As a response to the growing influence of independent churches, some denominational churches were motivated to make certain changes in their ministry. The denominational churches realized that pastors in their churches did not have the independence to minister to the rural congregations depending on the need and context of the people. They also recognized that their political and administrative structures and their administrative responsibilities limited their freedom to reach people in their given context and spirituality.

In order to give more independence to the rural pastors in terms of their ministry and methods, Andhra Evangelical Lutheran Church introduced a new category of ministers apart from the pastors, called "Licensed catechist." They have been given freedom to administer the sacraments, and to preach and teach in an indigenous way. In the first two years of introduction of this ministry, it was noticed that "there was hundred percent growth in stewardship and significant growth in numbers in nearly all the parishes served by licensed catechists."[61] Later, however, the ministry did not continue in the same manner.

The Church of South India (CSI) has tried to implement some measures that are culturally appropriate to the context. In one of their programs, called "Vision for Equipping the Local Congregation for Mission" (VELCOM), a love feast, similar to that of the Assemblies, was suggested

---

Guntur in Andhra Pradesh. In Guntur and surrounding places, at that time, the group church movement was very active. Brother Bakht Singh, a convert from Sikhism, has started several big groups, including, among others those called Elim and Jehova-shama, and many young and old people from my church, the Lutheran Church, began to join his fellowship. The local pastors of the mainline churches were very much concerned for the losses in their ranks." Raj, *Christian Folk Religion*, 14.

60. Conversations with mainline church members. See Raj, *Christian Folk Religion*, 6–7.

61. Bergquist and Manickam, *Crisis of Dependency*, 74–75.

by the bishop. The bishop clearly stated the reason for recommending the program. He wrote:

> The Table fellowship-*agape* suggested in VELCOM programme enhances local fellowship and breaking down of dividing walls of prejudice and caste discrimination in every local community. Eating together is the highest form of building relations among the otherwise antagonized groups in our Land. Jesus ate with the publicans and sinners to the utter dismay of the elite and religious leaders. Eating together helps building fellowship, friendship and commitment to each other.[62]

In some of the CSI churches they have started distributing promise cards during the Watch Night Service on the 31st of December. Some have kept churches open for mid-week Bible studies, fasting and all-night prayer meetings, which in earlier years was not common in the denominational churches.[63]

Most of the independent, nondenominational assemblies follow the pattern of Bakht Singh Assemblies. Their worship, architecture and practices are adopted from the Assemblies. Some of the independent charismatic churches were started by individuals who were originally members of the Assemblies. Some, such as Zac Poonen, were even nurtured by Bakht Singh.[64] Bakht Singh has paved the way for the indigenous Christian movement to take momentum. In the sense people felt free to establish churches in their own way of worship and to their own people. The concept of establishing nondenominational churches by lay leaders was in fact introduced and promoted by Bakht Singh, thus making him the main architect of the independent church movement in India.

---

62. P. Victor Premasagar, "Gospel and Culture," in *The Goodnews of Jesus Christ in the Indian Setting*, ed. T. Dayanandan Francis (Chennai: Christian Literature Society, 2000), 139.
63. Church of South India, Kurnool, Andhra Pradesh.
64. Bergunder, *South Indian Pentecostal Movement*, 288.

Union of Evangelical Students of India (UESI)

Bakht Singh was indirectly instrumental in the formation of the Union of Evangelical Students of India, one of the premier interdenominational student Christian organizations in the country. In 1946, Bakht Singh was the keynote speaker at the Urbana Conference of the InterVarsity Christian Fellowship. There, Singh met some of the student organizers who later went out as missionaries to different parts of the world. One of them was T. N. Sterrett who worked as a missionary in Jhansi, North India. In South India, three different groups of students met independently for Bible studies in Madras, Vellore and Coimbatore respectively. H. Enoch, who belonged to the Assembly of Bakht Singh, was the leader of the Madras group. Bakht Singh introduced Sterrett, who was in India then as a representative of the International Fellowship of Evangelical Students, to H. Enoch. Later, the three groups merged to form the UESI. T. N. Sterrett was one of the first staff workers, and H. Enoch was the founding member of the UESI.[65] Thus, behind the scenes, Bakht Singh was responsible for the formation of UESI.

Bakht Singh also worked very closely with H. Enoch. The *Hebron Messenger* carried a regular prayer item for the ministry of H. Enoch. Bakht Singh frequently ministered in the meetings of the UESI. In fact, the financial policy of UESI was influenced by the faith policy of Bakht Singh. UESI also has the policy not to accept funds from foreign agencies and totally depend upon God for its needs. Its teaching on "finding God's will" and that believers should marry only believers are some other strong affinities between the Assemblies and the UESI.

Foreigners as Coworkers

Although Bakht Singh was highly critical of the missionary model of the churches and the kind of Christianity that was practiced in the mainline churches, he was not against working with independent missionaries who agreed with his understanding of the nature of the church. Missionaries

---

65. Information furnished by Sathkeerthi Rao and Dr R .E. Dhanaraj. See P. T. Chandapilla, "T. N. Sterrett," in *Dictionary of Asian Christianity*, 798; and Prema Fenn, "Union of Evangelical Students of India," in *Dictionary of Asian Christianity*, 864.

Religious Culture of the Assemblies and Its Impact on Christianity in India 215

from the Honor Oak Fellowship, for instance, worked with Bakht Singh from the beginning of the Assemblies. Later he was joined by independent foreign missionaries, mostly from the open Brethren[66] and Baptist backgrounds. Daniel Smith notes, "In that fellowship there is no dependence on the West; but there is fellowship with Westerners and also a place for their help and ministry, if they have ought worthy to give."[67]

Some of the foreign missionaries who observed the work of Bakht Singh left their mission organizations and joined Bakht Singh and became his coworkers, living a life of faith. Leslie Carter, who originally belonged to "India Mission," was with Bakht Singh from 1943–1959. In 1943 Wilfred Durham, who was a Brethren missionary, joined Bakht Singh in his literature ministry. Durham founded the Gospel Literature Service (GLS) in Bombay in 1943. GLS published most of Bakht Singh's booklets during the initial stages of the movement and it was instrumental in spreading the work of Singh beyond India. Bakht Singh was one of the members of the GLS Trust from 1952 until the late 1980s.[68]

While Bakht Singh did not officially associate himself with any of the denominational churches either in India or abroad, he did work very closely with some interdenominational organizations. Missionaries, both men and women, who belonged to the Worldwide Evangelization Crusade from the UK, Canada and Australia, worked with Bakht Singh in the Assemblies. Most of the missionaries were involved in taking Bible studies and teaching in the Assemblies.

George Verwer and his organization, Operation Mobilization (OM), had a very close working relationship with Bakht Singh. OM was involved in evangelization through literature distribution and door-to-door evangelism through teams that went out all over the country. While OM supplied trucks, drivers and leaders for the ministry, Bakht Singh provided the members for the teams that did the field evangelism from the Assemblies. Bakht Singh also traveled in other countries ministering in different places.

---

66. In Pakistan the Brethren Assemblies work in unity with the Assemblies of Bakht Singh. They do not have separate churches as in India and other countries. The Assemblies of Bakht Singh in Pakistan are known as "Brethren Churches." See Koshy, *Brother Bakht Singh of India*, 356–366.

67. Smith, *Bakht Singh of India*, 50.

68. Koshy, *Brother Bakht Singh of India*, 93–95.

These contacts resulted in establishing similar Assemblies in various other countries. Thus, the movement spread to other countries making it an international one.[69]

By developing a "New Testament pattern" church that was truly Indian, Bakht Singh was required to interact with the biblical culture as well as the Indian cultural context. His struggle to maintain a distinctly Indian form of Christianity, on the one hand, made Christianity Indian to a large extent, and on the other, brought an Indian subculture into the already westernized Indian Christian culture. Bakht Singh was able to create a lifestyle within the Assemblies that was defined by witness and evangelism. This, in fact, has led to the development of the movement wherever the members of the Assemblies have gone. These members developed a strong sense of spirituality that not only gave them an identity, but also separated them from other Christians who belonged to the denominational churches. The sense of brotherhood within the Assemblies also sustained the movement in the face of opposition from other denominations.

The lack of a systematic structure scattered the churches far and wide and also created a house church movement in India, where there was proliferation of independent churches in many parts of South India. While the current situation of the Assemblies is a debatable issue and a topic for further research, the fact that the model established by Bakht Singh continues to influence the shape of spirituality and worship in many non-Pentecostal, independent churches in India and elsewhere is a tribute to the legacy of the work and ministry of Bakht Singh and the movement started by him.

---

69. See Koshy, *Brother Bakht Singh of India*, 311–400 for the spread of the movement in other countries.

Conclusion

Any religion or religious movement evolves within a given social, cultural, political, and religious context. Bakht Singh's movement had its roots within the political and religious context of the nationalism and freedom struggle when Indians fought for independence from colonial rule, and Indian Christians sought independence from an alien form of Christianity as well as "missionary imperialism." The intellectual and dogmatic Christianity that was introduced into India by the historic denominational churches failed to address the common person's quest for a deeper spiritual religion that covered one's entire life. In an already socially stratified and religiously constrained society, the institutionalized structures or system of the church posed a difficult challenge for Christians, as well as an additional restraint on their freedom to understand and worship God.

The Assemblies established by Bakht Singh originated as a protest movement to the prevailing situation in the historic denominational churches. Although it originated as a protest movement, the challenge they had to face was to find an alternate model to the existing denominational structures. In order to accomplish this, Singh turned to the Scriptures, to his personal religious experience as a Christian, and to his pre-Christian religious heritage as a Sikh, and to other likeminded Christian movements that arose out of similar contexts in other parts of the world.

Anchored in the Scriptures, Bakht Singh's personal encounter with Christ formed the basis for his theology and life. This encounter with Christ took place within a context that was already steeped in the spiritual ethos and mindset of the Sikh *Bhakti* tradition in which he grew up. While the similarities between Sikhism and Christianity were substantial, the differences between them were fundamental. In a way, the similarities as well as the differences served as a basis for Bakht Singh's understanding and willingness to accept the new religion – Christianity. But instead of eliminating the existing pre-Christian worldview, Bakht Singh transformed it, thereby making it a channel to allow for the incarnation of Christianity in a uniquely Indian form.

The creative genius of Bakht Singh is visible in the way he analyzed the deficiencies in the historic denominational churches and in the way that he was able to utilize the resources that were available from his pre-Christian faith, which he could then synthesize into a new biblical understanding that was clothed in the religious culture of the Indian people. Thus, aided by his own understanding of the Bible, his own spiritual experience, and his knowledge of both western and Indian religion and culture, Bakht Singh translated the gospel in such a way that it met the wide-ranging needs of the culture and the context.

Bakht Singh was able to address certain issues that he perceived to be hindrances to the translatability[1] of the Christian faith into the Indian context. The first of these issues was what he perceived to be the utter neglect of the place of spiritual experience by the historic denominational churches. Coupled with this was his criticism of their emphasis on the intellectual assent to a set of dogmas and traditions that he saw as being imposed upon the Christians of India from the outside. Second, Bakht Singh also recognized that the members of the historic denominational churches possessed a religious or intellectual affiliation to their faith but because of their emphasis upon the intellectual side of faith, they seemed to lack a genuine experience of being born again.

Bakht Singh contended that being a believer or having a true Christian experience involved a confession of faith in and a commitment to Jesus Christ as personal Savior, and the development of an ongoing relationship with him. This relationship was to be defined by the believers' dependence upon Scripture and a life controlled by the guidance of the Holy Spirit. This position also led Singh to maintain that the members of the historic denominational churches or those that he termed as "unbelievers" or "nominal Christians," had not surrendered their self to the Lordship of Christ. At the same time Bakht Singh was aware that the experience of

---

1. The term is borrowed from Lamin Sanneh. See Lamin Sanneh, *Translating the Message: The Missionary Impact on Culture* (Maryknoll, NY: Orbis, 1989).

a personal God such as he taught, held more in common with the kind of spiritual perception and religious background from which he and other Indians Christians in India had been uprooted – an experience which many Indians sought. As a result, Bakht Singh was able to connect his own personal experience with Christ to the phenomenon of "religious or spiritual experience through a relationship or devotion to a personal God" related to *Bhakti* that could be found within Indian spirituality.

As Bakht Singh exercised *Bhakti* within his own personal expression of spirituality, he was also able to articulate it while engaging the biblical idiom, thereby making it possible for the *Bhakti* tradition to become integrated into a viable expression of the Christian faith. To the Indian mind, this gave significance to the experience of God within religious life. In this way, Bakht Singh's teaching of a personal relationship and experience of Jesus Christ was naturally appealing. His pre-Christian religious tradition that provided the root and dynamic for the main components of his Sikh heritage were readily transformed or reinterpreted into a biblical theology. In a sense, then, Bakht Singh made *Bhakti* a biblical religion that was also the desired religion of the people of India. At the same time, he made Christianity an Indian religious faith, which no longer has to suffer from its alien form and theology. In this way he was able to get rid of the western forms that were not appropriate to the context.

Another issue that Bakht Singh confronted involved the structures and tradition found within mainline Christianity. He saw the system and structures in the historic denominational churches not only as constraining the freedom of the people to worship God in their own way, but as replacing God and his word in the life of the believer and the church. In order to rectify this situation, he strove to introduce a new emphasis upon the primacy of the word of God and its importance in the daily life of the individual believer and the church as a whole. Bakht Singh's background as a Sikh, taken together with his experiences as a Christian, must have suggested to him that the Scriptures and a personal experience of God through devotion are intimately connected and are, therefore, essential to sustain the spiritual nature of the church and the spirituality of the congregation.

Bakht Singh insisted on the headship of Christ over the church and on the spiritual nature of the church. Since Christ is the head of the church, the duty of the believers is to follow the directives given by God that allow God to govern his church. This understanding of the dynamic nature of the church demands a continuous relationship with God as well as an ongoing dependence upon the word of God for guidance which is intended to provide for the smooth functioning of the Assemblies. This idea was so important to Singh's understanding, that listening to the voice of God and discerning the will of God became imperative for the very existence of the believer and of the church. By advocating dependence upon God, Bakht Singh tried to dispense with the centralized control and hierarchical structure, although to a large extent he was viewed as the sole authority for a long time.

Bakht Singh's understanding of what constituted the dynamic control of the Spirit and the specific guidance of the Holy Spirit for the day-to-day existence of each congregation was one of the most significant reasons that he encouraged the autonomy of each local congregation. Bakht Singh also maintained that the autonomy of the local Assemblies relieved them from the bondage and the ill effects of being under an institutionalized system or structure and a tradition and gave people the freedom to worship God in an Indian way.

Bakht Singh recognized that the incarnation of the gospel should take place both in the ideas and truths, and in the way that those truths are lived out. He recognized that the translatability of the gospel was not only in the conceptual realm, but also in the practical realm of living out one's faith. Here again, Bakht Singh noticed the cultural dichotomy that prevailed in the worship, lifestyle and practices that were to be found within the historic denominational churches. Once again, he turned to his earlier religious heritage that offered a workable model, but at the same time, did not contradict the Christian faith or Christian practice. Thus, he introduced some practices into the Assemblies that could also be found in Sikhism, thereby bringing the practice of Christian faith nearer to the Indian spiritual practices in other religions. By introducing the age-old customs such as leaving footwear outside the Assembly building, kneeling down for prayer, women covering their head in the Assemblies, upholding the importance of the word of God, and affirming the importance and role of the individual believer, for example, Bakht Singh was able to retain the devotion and sanctity of the Christian worship and worship place in the church that was viewed by other religious groups in India as being absent from the historic denominational churches.

Although the emphasis on personal spiritual experience makes possible an individualistic approach to Christian faith and practice, Bakht Singh stressed the congregational aspect of spirituality as well as the communitarian aspect of the church. Spiritual exercises such as prayer, meditation on the word of God, and worship were common to the individual and to the congregation. The concepts of fellowship, equality, and care for one another were exemplified through the practices of the love feast, holy convocations and the teaching that the importance of every believer in the congregation is responsible for the sustenance and survival of the whole Assembly. In these ways, then, both individual and corporate aspects were seen holistically, without any separation. The drumbeat in his teaching, however, was on the personal and the inward.

By emphasizing the spirituality of the individual believer as foundational for the establishment and proper functioning of the Assemblies, Bakht Singh minimized the importance of academic and theological training for "God's servants." This seems to be a major weakness in the solution that Bakht Singh sought for the church in India. By adopting this position, Singh failed to encourage the Assemblies to grow much further than the personal experiential level of spirituality. Similarly, he did not encourage the Assemblies to explore ways to address the sometimes complex intellectual issues faced by the members of the congregations. As a result, with their spirituality, the Assemblies now stand in definite need of finding a way to enhance their theological training in order to meet the needs of their better informed and educated members. If they cannot do so they run the risk of losing these members to other groups, or to no group at all.

The heavy emphasis that Bakht Singh placed on the individual and spiritual side of things may give the impression that he was oblivious to the social needs and issues of his day, and that he did not address issues related to social justice. This impression, however, is not borne out when one looks more closely at his work. When issues of ethics were concerned, Bakht Singh integrated both the temporal and spiritual issues. He did not see them as separated from each other as is often the case in some western dualistic forms. For example, Singh mitigated the barriers of caste and of class in the Assemblies, by teaching and practicing the equality of all believers as the children of God. His emphasis on *Bhakti* was also a unifying factor that helped him to diminish the barriers of caste and class and promote an understanding of equality shared by all believers by giving them a common identity and relationship of being brothers and sisters in Christ. He also advocated that living a modest lifestyle was fitting in order that the believer should become a useful witness, and a model of Christ's calling. In this way the problem of materialism and class distinctions were also addressed.

However much Bakht Singh was sensitive to the Indian culture when it was helpful to him for the spread or incarnation of the gospel, he also understood that the following of certain cultural traditions was nothing more than idolatry, and thus, it was to be avoided by the believer. In a way this understanding has resulted in the development of a kind of subculture within the Assemblies. At the same time, it has increased the distance between the Assemblies and the historic denominational churches. Bakht Singh's claim that the Assemblies were based on a direct vision from the word of God and that they follow the New Testament pattern, is a primary example of this, because in a way it detached them from the historic Christian tradition. In this regard, then, it fails to promote the cause of ecumenism. Moreover, Bakht Singh's running critique of other churches inevitably suggests a reactionary fixation. This has had some long-term negative consequences in terms of Christian unity and mutual respect.

Bakht Singh's movement arose in response to the negative effects of the apparently static structures and traditions that could be found within the denominational churches. It lifted up the place of a living form of spirituality as an alternative to what he viewed as the lifeless and static dogmas and constitutions. The current state of the Assemblies, however, now reveals a significant negative consequence that taking this position has produced. While lifting up a living form of spirituality may have been a much needed corrective within the denominations found within the Indian context, his failure to understand fully or to appreciate the need for a clear organizational structure resulted in Singh's failure to assure the ongoing life of his congregations in an undisputed manner. While not appointing a successor fits into Bakht Singh's understanding of the personal guidance of the Holy Spirit, and not bringing the Assemblies under a structure and a centralized system in order to maintain the autonomy of the local Assemblies, Bakht Singh left the door open to the current strife and dissent that permeates the Assemblies today. Thus, the onus now rests on the Assemblies to find a way to carry out the vision of Bakht Singh while maintaining an equally spiritual yet organized structure for the ongoing life of the Assemblies.

In a context of diverse cultures, religions, and languages the most unifying dynamic in Indian spiritual ethos was *Bhakti*. By adopting *Bhakti* not only at an intellectual or conceptual level, but also by practicing it both in the individual and in the corporate realms of the Christian life, Singh was able to draw a common spiritual ethos within Christianity that could be appropriated and identified by any seeker of religion in India. He also redeemed Christianity from the monopoly of the western denominations and missions and made it a religion of the people of India. By establishing local Assemblies that are both autonomous and financially independent, Bakht Singh further affirmed that the Indian church could succeed on its own without outside help, with its own theology, ecclesiology, and government, and with spirituality or *Bhakti* providing the unifying factor of Christians around the world. It is in these ways that Bakht Singh has made a substantial contribution to the church and to the life of the church as it is expressed within Indian culture among the people of India today and thereby brought an "Indian" church into being thus deserving the title, "The Father of the Independent Indian Christian church movement."

Glossary

Adi Granth: Sikh scriptures
Ardas: Sikh prayer used at the conclusion of the service or private devotions.
Bani: Speech. Hymns included in the Guru Granth Sahib.
Bhakti: Devotion or loving devotion to a personal god.
Bhakta: Devotee
Bhagat: A devotee or exponent of *bhakti*.
Bhai: Brother, a title applied to Sikhs of outstanding piety and learning.
Bhava: Attitude or feeling.
Granth: Book. The Adi Granth or Guru Granth Sahib
Granthi: One who looks after the Guru Granth Sahib. A reader of the Granth in the *gurudwara*.
Gurbani: Guru's teaching, the content of the Adi Granth.
Gurudwara: Sikh temple
Gurmukh: Follower of the *guru*.
Guru: A spiritual preceptor. One who delivers a person from darkness to light.
Haumai: Self or self-centeredness
Hukam: Order, command
Karma: Consequences based on actions leading to transmigration of souls.
Kesh: Uncut hair
Keshdhari: One who wears the hair uncut.
Khalsa: The Sikh order, brotherhood instituted by Guru Gobind Singh.
Kirtan: The singing of songs in praise of God to the accompaniment of music.
Langar: Community kitchen
Mul Mantra: Creedal statement of Sikhism
Nam: The divine name
Nam Japo: Repetition of God's name
Nam Simaran: Meditation upon God's name
Nirguna: Without qualities or attributes.
Panth: Sikh community
Pir: The head of a *Sufi* order, a *Sufi* saint.
Sabad/Shabad/Sabda: Word. Hymn of the Adi Granth

Sadhu: Mendicant, ascetic
Saguna: With qualities or attributes
Sangat: Gathering, assembly, congregation.
Sant: Synonymn of *sadhu*, member of a North Indian religious tradition, e.g. Kabir.
Satguru: The true Guru, God.
Sati Nam: The true name
Satsang: Fellowship of true believers.
Seva: Service, service on behalf of the Sikh community.
Sruti: Hearing, scriptures.
Sufi: Muslim mystic.

Bibliography

Primary Sources

Austin-Sparks, T. *The Church Which Is His Body*, revised edition. Tulsa, OK: Emmanuel Church, 2000.

———. *The Cross, the Church and the Kingdom*. Tulsa, OK: Emmanuel Church, 2008.

———. "Explanation of the Nature and History of 'This Ministry.'" Tulsa, OK: Emmanuel Church, 2004.

———. *God's Spiritual House*. Tulsa, OK: Emmanuel Church, n.d.

———. *The Nature of the Dispensation in Which We Live*. Online Library of T. Austin-Sparks. Available from www.Austin-Sparks.Net.

———. *What Is the Church*. Online Library of T. Austin-Sparks. Available from www.Austin-Sparks.Net.

———. *What It Means to Be a Christian*. Tulsa, OK: Emmanuel Church, n.d.

———. *Worship*. Online Library of T. Austin-Sparks. Available from www.Austin- Sparks.Net.

Hebron Messenger. Hyderabad: Hebron.

Llewellyn, Eleanore H. "Bakht Singh of India." In *Unforgettable Disciples*. New York: Board of Foreign Missions of the Presbyterian Church in the United States of America, 1942.

Minutes of the Proceedings of the Principal Trustee, Bro. Bakht Singh, of the Society of Trustees of Indigenous Churches in India, Hebron, Golconda Cross Roads, Hyderabad 500020. 24 February 1983.

Nee, Watchman. *The Body of Christ: A Reality*. New York: Christian Fellowship Publishers, 1978.

———. *Further Talks on the Church Life*. Los Angeles, CA: Stream Publishers, 1969. Reprint, 1974.

———. *The Glorious Church*. 2nd Indian edition. Anaheim, CA: Living Stream Ministry, 2005.

———. "Narration of the Past." In *Notes on Scriptural Messages*: *The Collected Works of Watchman Nee*, vol. 18. Anaheim, CA: Living Stream Ministry, 1992.

———. *The Orthodox Tradition of the Church*. Taiwan: Gospel Boon Room, 1963.

Rajamani, Rayappan R. *Monsoon Daybreak*. London: Open Books, 1971.

———. *Monsoon Daybreak*. Fort Washington, PA: Christian Literature Crusade, 1971.

"Report of the Commission on Christian Doctrine." Appointed by the Archbishops of Canterbury and York in 1922 and entitled Doctrine in the Church of England in *The Madras Diocesan Magazine* 33, no. 2 (February 1938): 55–57.

Singh, Bakht. *Behold I Will Do a New Thing*. 4th ed. Hyderabad: Hebron, 1994.

———. *Bethany*. Reprinted. Hyderabad: Hebron, 2002.

———. *Come Let Us Build*. 3rd edition. Hyderabad: Hebron, 1994.

———. *David Recovered All*. Reprint. Hyderabad: Hebron, 2002.

———. *Fellowship of the Mystery or All One in Christ Jesus* (message online). Available from www.brotherbakhtsingh.com.

———. *Forty Mountain Peaks*. Hyderabad: Hebron, 1971.

———. *Fullness of God*. 4th edition. Hyderabad: Hebron, 2003.

———. *God's Dwelling Place*. Mumbai: Gospel Literature Service, 1957.

———. "Guidelines for Appointing Elders." (Manuscript on the decision taken in a meeting during the last week of January 1983.)

———. *High Way to Victory*. 4th edition. Hyderabad: Hebron, 2005.

———. *The Holy Spirit: His Work and Significance*. Hyderabad: Hebron, 2001.

———. *The Joy of the Lord*. Hyderabad: Book Room, 2003.

———. *The Lamb upon the Throne*. Hyderabad: Hebron, 2005.

———. *Looking unto Jesus*. 4th edition. Hyderabad: Hebron, 2005.

———. *My Chosen*. Hyderabad: Book Room, 1964.

———. *The Overcomers' Secret*. Hyderabad: Hebron, 1981.

———. *Return of God's Glory*. Hyderabad: Hebron, 2006.

———. *The Skill of His Loving Hands*. Bombay: Gospel Literature Service, 1975.

———. *The Strong Foundation*. Hyderabad: Hebron, 1983.

———. *True Liberty*. Hyderabad: Hebron, 1994.

———. *The True Salt*. Hyderabad: Hebron, 2003.

———. *Unsearchable Greatness of the Salvation*. 2nd edition. Hyderabad: Hebron, 1984.

———. *The Voice of the Lord*. Hyderabad: Hebron, 1970.

———. *Walk before Me*. 29th reprint. Hyderabad: Hebron, 2005.

———. *What Happened on the Day of Pentecost* (message online). Available from www.brotherbakhtsingh.com.

———. *Write the Vision.* Unpublished Manuscript.

Correspondence

Chhabra, Amar Nath, email to T. E. Koshy on 16 February 2001.
Flack, A. J. (Fred), to author on 13 December 2006.
Flack, A. J. (Fred), to author on 13 March 2007.
Golsworthy, Raymond, to T. E. Koshy on 6 April 2000.
McCumber, Brinda, email to author on 23 March 2009.
McCumber, Brinda, email to author on 26 March 2009.

Interviews

Amrutharaj, Selvi. Interview by author, 18 December 2007, Bangalore.
Benjamin, G. T. Interview by author, 13 January 2008, Hyderabad.
Chhabra, Shrichand. Interview by author, 29 November 2007, Delhi.
    Tape recording.
Christopher. Interview by author, 13 September 2007, Syracuse, USA.
Christopher, Ruth. Interview by author, 13 September 2007, Syracuse, USA.
Daniel, S. A. Interview by author, 21 December 2007, Hyderabad.
Devadatta, Joe. Interview by author, 11 December 2007, Vellore, India.
Dhanaraj, Earnest. Interview by author, 12 December 2007, Vellore, India.
Dhanaraj, Mrs Interview by the author, 12 December 2007, Vellore, India.
Flack, A. J. (Fred). Interview by author, 16 November 2006. Telephone.
Hansdar, Samuel. Interview by author, 21 December 2005, Kalimpong, India.
Isaac, M. Interview by author, 13 January 2006, Hyderabad, India.
Jaya. Interview by author, 19 December 2005, Kalimpong, India.
Jayakumar, David. Interview by author, 24 August 2009, Pasadena, California.
Joshi, Sarala. Interview by author, 23 October 2008. Telephone.
Kalyani. Interview by author, 11 October 2007, Hebron, Hyderabad, India.
Koshy, T. E. Interview by author, 13 September 2007, Syracuse, USA.
Lepcha, D. Wangdi. Interview by author, 21 December 2005, Kalimpong, India.
Mercy. Interview by author, 6 December 2007, Tirupati, India.
Panchnath. Interview by author, 20 December 2005, Kalimpong, India.
Rai, Daniel. Interview by author, 22 December 2005, Kalimpong, India.
Rao, Sathkeerthi. Interview by author, 25 September 2008, Pasadena, California.
Rao, Sathkeerthi. Interview by author, 14 November 2007, Hyderabad, India.
Singh, Bakht. Interview by T. E. Koshy, 1970.
Stephen. Interview by author, 21 November 2007, Delhi.
Tamang, D. B. Interview by author, 21 December 2005, Kalimpong, India.

Tendoop. Interview by author, 20 December 2005, Kalimpong, India.
Vani, Sree. Interview by author, 28 November 2007, Delhi.
Vedanayagam, Joseph. Interview by author, 19 December 2007, Hyderabad.
Vedanaygam, Sumathi. Interview by author, 19 December 2007, Hyderabad.

Secondary Sources

Abbiss, G. G. "Training in Hebron." *India Church Growth Quarterly* 6, no. 1 (January–March 1984): 9–12.

Ahluwalia, Jasbir Singh. *The Sovereignty of the Sikh Doctrine: Sikhism in the Perspective of Modern Thought*. New Delhi: Bahri Publications, 1983.

Airan, C. Daniel. *Kalgara Subba Rao: The Mystic of Munipalle*. Vijayawada: M/s N. Kutumba Rao & Co., n.d.

Alphonse, Martin. *The Gospel for the Hindus: A Study in Contextual Communication*. Chennai: Mission Educational Books, 2003.

Anand, Subhash. "The Liberative Potential of Popular Religious Traditions." In *Re-Visioning India's Religious Traditions: Essays in Honour of Eric Lott*, edited by David C. Scott and Israel Selvanayagam, 99–118. Delhi: ISPCK, 1996.

———. *The Way of Love: The Bhagavata Doctrine of Bhakti*. New Delhi: Munshiram Manoharlal Publishers, 1996.

Appasamy, A. J. *Christianity as Bhakti Marga*, 3rd edition. Madras: Christian Literature Society, 1991.

———. *The Theology of Hindu Bhakti*. Madras: Christian Literature Society, 1970.

Asirvatham, Eddy. *Christianity in the Indian Crucible*. Calcutta: YMCA Publishing, 1957.

Baago, Kaj. *The Movement around Subba Rao*. Madras: Christian Literature Society, 1968.

———. *Pioneers of Indigenous Christianity*. Madras: CISRS & CLS, 1969.

Bailey, G. M., and I. Kesarcodi-Watson, eds. *Bhakti Studies*. New Delhi: Sterling Publishers, 1992.

Banerjee, Anil Chandra. *Guru Nanak and His Times*. Patiala: Punjabhi University, 1971.

Barrett, David B., George T. Kurian, and Todd M. Johnson, eds. *World Christian Encyclopedia*. 2 Vols. Oxford: Oxford University Press, 2001.

Basu, Shobarani. "Some Religious Concepts in Hinduism and Sikhism: Guru and Sabda." In *Perspectives on Guru Nanak: Seminar Papers*, edited by Harbans Singh, 124–135. Patiala: Punjabi University, 1975.

Bebbington, David W. *Evangelicalism in Modern Britain: A History from the 1730s to the 1980s*. London: Routledge, 1989.

Beck, Rex G. *Shaped by Vision: A Biography of T. Austin-Sparks.* Cleveland, OH: Greater Purpose Publishers, 2005.

Bergquist, James A., and P. Kambar Manickam. *The Crisis of Dependency in Third World Ministries: A Critique of Inherited Missionary Forms in India.* Madras: Christian Literature Society, 1976.

Bergunder, Michael. *The South Indian Pentecostal Movement in the Twentieth Century.* Grand Rapid, MI: Eerdmans, 2008.

Bhatia, H. S. "Sikhism and Sri Guru Granth Sahib." *Journal of Dharma* 21, no. 4 (October–December 1996): 378–394.

Blair, Colin. "Communicating to Hindus and Muslims in India," ThM Thesis, Fuller Theological Seminary, 1983.

Boyd, R. H. S. *India and the Latin Captivity of the Church: The Cultural Context of the Gospel.* London: Cambridge University Press, 1974.

———. *An Introduction to Indian Christian Theology.* Madras: Christian Literature Society, 1969.

———. *Khristadvaita: A Theology for India.* Madras: Christian Literature Society, 1977.

Callahan, James Patrick. *Primitivist Piety: Ecclesiology of the Early Plymouth Brethren.* Lanham, MD: Scarecrow Press, 1996.

Carner, Gerald L. "The Testimony of an Illiterate, Nargaon, East Khandesh, India." *The Alliance Weekly: A Journal of Christian Life and Mission* 78, no. 16 (1943): 249.

Chandapilla, P. T. "T. N. Sterrett." In *Dictionary of Asian Christianity*, edited by Scott W. Sunquist. Grand Rapids, MI: Eerdmans, 2001.

Chatterji, Saral K. "Indigenous Christianity and Counter-Culture." *Religion and Society* 36, no. 1 (December 1989): 3–17.

Chaubey, B. B. "The Nature of Guruship according to the Hindu Scriptures." In *The Nature of Guruship*, edited by Clarence O. McMullen, 9–25. Delhi: ISPCK, 1982.

Chetti, O. Kandaswami. "'Why I Am Not a Christian': A Personal Statement." In *Pioneers of Indigenous Christianity*, edited by Kaj Baago, 207–214. Madras: CISRS & CLS, 1969.

Cheung, James Mo-oi. *The Ecclesiology of Watchman Nee & Witness Lee.* Fort Washington, PA: Christian Literature Crusade, 1972.

Clarke, Sathianathan. "Viewing the Bible through the Eyes and Ears of the Subalterns in India" (article online). Available from www.brill.nl.

Clement, Kuchipudi. "Bakht Singh." In *A Dictionary of Asian Christianity*, edited by Scott W. Sunquist. Grand Rapids, MI: Eerdmans, 2001.

Clough, John E. *Social Christianity in the Orient.* Philadelphia, PA: American Baptist Publications, 1915.

Cole, W. Owen. *The Guru in Sikhism*. London: Darton, Longman & Todd, 1982.
Cole, W. Owen, and Sambhi, Piara Singh. *Christianity and Sikhism: A Comparative Study*. New York: St Martin's Press, 1993.
———. *The Sikhs: Their Religious Beliefs and Practices*. 2nd revised edition. Brighton: Sussex Academic, 1998.
Das, Sisir Kumar. *The Shadow of the Cross*. New Delhi: Munshiram Manoharlal Publishers, 1974.
Devadoss, D. R. *And They Continued Steadfastly . . . Acts 2:42* (article online). Available from www.brotherbakhtsingh.com.
Devasahayam, V. *Frontiers of Dalit Theology*. Madras: Gurukul, 1996.
Dhavamony, Mariasusai. *Love of God according to Saiva Siddhanta*. Oxford: Clarendon Press, 1971.
Dhillon, Balwant Singh. "Guru Granth Sahib as Eternal Guru." In *Guru Granth Sahib and Its Context*, edited by J. S. Neki, 95–102. New Delhi: Bhai Vir Singh Sahitya Sadan, 2007.
Dhillon, Dalbir Singh. "The Institutions of Guru (Guruship), Gurudwara, Sangat and Langar." In *Guru Nanak: Ideals and Institutions*, edited by H. S. Soch and Madanjit Kaur, 202–225. Amritsar: Guru Nanak Dev University, 1998.
———. *Sikhism Origin and Development*. New Delhi: Atlantic, 1988.
Dunn, Robert Bernard. *Father of Faith Missions: The Life and Times of Anthony Norris Groves*. Waynesboro, GA: Authentic, 2004.
Embree, Ainslie T. *Sources of Indian Tradition. Volume One: From Beginning to 1800*, 2nd edition. New York: Columbia University Press, 1988.
Fenn, Prema. "Union of Evangelical Students of India." In *Dictionary of Asian Christianity*, edited by Scott W. Sunquist. Grand Rapids, MI: Eerdmans, 2001.
Forrester, Duncan B. *Caste and Christianity*. London: Center for South Asian Studies School of Oriental and African Studies, 1980.
Fountain, David G. *Contending for the Faith: E. J. Poole-Connor – A Prophet amidst the Sweeping Changes in English Evangelicalism*. London: Wakeman Trust, 2005.
Francis, T. Dayanandan. *The Christian Bhakti of A. J. Appasamy: A Collection of His Writings*. Madras: Christian Literature Service, 1992.
Ghurye, G. S. *Foundations of Culture: Religious Consciousness*. Bombay: Popular Prakashan, 1965.
Gill, Pritam Singh. *Trinity in Sikhism*. Jullunder: New Academic, 1973.
Gladstone, J. W. "Mission and Evangelism in India: Historical Perspectives." In *The Community We Seek: Perspectives on Mission*, edited by Jesudas M. Athyal, 125–135. Tiruvalla: Christava Sahitya Samithi, 2003.

———. *Protestant Christianity and People's Movement in Kerala*. Trivandrum: Kerala United Theological Seminary, 1984.

Grewal, J. S. *Guru Nanak in History*. Chandigarh: Punjab University, 1969.

Guha, Ranajit. "On Some Aspects of the Historiography of Colonial India." In *Selected Subaltern Studies*, edited by Ranajit Guha & Gayatri Chakravarti Spivak, 1–8. New York: Oxford University Press, 1988.

Gunn, Angus. *Theodore Austin-Sparks: Reflections on His Life and Work*. Toronto: Clements, 2001.

Hastings, Adrian. *A History of English Christianity 1920–1990*. London: SCM Press, 1991.

Hedlund, Roger E. *Quest for Identity: India's Churches of Indigenous Origin: The "Little Tradition" in Indian Christianity*. Delhi: ISPCK/MCCS, 2000.

Hoefer, Herbert E. *Churchless Christianity*. Pasadena, CA: William Carey Library, 1991.

Hoerschelamnn, Werner. *"Christian Gurus": A Study on the Life and Work of Christian Charismatic Leaders in South India*. Chennai: Gurukul Lutheran Theological College and Research Center, 1998.

Hollenweger, Walter J. *Pentecostalism Origins and Developments Worldwide* Peabody, MA: Hendrickson, 1997.

Hunt, Dave with update by John S. Gupta. *God of the Untouchables*. Honolulu, HI: Straight Street, 1999.

Islam, Md. Sirajul. *Sufism and Bhakti: A Comparative Study*. Washington DC: Council for Research in Values and Philosophy, 2004.

Johnson, Stephen C. *The Spirituality of Watchman Nee, Its Sources and Its Influences* (book online). Available from www.tren.com.

Jones, Kenneth W. *Socio-Religious Reform Movements in British India*. Cambridge: Cambridge University Press, 1989.

Jorgensen, Jonas Adelin. *Jesus Imandars and Christ Bhaktas: Two Case Studies of Interreligious Hermeneutics and Identity in Global Christianity*. Frankfurt: Peter Lang, 2008.

Kadankavil, Thomas. "Sikhism: A Sacrament of Steel." *Journal of Dharma* 14, no. 3 (July–September 1989): 298–306.

King, Richard. *Orientalism and Indian Religions*. London: Routledge, 1999.

Kinnear, Angus. *Against the Tide: The Story of Watchman Nee*. Fort Washington, PA: Christian Literature Crusade, 1973.

Koshy, T. E. *Brother Bakht Singh of India: An Account of 20th Century Apostolic Revival*. Secunderabad: OM Books, 2003.

Kumaradoss, Y. Vincent. "Creation of Alternative Public Spheres and the Church Indigenization in the Nineteenth Century Colonial Tamilnadu: The Hindu Christian Church of Lord Jesus Christ and the National Church of India."

In *Christianity Is Indian: The Emergence of an Indigenous Community*, edited by Roger E. Hedlund, 3–22. Delhi: ISPCK, 2004.

Kumari, M. Santha. "Contextualization of Christianity in India: A Critical Study of the Contribution of Bakht Singh and His Assemblies." M.Phil. dissertation, University of Madras, 2006.

Lee, Joseph Tse-Hei. "Watchman Nee and the Little Flock Movement in Maoist China." *Church History* 74, no. 1 (March 2005), (journal online). Available from http://proquest.umi.com.Lele, Jayant. "The *Bhakti* Movement in India: A Critical Introduction." In *Tradition and Modernity in Bhakti Movements*, 1–15. Leiden: E. J. Brill, 1981.

Lie, Geir. "Poul Madson and the Danish Kristent Fælleskab Movement." *The Journal of the European Pentecostal Theological Association* 28, no. 1 (2008): 34–48.

———. *T. Austin-Sparks: A Brief Introduction*, (article online). Available from www.reflekspublishing.com.

Lorenzen, David N. "Introduction: The Historical Vicissitudes of Bhakti Religion." In *Bhakti Religion in North India: Community Identity & Political Action*, edited by David N. Lorenzen, 1–32. Albany, NY: State University of New York Press, 1995.

Luke, P. Y., and John B. Carman. *Village Christians and Hindu Culture: Rural Churches in South India*. New York: Friendship Press, 1968.

Lyall, Leslie. *Three of China's Mighty Men*. Dunton Green, Sevenoaks: Hodder & Stoughton, and Overseas Missionary Fellowship, 1980.

May, Grace Y. "Watchman Nee and the Breaking of Bread: The Missiological and Spiritual Forces that Contributed to an Indigenous Chinese Ecclesiology." Th.D. Thesis, Boston University School of Theology, 2000.

Manikam, Rajah B., ed. *Christianity and the Asian Revolution*. Madras: The Joint East Asia Secretariat of the International Missionary Council and the WCC, 1954.

McCumber, Brinda. "Midwest and Tuscola History." Available from http://www.geftakysassembly.com/Articles/PersonalAccounts/MidwestAndTuscola.htm.

McLeod, W. H. "Bhai." In *Encyclopaedia of Sikhism* vol. 1, edited by Harbans Singh. Patiala: Punjabi University, 1992.

———. *Exploring Sikhism: Aspects of Identity, Culture and Thought*. New Delhi: Oxford University Press, 2000.

———. *Guru Nanak and the Sikh Religion*. New Delhi: Oxford University Press, 1998.

———. *Textual Sources for the Study of Sikhism*. Totowa, NJ: Barnes & Noble Books, 1984.

Melton, J. Gordon. "Local Church Movement." In *Encyclopedia of American Religions*, 5th edition. Available from www.localchurches.org.

Meyer, U. "Indigenisation – A Critical Review of the Discussion in India 1942–65." *Indian Church History Review* 7, no. 2 (1973): 91–120.

Mishra, Vijay. "Kabir and the Bhakti Tradition." In *The Sants: Studies in the Devotional Tradition of India*, edited by Karine Schomer and W. H. McLeod, 182–235. Berkley: Berkley Religious Studies Series; Delhi: Motilal Banarsidass, 1987.

Mokashi-Punekar, Rohini. "*Bhakti as Protest*." (article online). Available from http://www.arts.ualberta.ca/cms/punekar.pdf.

Mundadan, Mathias. "Changing Approaches to Historiography." *Indian Church History Review* (June 2001): 28–61.

———. *History of Christianity in India*. Vol. 1. Bangalore: CHAI, 1984.

Muttickal, James. "Mystic Poets of *Bhakti* Movement." In *Journal of Dharma* 29, no. 3 (July–September 2004): 337–350.

Narulla, Sushil. "Striking New Roots." *Indian Journal of Gender Studies* 6, no. 2 (1999): 175–190.

Neki, Jaswant Singh. "Bhakti and Sikhism." In *Encyclopaedia of Sikhism* vol. 1, edited by Harbans Singh, 335–337. Patiala: Punjabi University, 1992.

Nelson, Amirtharaj. *A New Day in Madras: A Study of Protestant Churches in Madras*. Pasadena, CA: William Carey Library, 1975.

Nirmal, A. P. *A Reader in Dalit Theology*. Madras: Gurukul, 1992.

Oberoi, Harjot S. *The Construction of Religious Boundaries: Culture, Identity, and Diversity in the Sikh Tradition*. Chicago, IL: University of Chicago Press, 1994.

———. "From Ritual to Counter-Ritual: Rethinking the Hindu-Sikh Question, 1884–1915." In *Sikh History and Religion in the Twentieth Century*, edited by Joseph T. O'Connell et. al., 136–158. New Delhi: Manohar Publications, 1990.

———. "Popular Saints, Goddesses, and Village Sacred Sites: Rereading Sikh Experience in the 19th Century," in *History of Religions* 31 (1992): 363–384.

Oddie, G. A. "Christian Conversion in Telugu Country, 1860–1900: A Case Study of One Protestant Movement in the Godavary-Krishna Delta." *Indian Economic and Social History Review* 12, no. 1 (1975).

Oommen, George. "Historiography of Indian Christianity and Challenges of Subaltern Methodology." *Journal of Dharma* 28, no. 2 (April–June 2003): 212–231.

———. "Is Indian Christianity Both Indian and Christian." Paper presented at the consultation on "How Do People of Other Faiths Perceive Christianity in India," EFI Theological Commission, 4 December 2002.

Pamudji, Peterus. *Little Flock Trilogy: A Critique of Watchman Nee's Principal Thought on Christ, Man, and the Church*. Ann Arbor, MI: University Microfilms International, 1986.

Philip, T. V. "Chakkarai and the Indian Church," in *Society and Religion Essays in Honour of M. M. Thomas*, edited by Richard W. Taylor. Madras: Chistian Literature Society, 1976.

———. "Church History in Ecumenical Perspective." In *The Teaching of Ecumenics*, edited by Samuel Amirtham and Cyris H. S. Moon, 417–429. Geneva: WCC Publications, 1983.

———. *Edinburgh to Salvador Twentieth Century Ecumenical Missiology: A Historical Study of the Ecumenical Discussions on Mission*. Delhi: CSS & ISPCK, 1999.

———. "Protestant Christianity in India since 1858." In *Christianity in India*, edited by H. C. Perumalil and Hambye, 267–299. Alleppy: Prakasam Publications, 1972.

———. *Reflections on Christian Mission in Asia*. Delhi: ISPCK/CSS, 2000.

———. "Theological Tradition in India." *ICHR* 21, no. 1 (June 1987): 28–56.

Pollock, J. C. *The Keswick Story*. Chicago, IL: Moody, 1964.

Poole-Connor, E. J. *Evangelicalism in England*. London: Fellowship of Independent Evangelical Churches, 1951.

Prabhakar, M. E. "Christians in Andhra Pradesh: Some Issues for Church Growth and Church-Planning." *India Church Growth Quarterly* 12, no. 1 (Jan–Mar 1990): 74–80.

Prakash, P. Surya. "The Contribution of Sadhu Sundar Singh: Preacher and Theologian." *Bangalore Theological Forum* 31, no. 1 (July 1999): 101–116.

Premanandam, Moses. "God-Chosen Movement for India." In *Christianity Is Indian: The Emergence of an Indigenous Community*, edited by Roger E. Hedlund. Delhi: ISPCK, 2004.

Premasagar, P. Victor. "Are Indigenous Churches a Silent Protest against the So-Called Mainline Churches?" In *The New Wine Skins: The Story of the Indigenous Missions in Coastal Andhra Pradesh, India*, edited by P. Solomon Raj, 163–170. Delhi: ISPCK/MIIS, 2003.

———. "Gospel and Culture." In *The Good News of Jesus Christ in the Indian Setting*, edited by T. Dayanandan Francis, 128–139. Chennai: Christian Literature Society, 2000.

Price, Charles, and Ian Randall. *Transforming Keswick*. Carlisle, Cumbria: OM Publishing, 2000.

Puri, Sunita. *Advent of Sikh Religion: A Socio-Political Perspective*. New Delhi: Munshiram Manoharlal Publishers, 1993.

Raj, P. Solomon. *A Christian Folk Religion in India*. Frankfurt: Verlag Peter Lang, 1986.

———. *New Wine Skins: The Story of the Indigenous Missions in Coastal Andhra Pradesh, India*. Delhi: ISPCK/MIIS, 2003.

Randall, Ian M. *Evangelical Experiences: A Study in the Spirituality of English Evangelicalism 1918–1939*. Carlisle, Cumbria: Paternoster, 1999.
Randhawa, G. S. *Guru Nanak's Japu Ji: Text, Translation & Study*, 4th edition. Amritsar: Guru Nanak Dev University, 1996.
Rao, B. S. L. Hanumantha. *Religion in Andhra*. Guntur: Tripura Sundari, 1973.
Rao, P. A. Susheel. "Bakht Singh Movement: A Case Study." In *The Community We Seek: Perspectives on Mission*, edited by Jesudas M. Athyal, 152–154. Tiruvalla: Christava Sahitya Samithi, 2003.
Rao, R. R. Sundara. *Bhakti Theology in the Telugu Hymnal*. Bangalore: CISRS, 1983.
Roberts, Dana. *The Newest Book on Watchman Nee: Understanding Watchman Nee*. Plainfield, NJ: Haven Books, 1980.
Rosem, Lal. *Brother Bakht Singh*. Delhi: ISPCK, 2002.
Said, Edward W. *Orientalism*. New York: Pantheon, 1978.
Sambhi, Piara Singh. "Living in a Multi-Cultural Society: A Sikh Looks at the Christian Church." *The Expository Times* 88 (July 1977): 292–295.
Samuel, Reddimala. "A Study of Bakht Singh Movement, Its Origins and Growth especially in Andhra Pradesh." BD thesis, The United Theological College, Bangalore, 1971.
Sanneh, Lamin. *Translating the Message: The Missionary Impact on Culture*. Maryknoll, NY: Orbis Books, 1989.
Sarkar, Sumit. *Writing Social History*. New Delhi: Oxford University Press, 2000.
"A Scheme for a Comprehensive History of Christianity in India." *Indian Church History Review* 8 (1974): 89–90.
Schomer, Karine. "Introduction: The Sant Tradition in Perspective." In *The Sants: Studies in the Devotional Tradition of India*, edited by Karine Schomer and W. H. McLeod, 1–17. Berkley, CA: Berkley Religious Studies Series; Delhi: Motilal Banarsidass, 1987.
Sen, Amiya P. "Bhakti Paradigms, Syncretism and Social Restructuring in Kaliyuga: A Reappraisal of Some Aspects of Bengali Religious Culture." *Studies in History* 14, no. 1 (1998): 89–126.
Sharma, Krishna. *Bhakti and the Bhakti Movement: A New Perspective*. New Delhi: Munshiram Manoharlal Publishers, 1987.
Shenk, Wilbert R. "Toward a Global Church History." *International Bulletin of Missionary Research* (April 1996): 50–57.
Shuff, Roger. *Searching for the True Church: Brethren and Evangelicals in Mid-Twentieth-Century England*. Carlisle, Cumbria: Paternoster, 2005.
Singh, Daljeet. "The Essentials of Sikh Bhakti and Hindu Bhakti." *Dialogue and Alliance* 5, no. 3 (Fall 1991): 21–35.
Singh, Darshan. *Indian Bhakti Tradition and Sikh Gurus*. Chandigarh: Punjab Publishers, 1968.

Singh, Gopal. *The Religion of the Sikhs*. New York: Asia Publishing, 1971.
Singh, Gurnek. "Bhai." In *Encyclopaedia of Sikhism* vol. 1, edited by Harbans Singh, 331–333. Patiala: Punjabi University, 1992.
Singh, Harbans, ed. *Encyclopaedia of Sikhism,* 4 vols. Patiala: Punjabi University, 2002.
Singh, Harmandar. "*Gurpurb*." In *The Encyclopaedia of Sikhism* vol. 2, edited by Harbans Singh, 194–195. Patiala: Punjabi University, 1992.
Singh, Jodh. *Gurmati Niranay, Chs. 1, 2, 6 and 8, Passim*. In *Textual Sources for the Study of Sikhism,* translated and edited by McLeod, 136–141. Totowa, NJ: Barnes & Noble, 1984.
———. "Guru Nanak's Concept of Sabad as Guru." *Studies in Sikhism and Comparative Religion* 1, no. 1 (October 1982): 37–51.
Singh, K. Jagjit. "Sangat." In *Encyclopaedia of Sikhism* vol. 4, edited by Harbans Singh, 41–43. Patiala: Punjabi University, 1992.
Singh, Kushwant. *The History of the Sikhs: Volume 2:1839–1974*. Delhi: Oxford University Press, 1977.
Singh, Pashaura. "Early Markers of Sikh Identity: A Focus on the Works of First Five Gurus." In *Sikh Identity: Continuity and Change*, edited by Pashaura Singh and N. Gerald Barrier, 69–92. New Delhi: Manohar, 1999.
Singh, Parkash. *Community Kitchen of the Sikhs*. Amritsar: Singh Brothers, 1994.
———. "Guru Ka Langar." In *Encyclopaedia of Sikhism* vol. 2, edited by Harbans Singh, 207–209. Patiala: Punjabi University, 1992.
Singh, Ravindra Raj. "The Pivotal Role of *Bhakti* in Indian World Views." *Diogenes* 156 (Winter 1991): 65–81.
Singh, S. Kapur. "Guru Nanak: His Place in History." In *Sikh Gurus and the Indian Spiritual Thought*, edited by Taran Singh, 109–147. Patiala: Punjab University, 1981.
Singh, Sahib. "Sri Guru Granth Sahib Darapan." In *Textual Sources for the Study of Sikhism,* translated and edited by McLeod, 144–146. Totowa, NJ: Barnes & Noble, 1984.
Singh, Taran. "The Nature of Guruship in the Guru Granth." In *The Nature of Guruship*, Christian Institute of Sikh Studies, 26–32. Delhi: ISPCK, 1976.
Singh, Teja. *Asa di Var da bhav prakasani tika*, (Amritsar). In *Textual Sources for the Study of Sikhism,* translated and edited by McLeod, 24–28. Totowa, NJ: Barnes & Noble, 1984.
Singh, Wazir. *The Sikh Vision: Problems of Philosophy and Faith*. New Delhi: Ess Publications, 1992.
Smith, Daniel. *Bakht Singh of India*: *A Prophet of God*. Washington, DC: International Students Press, 1959.
Staal, Frits. "The Concept of Scripture in Indian Tradition." In *Sikh Studies*: *Comparative Perspectives on Changing Tradition*, edited by Mark

Juergensmeyer and N. Gerald Barrier, 121–124. Berkley, CA: Berkley Religious Studies Series GTU, 1979.

Stanford, Miles J. *Plymouth Brethren Emulators (circa 1970)*, (article online). Available from www.withchrist.org.

Talib, Gurbachan Singh. "The Concept of Guruship in the Sikh Tradition." In *The Nature of Guruship*, Christian Institute of Sikh Studies, 90–100. Delhi: ISPCK, 1976

———. "Sikhism." In *The Encyclopaedia of Sikhism* vol. 4, edited by Harbans Singh, 148–155. Patiala: Punjabi University, 1992.

———. "Vahi Guru ji ka Khalsa Vahi Guru ji ki Fatheh." In *The Encyclopaedia of Sikhism* vol. 4, edited by Harbans Singh, 400–402. Patiala: Punjabi University, 1992.

Taylor, Richard W. "Communication through Art Forms." In *Christian Communication in India: Problems and Prospects*, edited by Mathai Zachariah, 47–55. Delhi: ISPCK, 1981.

Thomas, George. *Christian Indians and Indian Nationalism 1885–1950: An Interpretation in Historical and Theological Perspectives*. Frankfurt: Verlag Peter D. Lang, 1979.

Thomas, V. V. "Subaltern Historiography and Post-Colonial Theory: The Case of Dalit Pentecostalism in Kerala." *Religion and Society* 49, no. 2 & 3 (June & September 2004):121–139.

Tripathi, R. K. "Teachings of Guru Nanak Dev." In *Sikh Gurus and the Indian Spiritual Thought*, edited by Taran Singh, 205–240. Patiala: Publication Bureau, Punjabi University, 1981.

Uberoi, J. P. Singh. "The Five Symbols of Sikhism." In *Sikhism*, edited by Fauja Singh et. Al., 359–365. Patiala: Punjabi University, 1969.

"Vaisakhi," *Wikipedia* (article online). Available from http://en.wikipedia.org/wiki/Vaisakhi

Vasantharao, Chilkuri. *Jathara: A Festival of Christian Witness*. Hyderabad: Liturgy and Literature Committee, CSI Diocese of Medak, 1997.

Vyas, R. N. *Melody of Bhakti and Enlightenment*. New Delhi: Cosmo Publications, 1983.

Webster, J. C. B. *The Christian Community and Change in Nineteenth Century North India*. Delhi: Macmillan, 1976.

Wickeri, Philip L. *Seeking the Common Ground: Protestant Christianity, The Three-Self Movements and China's United Front*. Maryknoll, NY: Orbis Books, 1988.

Langham Literature and its imprints are a ministry of Langham Partnership.

Langham Partnership is a global fellowship working in pursuit of the vision God entrusted to its founder John Stott –

> *to facilitate the growth of the church in maturity and Christ-likeness through raising the standards of biblical preaching and teaching.*

Our vision is to see churches in the majority world equipped for mission and growing to maturity in Christ through the ministry of pastors and leaders who believe, teach and live by the Word of God.

Our mission is to strengthen the ministry of the Word of God through:
- nurturing national movements for biblical preaching
- fostering the creation and distribution of evangelical literature
- enhancing evangelical theological education

especially in countries where churches are under-resourced.

Our ministry

Langham Preaching partners with national leaders to nurture indigenous biblical preaching movements for pastors and lay preachers all around the world. With the support of a team of trainers from many countries, a multi-level programme of seminars provides practical training, and is followed by a programme for training local facilitators. Local preachers' groups and national and regional networks ensure continuity and ongoing development, seeking to build vigorous movements committed to Bible exposition.

Langham Literature provides majority world preachers, scholars and seminary libraries with evangelical books and electronic resources through publishing and distribution, grants and discounts. The programme also fosters the creation of indigenous evangelical books in many languages, through writer's grants, strengthening local evangelical publishing houses, and investment in major regional literature projects, such as one volume Bible commentaries like *The Africa Bible Commentary* and *The South Asia Bible Commentary*.

Langham Scholars provides financial support for evangelical doctoral students from the majority world so that, when they return home, they may train pastors and other Christian leaders with sound, biblical and theological teaching. This programme equips those who equip others. Langham Scholars also works in partnership with majority world seminaries in strengthening evangelical theological education. A growing number of Langham Scholars study in high quality doctoral programmes in the majority world itself. As well as teaching the next generation of pastors, graduated Langham Scholars exercise significant influence through their writing and leadership.

To learn more about Langham Partnership and the work we do visit **langham.org**

www.ingramcontent.com/pod-product-compliance
Lightning Source LLC
Chambersburg PA
CBHW051539230426
43669CB00015B/2651